The Tropic of Cracker

THE FLORIDA HISTORY AND CULTURE SERIES

Al Burt

Foreword by Raymond Arsenault and Gary Mormino

THE *Tropic* OF CRACKER

University Press of Florida

Gainesville · Tallahassee · Tampa · Boca Raton · Pensacola · Orlando · Miami · Jacksonville

Al Burt's Florida: Snowbirds, Sand Castles, and Self-Rising Crackers, by Al Burt (1997)

Black Miami in the Twentieth Century, by Marvin Dunn (1997)

Gladesmen: Gator Hunters, Moonshiners, and Skiffers, by Glen Simmons and Laura Ogden (1998)

"Come to My Sunland": Letters of Julia Daniels Moseley from the Florida Frontier, 1882–1886, by Julia Winifred Moseley and Betty Powers Crislip (1998)

The Enduring Seminoles: From Alligator Wrestling to Ecotourism, by Patsy West (1998)

Government in the Sunshine State: Florida Since Statehood, by David R. Colburn and Lance deHaven-Smith (1999)

The Everglades: An Environmental History, by David McCally (1999)

Beechers, Stowes, and Yankee Strangers: The Transformation of Florida, by John T. Foster and Sarah Whitmer Foster (1999)

The Tropic of Cracker, by Al Burt (1999)

Library of Congress Cataloging-in-Publication Data
Burt, Al.
The tropic of cracker / Al Burt : foreword by Raymond Arsenault and Gary
Mormino.
p. cm.—(The Florida history and culture series)
Includes bibliographical references
ISBN 0-8130-1695-9 (alk. paper)
1. Florida—Social life and customs—Anecdotes. 2. Florida—Biography—Anecdotes.
3. Florida—Description and travel—Anecdotes. 4. Country life—Florida—
Anecdotes. 5. Natural history—Florida—Anecdotes. I. Title. II. Series.
F316.2.B84   1999
975.9'063—dc21   99-18371

The University Press of Florida is the scholarly publishing agency for the State
University System of Florida, comprising Florida A&M University, Florida Atlantic
University, Florida International University, Florida State University, University of
Central Florida, University of Florida, University of North Florida, University of
South Florida, and University of West Florida.

University Press of Florida
15 Northwest 15th Street
Gainesville, FL 32611-2079
http://www.upf.com

For Joan and James F. Hutchinson, whose paintings
depict the Tropic of Cracker at its best, and
for the good Crackers of Florida

Contents

Illustrations

Foreword

The Tropic of Cracker is the ninth volume in a new series devoted to the study of Florida history and culture. During the past half century, the burgeoning population and increasing national and international visibility of Florida have sparked a great deal of popular interest in the state's past, present and future. As the favorite destination of countless tourists and as the new home for millions of retirees and other migrants, modern Florida has become a demographic, political and cultural bellwether. Unfortunately, the quantity and quality of the literature on Florida's distinctive heritage and character have not kept pace with the Sunshine State's enhanced status. In an effort to remedy this situation—to provide an accessible and attractive format for the publication of Florida-related books— the University Press of Florida has established the Florida History and Culture Series.

As coeditors of the series, we are committed to the creation of an eclectic but carefully crafted set of books that will provide the field of Florida studies with a new focus and that will encourage Florida researchers and writers to consider the broader implications and context of their work. The series will continue to include standard academic monographs, works of synthesis, memoirs, and anthologies. And, while the series will feature books of historical interest, we encourage authors researching Florida's environment, politics, literature and popular or material culture to submit their manuscripts for inclusion in the series. We want each book to retain a distinct personality and voice, but at the same time we hope to foster a sense of community and collaboration among Florida scholars.

In 1997, the University Press of Florida published *Al Burt's Florida: Snowbirds, Sand Castles, and Self-Rising Crackers* as the inaugural volume of the Florida History and Culture Series. The popular response to Burt's engaging folk history has been gratifying to everyone involved in the production of the book. Readers and reviewers who have traveled with Al Burt along the backroads and cultural byways of Florida have marveled at the wit and wisdom of one of America's great storytellers. Burt's unique style, his uncanny sense of place and his consummate mastery of the regionalist genre set him apart from the host of other writers who have tried to capture the essence of twentieth-century Florida. He is the rarest of writers, an author who challenges his readers yet invariably leaves them begging for more.

More—indeed, much more—is what Al Burt gives us in *The Tropic of Cracker*. Mixing new and old essays, he takes us on an unforgettable journey through the personal homeplaces and cultural thickets of the Tropic of Cracker, a realm that, as he puts it, "exists more in mind than in geography, more in the memory than in the sight, more in attitude than in the encounter." Drawing upon his long career as a roving Florida journalist, Burt uses a series of vivid biographical profiles to explore the full range of "crackerdom," from the good old boys and "pork chopper" politicians of the Panhandle to the native Conchs of Key West. Perhaps most impressive, he brings these endangered subcultures to life without resorting to sensationalist caricature or lapsing into nostalgic revery. Cracker Florida, which surely has suffered more than its share of condescension and misunderstanding, has finally found its laureate. Burt, a truth-telling semi-native (though his parents were then Florida residents, his mother went back home to Georgia for a two-week visit at the time of his birth), has a glorious gift of telling memory and artful reflection.

Raymond Arsenault and Gary R. Mormino, Series Editors

Preface

The Tropic of Cracker survives in myth, memory and love of natural Florida. It exists more in the mind than in geography, more in the memory than in the sight, more in attitude than in the encounter. It thrives in the sprinklings of people who still honor a multifaceted heritage rooted in the appreciation of a place and the understanding of customs that harmonized with its peculiar blessings. It tolerates and explains the humanly dimensioned heroes and the heroically flawed rogues who give it voice.

This book tells you about one man's vision of a state struggling to remain true to itself. It mixes new essays with a span of earlier ones written during nearly a quarter century of roving the state as a columnist for *The Miami Herald*. All of them, in sum, help illuminate and explain the Tropic of Cracker.

PART I THE TROPIC OF CRACKER

A Celebration of Natural Florida

In the Tropic of Cracker there are no parallels staked out, circling the earth at certain degrees and so many minutes above the equator, marking a zone and rendering scholarly identification of the climate and range of life. The Tropic of Cracker has no boundaries. In Florida it simply occurs, as unbidden as sandspurs or wildflowers, rooting in the minds of Floridians who have links to their past and kinship to their native heritage. Without forgetting practicality, it lifts spirits and fires imaginations.

Sometimes discomforting things invoke the Tropic of Cracker—bugs and weeds and thunderstorms and heat and humidity—and sometimes it wafts in on the stimulation of things more majestic. It can arrive, for example, with one of those Florida sunsets so awesome that if they happened in just one place and at just one time each year, rather than all over the state every evening, they would be tourist attractions all by themselves. If there were only one annual Florida sunset it would be worth traveling hundreds of miles to see, as are the brilliant changes of leaf color each fall in the Blue Ridge Mountains.

Wildflowers splashing a simple trail of color across a drab field can induce it. Individual sensitivities determine it. Whatever brings to the mind a confirming identification with native Florida, whatever reassures that there can be natural beauty and treasured culture among common folk and in common places can conjure up the Tropic of Cracker.

It has no created facade. It was not invented to please a stranger for the purpose of taking his money, though that might be a side benefit. It simply celebrates native Florida, the full scope of it, the free-flowing rivers and the beautifully framing beaches and the clear springs, the mythic swamps where only the sound of the wind or the cry of an animal breaks the silence, the great stretches of forests where night falls black without the interruption of halogen lamps. It revels in the sights and songs of untamed things, the yodel and gobble of sandhill cranes cruising the prairies and pastures, the bob-white call of a quail or the mourning coo of a dove, pelicans squawking on a Keys dock or gulls lobbying fishing boats for a handout, exuberant mullet jumping clear in the bays, pursued shrimp skittering across the surface of inlets, buzzards poetically circling over a downtown courthouse.

From nurtured backyard jungles to the great vistas of the Everglades, from the magical Keys to the thousands of clear lakes socketed into central Florida sandhills, from river-sweetened estuaries to dune-guarded beaches where Spanish conquistadores once splashed ashore, the Tropic of Cracker represents what remains of the Florida that needed no blueprint or balance sheet for its creation, that was here before there was a can opener or a commercial or a real-estate agent.

Crackers inhabit the Tropic of Cracker, and they are called that either because they are natives of Florida or because they so love the native things of Florida that they have been naturalized by experience and exposure. People argue about the use of the word "Cracker," but it does not matter. In Florida, the word comes out of state history. Old-time cow hunters drove great herds of cattle across Florida to shipping points, popping long cowhide whips so loudly that they could be heard miles ahead. Because of this, they became known as Crackers. The Florida definition has nothing to do with race. It is a tribal feather, not a street slur. Some Snowbirds, some newcomers who arrive wanting to teach Florida lessons rather than to learn the lessons of Florida, have trouble with that. Let them learn. They probably did not understand about aquifers or sinkholes or kumquats or gopher tortoises when they arrived, either. They have a treat in store. We are willing to share.

Crackers come in all sizes and shapes and backgrounds and beliefs. As Florida leapfrogged from a frontier to a megastate on wave after wave of migration, backwoods Crackers whose families had seeped

A pair of Cracker farmers: the Crews brothers of Baker County. Photo by the author, 1973.

down across the borders from Alabama or Georgia chasing one of the booms dwindled from dominance, but not from influence.

The life of John DeGrove tells the best side of Cracker history. The distinguished Dr. DeGrove, known as the "father of growth management" in Florida, is a fifth-generation native of this state. He grew from a boyhood in backwoods Palm Valley, where he fed his mule with dried moonshine mash, to become one of the state's most distinguished educators. His story and vision are told in the last section, "The Next Florida."

Lawrence Atkinson told a typical Florida story. In 1926 his family lived in Madison, Georgia. There were seven children in the family. When the boll weevil hit and wiped out the cotton crops around Madison, times became desperate. A brother who had gone south to Florida wrote back home that there were good-paying jobs in Florida, and off the Atkinsons went. Lawrence said that they drove as far as Umatilla, a town sitting among landlocked lakes in central Florida's Lake County, when a tire blew out on the old car. "So we stayed," Atkinson said. They arrived in September of 1926, just before a severe hurricane hit south Florida and barely three years ahead of the Depression. They first tried raising cotton, then watermelons, then (because they had two teams of mules) began to hire out to work in the citrus groves. Nearly 50 years later (1974) when I talked to him, he was a prosperous Cracker with his own citrus grove service looking after 3,000 acres of fruit, including 300 acres of his own. As it was for so many others, the Florida dream was good for the Atkinsons.

In the quarter century after World War II, when migration at its peak brought in a net gain of 1,000 new Floridians per day, a new kind of urban or suburban Cracker began to emerge. These typically were the old Crackers with the rough edges buffed off, or the sons and daughters and grandchildren of those old Crackers, far enough removed that they could look back on the hard times of the earlier years and see them as quaint, or even romantic. Attitudes changed, interests diversified, horizons broadened. Like almost everybody else in America, the Crackers too grew up.

Appreciative natives—folklife historians, environmentalists, naturalists and their kin, simple defenders of the feel and flavors of an old

E. L. Atkinson. Photo by the author, 1974.

Florida lifestyle, but not of the narrower social outlook—became the new Crackers. They were simply proud Floridians, housebroken and optimistic, perturbed by swamping new growth that changed the landscape and wiped out familiar vistas and landmarks. They were chagrined to see the Florida landscape being crimped and bent to give it an ambience imported from some other place. Many of them became absorbed with saving the Florida they knew, with the ideal of a Florida that honored its own nature. These were citizens who clung to the hope that growth need not necessarily mean the trashing of a great state. For them, the Tropic of Cracker had the aura of truth.

The old Crackers did not fade without significant grumbling about the changes. Some of them just hated to give up their mules for tractors, and didn't. Others dwelled on a change in values and attitudes.

One summer day in 1976, Colon Harris tried to explain about mules. He had a 15-acre farm near Glen St. Mary on State Road 125 about 35 miles west of Jacksonville. He started each summer day by putting on a pair of overalls and going out to the barn to talk to his mule, Ginny. He would pull her ears and pet her while she nuzzled his pockets looking for a piece of candy or chewing gum. After a while, Harris would hitch Ginny to a plow and head for the fields. Together they would plod up and down long rows of corn and vegetables, leaving behind them furrows of dark, freshly turned earth.

Colon would flip the reins as he held on to plow handles that swept back like the long horns of a steer. While Ginny pulled, he walked behind her and talked. If he called, "Gee," Ginny would turn left; if he called, "Haw," she went right. "Whoa" would stop her, and "Back up" put her in reverse. Most of the time, though, they were a team that meshed without commands. They understood each other.

Colon Harris and his mule, Ginny. Photo by the author, 1976.

Harris, then 68, and his wife, both natives of Baker County, lived alone. Their four children had grown up and moved away. Occasionally, a grandchild would come and stay with them in the summer. He bought Ginny for $100, and later turned down an offer of $300 for her. "Bought her from a fella over in Lake Butler," Harris said. "He was a Northern fella, I think. He named her Ginny. He stayed by hisself, and he just had her for a pet. That's how come she's so spoiled."

"Whooooo, yes," said Mrs. Harris, laughing. "She won't even drink water less'n you give it to her fresh and cool. She won't work but half a day, neither. He'll get out there and work *her* half a day, and then he'll get out there and work by himself the rest of the day."

Harris defended Ginny. "She's just now getting full grown," he said. "She wasn't much more'n a colt when I bought her. Never had a bridle on her before." He began to train Ginny for work by leading her behind a slow-moving car and gradually worked up to putting her in front of a plow. "What I done was pull on the lines and talk to her all the time. It's just like teaching a young'un something. Takes patience. She didn't know what I wanted at first and she'd set back on me. She was scared. She'd go to fighting the lines. I'd talk to her just like I talked to somebody and just lead her along. Pretty soon she got where she'd do most anything I said. She just had to understand first. She was the easiest to catch on of any mule I ever met."

Harris thought it was a shame that a fine mule like Ginny had come to be a symbol of the past. "I was raised to the mule. I worked one practically all my life," he said. "Like to have one around. Tractor's all right for turning a big piece of ground, but on a small one it don't do the job like a mule. I can plow in closer with Ginny. Keeps the grass down. I never had to go back and hoe my rows last year, she did so good. I give her two quarters of grain a day and one bale of hay a week. Don't have to buy that. I grow it. If I throw in a piece of candy or some chewing gum now and then, she's happy."

The mule, Colon Harris argued, was a craftsman in the furrows and had earned a place. As far as he was concerned, if the sight of a farmer and his mule was fading from the Florida scene, it was not because the mule got sloppy or lazy; the farmer did.

Noah Oswald Cook, an old-timer with a different complaint about changing times in Florida, lived in Carrabelle on the Panhandle coast. He had been mayor until the voters and their changing values elected somebody else. He was devoted to the past. "You don't know a person anymore," he said. "You know of them. Back in my days our vocabulary was small. Now it's growed to a tremendous vocabulary, but it's kinda like teaching a parakeet to talk. He talks and that's as far as it can go. No action. Makes it bad. Carrabelle's like all other small towns, except there's not another small town in the world like Carrabelle." He paused. "The Good Book says speak in parables, and that's what I do. People that don't think on my lines can't figure out what I'm talking about. I'm misunderstood in a lot of cases."

Nobody around Carrabelle ever thought that a few rules and regulations would topple Noah Cook. He was a master of the way things worked in the Panhandle. He did not let the new Lilliputians and their entanglements stop him. Still, he fell. One month he was in the hospital with a heart problem, "and it seemed like everybody in town was praying for the Lord to spare me." The next month 62 percent of the voters bounced him out of the mayor's office, which had been his on and off since 1963.

As such entrenched old-timers passed from the public scene, falling like battered pilings before an incoming tide, the outlines of Florida's evolution became clearer. Many saw this as progress, but in 1979 that was not the view from Cook's fish market.

"It's pitiful to me how people's got education and all that book learning and still don't know anything," Cook said. "The only people that thrived during the Depression was people that couldn't write their own name. They knowed how to make money, not paper business. Now everything's done on paper. I used to go to a city meeting and I probably had one paper in my hand, but now I go down to a meeting and I got to have one of those 100-pound fish boxes full of paper stuff. The good lumber they're putting in all this paper should be put into houses."

Cook was a big man, heavy and deliberate of manner. That day he sat on a folding chair in one corner of his aromatic little market, a corrugated tin structure fronting on u.s. 98, Carrabelle's main

Noah Cook. Photo by the author, 1979.

street. He was out of oysters, and he was struggling with his supply of patience, too. He wore suspenders and a straw hat and walked with a cane. In past years, some had called him the smartest man in Franklin County, but that election defeat and the full weight of his 79 years prompted him to ruminate sadly about the deteriorating condition of Florida and Floridians.

Carrabelle, founded in 1877 on the Gulf coast 50 miles from Tallahassee, historically lived off the seafood, timber and turpentine industries. A fine harbor, protected by Dog Island, lured sports fishermen as well. In a state where the population had grown from 1.6 million in 1930 to about 9 million in 1979, Carrabelle had grown from 920 to maybe 1,600. Noah Cook was born in 1901, the son of Maine seafarer Bert Cook, who with his brother sailed a four-master aground at the mouth of a nearby river. They shoveled the boat out of the sand, the brother sailed it back to Maine and Bert stayed to marry Noah's mother, Elvalee.

Noah Cook began politicking in the 1930s and never quit. He served in the Navy aboard tramp steamers (spending 14 months in China), labored in sawmills both locally and in Taylor County, worked in the prison system, opened the first motel in the area, owned restaurants, built boats and houses. He had retired and changed his mind five times.

As mayor, he did not care for directives on how to run his city. During his last campaign, attention focused on Cook's insistence upon following his own sanitation standards at his fish market, in opposition to the city planning and zoning board and the state Department of Environmental Regulation. "The only surprise," noted a *Carrabelle Times* editorial, "is that people got justifiably upset about it." That was unusual. Cook said it was another case of being misunderstood.

Cook was a man who longed for more practical times. He saw the world as a place being taken over by fast-talking parakeets lugging around huge boxes of paper. He had thrived in a commonsense day when a man with big feet paid more for his shoes, when smart men bought corner lots, when authority was never wrong and when a politician and his friends stayed hitched.

He foresaw disaster. "This history they spend billions of dollars on, for instance, don't mean a thing in the world except to read it," he complained. Change was reaching into all corners of the Panhandle, and Cook did not like it. "It's gon' be a terrible country," he said.

* * *

Changes wrought by Florida migration were daunting for almost all, even the reasonable. Throughout Florida history, wave after wave of newcomers invaded. One wave after the Civil War moved Florida's population from 140,000 in 1860 to 270,000 in 1880 (about 65 percent native born). Other waves came along during the 1920s boom, jumping the population to 928,000 in 1920 and to 1.5 million by 1930, during the Depression. In a post–World War II surge, the leaps became even larger, more than tripling in the next three decades to some 9 million in 1980 (up 564 percent since 1930), adding another 3 million in the 1980s (about two-thirds born somewhere else). As the year 2000 approached, Floridians numbered some 14 million plus 40 million or so tourists each year.

So the story of Florida in large part became a story of numbers, of the many from somewhere else who were so attracted to the extraordinary Florida nature that they stampeded here with their different notions of lifestyle, many wanting to mark it with their initials, to brand it with their own customs, to taste it and feel it and digest it and reshape it into all sorts of forms that had been favored in those other places where they had lived.

In a state like this, the Crackers began to understand, intelligent analysis could be made only if it were judged against itself, by its own standards and by its own natural treasures—not by the standards of some other place with far worse problems and a different history of how and why it arrived to them. It became a Cracker axiom that Florida couldn't truly measure its loss and gain and potential except by comparison with the good and bad of what life had been like here in Florida. Without remembering how it was, we could not know how it could be. Without remembering how it was, we could not know whether the new diversity, the new conveniences, the broadened horizons were worth what had been sacrificed for them. In some cases, they began to feel, the new job opportunities and the enlarged economy and the heightened awareness of the world took place at considerable cost. Florida began to lose some of its distinguishing peculiarities. Beaches grew crowded, traffic became congested, extraordinary natural vistas fell before bulldozers, the air and water began to suffer pollution, marine life was damaged, wading birds decreased, crime and stress went up, and the suicide and divorce rates shot up per capita among the leaders in the nation.

To preserve some sense of natural Florida and a lifestyle geared to it, there needed to be some spiritual first aid for the Cracker soul. One place it came from was such inventions as the Tropic of Cracker, paying homage to custom and mood and preference. It was like a pledge of allegiance, or maybe a prayer, for Florida.

Cracker faithful believed it was essential that Floridians keep in mind the special dimensions of Florida. They thought Floridians needed to understand this place if they were to live here and make reasonable decisions about it. They needed to understand that a sense of Florida depended upon assimilating all its brilliant points and counterpoints. They needed to remember that although a sandy spine anchors the middle of this peninsula that separates the Atlantic and the Gulf, almost everything that affects the interior makes its way to the water and affects the coast, and almost everything affecting the coast also impacts the interior.

Floridians needed to remember that as this state rises out of the beautiful subtropics and climbs into the temperate zone, immense change unfolds. Not only the weather and the temperatures change: The geography goes from sea level to hilly, the terrain from desert-like to swampy, the soil from sugar sands to muck and red clay. Each of those variations represents the preferences of living things, certain people and certain plants and certain animals, and each of those cluster to the parts they prefer. Within all that, almost everything moves and shifts and circles and returns in patterns—migrating human populations, ocean tides, birds and marine life. Florida thrives on mobility and change, and these affect all living things. In Florida, there are differences enough for all to find their special place.

If the Tropic of Cracker could be made real, by a Cracker Disney, all the houses would have front porches on which sat rockers. Every evening the family would sit there and wave to neighbors taking a walk. Everybody would smile a lot, because Crackers think a smile defines the breadth of the human dimension. They would try to charm the whole world, one yard at a time.

*   *   *

As long as you don't rile Crackers with nonsense about reshaping Florida into the facade of some other place, or by foisting off the exotic attitudes and practices of some other region on them, they usually remain calm, tolerant and compassionate. They recognize the frailty in others because it mirrors their own, and from experience they have learned that both humor and tragedy grow out of vulnerability, a universal flaw. Sharing that understanding can make strangers seem like family. At their best, Crackers are gentle, independent folk with their own ways and their own mindset about how the world ought to work. At their meanest and worst, they could make even a cottonmouth study etiquette, but the mean ones are arbitrarily exiled from the Tropic of Cracker.

When Crackers came to town, at least in the old days, worlds collided. The opportunity for misunderstanding was immense. Crackers once had their own version of the language, though that has diminished if not disappeared with the homogenizing influences of migration. Still, once they spoke in the stretched and softened accents of the South, Florida style, a bit less broad and mouthy than their Georgia cousins, but rounded and comfortable on the tongue. Nevertheless, the sounds could be confusing to the uninitiated.

Consider the true case of Mary, a shy girl long ago who wanted a new white pocketbook for the weekend square dance. On her Saturday trip into town, alone and determined, she entered a store and expressed herself to the saleslady. "Ah'm looking for a whyatt pocketbook," she said. Out came a variety of pocketbooks, all large and bulky, and none of them white. "No," said Mary, puzzled, "Ah want a whyatt one." More pocketbooks came out, still larger, and none with that splash of daintiness and purity that the dance required. Mary tried one more time. "Don't you have any whyatt ones at all?" The sales lady apologized. "Sorry," she said, "these are as wide as we have."

Sometimes I encountered misunderstandings that involved families. Once, a young Cracker wife in north Florida confided to me (while her husband nodded vigorous agreement) the story about the time her sister and brother-in-law brought a trailer down from Georgia and parked it out near the woods on the edge of their yard. The visitors quarreled so much it worried her. Late one night, a terrible scream woke her. She sat straight up in bed, trembling. She shook her husband awake. "That man is killing my sister," she said. "Get help."

There were no lights on in the trailer and the yard was dark. As her husband came out on the porch with a flashlight and a gun, she heard the scream again. "My God," the husband said, almost whispering. "Get back in here. That's a panther."

Next morning, things were a bit frosty around the house. The husband said you didn't need to worry about panthers, as a rule, but you shouldn't run out of the house in the middle of the night, practically on top of one. Anything might happen. She said when something woke you up screaming, she had a right to worry about her sister.

Meanwhile, they hadn't noticed that the visitors had packed up their things, hooked up the trailer and were preparing to leave. The sister stopped to say good-bye. She said she sure was sorry, but they had heard the screams in the night, and they didn't want to meddle because they knew how it was with young marrieds quarreling every now and then, but she thought it best that they leave. Maybe things would go better if there weren't any in-laws around to complicate things.

The resident sister never did tell them about the panther. She just waved good-bye.

* * *

Crackers love to tell panther stories. John Ferreira of Fernandina Beach told me a different one in 1976. He was 86 at the time and his father had been an engineer on the old cross-Florida railroad that ran from Fernandina to Cedar Key. "The train stopped anywhere a passenger wanted, wherever a horse and buggy waited," Ferreira said. "The engineer and the fireman ran the train by themselves, and the engineer had to take up the fares. When Dad found out that some passengers were getting off the train and running around to the other side to keep from paying, he began waiting until he got into the wild country out past Gainesville before he tried to collect. He would wait until he got into the middle of a Gulf hammock, out in the wild country where you could hear panthers screaming and there were all kinds of snakes and alligators, and then he would stop and collect. He didn't have to worry about anybody getting off then."

Ferreira remembered another bit of Cracker style as related by his father. In the old days, the local general store kept a barrel of whiskey. "When somebody paid his bill, he was offered a free gourd [dipper] of whiskey. If the bill was big enough, he might get two or three gourds, but whatever he got he had to drink down right there on the spot."

Ferreira, who was head of a local real-estate and insurance firm, was remembered around town as one of the men who almost cut up Fernandina's historic Fort Clinch to build a subdivision. According to Ferreira, he and some other men bought the fort property but ran short of money to develop it. With Cracker practicality, they began to tear down the old fort and sell the bricks to raise money. They dismantled part of the officers' quarters, but found the old mortar so tough that finally they gave up the job. Stymied, they sold the property to the state, and it became one of Florida's more interesting and historic oceanside parks.

* * *

Since 1974, I have lived in Melrose, a piece of old Florida hanging on in the outback of north central Florida. It is a good place. A good night's sleep there is more likely to be interrupted by the sound of an acorn rattling down a tin roof than by the wail of a police siren. There is probably less traffic on the nearest paved road to my house in one year than passes down I-95 or I-75 in one day. There is only one traffic light, and some may grumble but most are proud that we have it, because in late afternoon our capitol—Chiappini's cross-

Robin Chiappini behind the counter of Chiappini's, Melrose. Photo by the author, 1997.

roads general store and service station—gets crowded with commuters stopping off for refreshments on the way home. At Chiappini's, you can buy anything from live worms for fishing bait to Dom Perignon champagne, but the preferred libation is beer. That's true Cracker style.

The wry tastes of the Crackers extended to their kitchens.

Hugh Langdale was an expert on the Cracker menu, old style. One fine October day, he broke up a square of black earth next to his grocery store in Newport, south of Tallahassee not far from the Gulf, and planted his pot likker patch. In about six weeks, turnip greens and mustard greens and collard greens would begin poking up their leaves, ready for the pot. About that time, the mullet would start running. All would be in order.

"When it comes a full moon in November, right then's the big blow," Langdale said. "The fish are fixin' to spawn, the roe's starting to mature. Those mullet'll be butterball fat." Langdale then would harvest his garden, split and salt down the mullet in barrels, and look ahead to winter with confidence. "You can lick a bad winter with a pot likker patch and salt mullet," he told me. That was in 1975. Langdale, a tall, lean, crewcut fellow who had migrated in historic Cracker style from Georgia, ran the only general store in Newport, located a half hour south of Tallahassee on u.s. 98 near where it crossed the St. Marks River.

Langdale, a good-humored man of 65, once had driven a bus and would come down out of Georgia and drive through nearby Crawfordville, a regular stop. He liked what he saw of Florida. "Back in those days, I'd always see a bunch of fellows sitting around under the oak trees at the courthouse. Never did see 'em working. I asked somebody, 'Don't those fellows ever work?' He told me not to say that bad word. Somebody might hang me out of one of them trees. I always wanted to come down here and get me one of those jobs not working. Looked mighty good. I came, been right here 20 years, and now I'm too dang poor to get back to Georgia." He smiled at his joke.

In his store, Langdale started getting salt orders from the fishermen in October, getting ready for mullet season. In anticipation, he would stock about 1,000 pounds of salt. When the mullet came, would share in their catch.

"Mullet's not nobody's fool," he advised. "He's got that right eye to the shore all the time, if you don't scare him too much. They catch 'em in a gill net, split 'em and salt 'em and put 'em in barrels. That takes care of them. No refrigeration. When you go to cook 'em, pull 'em out the afternoon before and soak 'em in fresh water until the next morning. Eat 'em with grits. Won't taste like mullet. Salt mullet's as different from fresh as fresh pork from cured ham. Sop syrup and eat salt mullet. Just smell 'em cookin' and you get hungry."

Langdale also served a lot of other Cracker dinners at his general store, where all Newport's 43 families and a few passing strangers did business with him. "A Cracker dinner now, that's a can of sardines, some soda crackers and a plate of cheese and a red sody," he said, grinning widely. He did not recommend that kind of fancy eating as a regular thing, though. For good health, he preferred his pot likker garden and the mullet.

"That's your basics," he said. "The mullet won't spoil and the garden'll get better and better. You just thin it out, you know. Don't take it all at once. When you cook those greens, it takes a lot of juice. That's the pot likker. About Christmas you can start pulling the roots. Just throw 'em in with the greens. That'll get you through a hard winter."

Carl Allen, voted the No. 1 Cracker in the state in a survey taken by the Florida Bicentennial Commission in 1976, had different ideas about what a Cracker could eat. His specialty was fresh-fried rattlesnake. At his little board-and-batten restaurant in Auburndale, west of Lakeland down in Polk County, the walls and ceilings were lined with early Florida memorabilia—rifles, plows, Indian arrowheads, horse gear, lanterns. You sat at tables that once were sewing machines, drank iced tea from fruit jars and could order (in addition to rattlesnake) fried rabbit, armadillo, mullet, turtle, catfish and even ordinary chicken and cornbread.

Rattlesnakes were the prize entree, though. "I got some boys that hunt 'em for me. Bring 'em in alive. I kill 'em myself, so's I can guarantee they'll be fresh," he told me in 1977. He was 59 then and made a career out of being a Cracker. He was born in Auburndale, but his family migrated from Georgia. In 1976, in competition with 133 other nominees, Florida's Bicentennial Commission chose him as the No. 1 Cracker in the state. He loved the title.

"Most people don't know how to eat a rattlesnake," he said. "Got lots of bones, almost like a fish. Have to kind of pull the meat back off 'em. Good, though. Really good."

*　　*　　*

Prominent in the history of Cracker Florida are the stories of families who founded towns bearing the family name. Not all of them had Southern backgrounds. They came from the Midwest, the North, from wherever the word spread about the opportunities and the beauty in Florida. The Edgar family was an example. They were descendants of Scottish lairds who emigrated to America before the American Revolution. They made their way to Putnam County, Florida, and founded a dusty little company town that still bears their name, Edgar.

Until the 1870s, the Edgars had been farmers in Middlesex County, New Jersey, near the town of Metuchen. The family patriarch discovered clay on their farm, and his three sons began to mine it during the winter months when there were no crops to tend. They dug it with shovels, loaded it on wagons and hauled it 12 miles to Perth Amboy, where it was sold to scows heading for Trenton. They formed the Edgar Brothers Clay Co., and sold clay for use in making bricks and saggars (a fireproof form for enclosing ceramics during the firing process).

One of the boys, Charles S. Edgar, discovered that all clay for china was being imported from England, and he began looking for an American source. He explored the South, looking for white sand that might hide the kind of clay he needed. In 1880, when phosphate was discovered in Hawthorne, Florida, he got a break. Some geologists told him they had seen white kaolin.

In 1888, Edgar bought land among the low sand hills and sinkhole lakes of Putnam County, between Gainesville and Palatka, and founded a company. In 1892 it was incorporated as the Edgar Plastic

Allen Edgar. Photo by the author, 1974.

Kaolin Co., and its location became the town of Edgar. Another company later took over the original mines.

Allen C. Edgar, the grandson of Charles S. Edgar, was director of the Mid-Florida Mining Co. in Lowell, Florida (Marion County), in 1974. He talked about the founding of Edgar with a note of wonder in his voice. "When you think of a damn Yankee coming down to Florida in the mid-1880s and exploring it by mule and oxcart, you get an idea of the kind of thing he undertook. Nobody else had done it. He actually pioneered the kaolin industry in the United States. It was a two-day ride by mule then from Palatka to Gainesville. There was nothing at the place he picked but raw land. He had to create a town, build houses for the workers to live in, open a store where they could buy food, get a post office established for mail and set up a chapel for religious services."

There were other family-named towns, including Sebring, Destin, Macclenny, DeLand and many others. The unlikely dream of a Missouri farmboy created an extraordinary little village in a Cracker setting six miles west of Green Cove Springs in northeast Florida. James Cash Penney, Jr., son and grandson of Primitive Baptist ministers, built a chain of J. C. Penney stores across the country and then in the 1920s became entranced by Florida. He bought a home on Belle Isle in Miami, contributed to many charities and civic enterprises and invested heavily in the state. In 1925, at a sheriff's sale, he bought a 120,000-acre tract of cutover timberland six miles west of Green Cove Springs. First he set up an experimental cattle and dairy ranch, and then a retirement home for ministers dedicated to the memory of his mother and father. Though he suffered losses in the Depression, his creation survived in other hands and the retirement home remained open not only to church officials but also to laymen.

*　　*　　*

All those things are part of the collective Cracker memory and heritage. The Tropic of Cracker recalls a sense of it all—the landscape of old Florida and what there remains of it, quaintly tacky in many of its man-made aspects, natively ragged in nearly all ways, but still so purely beautiful it could inspire even a tourist to pray that this should last forever. It is not tourist Florida, not I-75 or I-95 or highrise Florida, not the TV-ad Florida behind tinted glass with soft lights and cool temperatures even in August, not the billboard Florida that issues maps locating the attractions with cute cartoon figures.

The Tropic of Cracker, in all its imaginary grandeur, is a matter of plain folk and an unashamed tethering to the land, an affection as pure as puppy dog love, love of Grandma and Grandpa, or love of a new baby in an old family. It is a thing of the mind, a matter of memories and appreciations, of recalling people and things and places that you would sacrifice to bring back, things whose value goes beyond the measure of numbers.

For some, the smell of an orange blossom triggers it. For others, the sight of Spanish moss hanging off the twisted black limbs of a live oak. For a few, reminders of the wild bring it alive—the roar of a bull gator, or maybe the leap of a dolphin between a swimmer and the shore, or a rattlesnake defensively coiling under a palmetto and flicking its forked tongue and angrily rattling its tail. The oddly sweetish taste of a fresh muscadine grape might do it, or the shock of a dive into the exhilaratingly cold waters of a deep spring where thousands of bubbles trail across the body and curious fish swim close to see the intruder. The sound of the first chuck-will's-widow in the spring could induce it, or the sight of lightning bugs bumping against the windows at night, flashing semaphore signals from the wild.

A tall white egret elegantly stalking the lakeshore, readying the spear of its beak for a quick snap at a live snack, calls it up; beach dunes rippled and silkened by the wind; those old rust-streaked oranges that scientists later made perfectly orange to please the Snow-birds; the distinctly wry and character-building taste of grapefruit that a Cracker could imagine eating up the cholesterol and strengthening the principles, but now sweet and tinted, like soda pop.

The Tropic of Cracker feeds a bit on nostalgia, sure, but there is more to it than that. There is the aspect of trying to defend home and trying to inspire others to help, of wanting to shuck off past evils and celebrate the good things of old Florida. It is the feeling that here there has been something special that should not be lost or forgotten, something not just confined to the library or to a museum or to a vault. There is a desire to cull the best of heritage and weave it back into daily life.

The Tropic of Cracker requires imagination, but it represents commitments blooded and boned into the lives of Floridians as they grew up. Those feelings become the idealized vision of home. Nothing can change them.

PART 2 FINDING A WAY

One More Cattle Roundup

John Olan Pearce, Sr., took up cattle ranching—the family business—at age 15. He came along when Florida still was a frontier, which was not that long ago in the Kissimmee River Valley. At 15, he had his own cattle brand and could burn it into the hide of a calf with joy. He rode and roped, cowboy style, and carried a .38 caliber pistol for shooting snakes. He could hit one at 20 feet. "I'd split one's nose," he said. "Get him up under a palmetto and split his nose."

All the Pearces of Okeechobee were cattlemen. Young Olan grew up listening to campfire stories of his great-grandfather, Capt. John Mizell Pearce, putting together cattle drives out of Polk County during the Civil War. He learned to believe in the beauty of work. He remembered the tales of his grandfather fleeing Polk County because it was getting too crowded, and moving to the open prairies around Fort Basinger on the Kissimmee River northwest of Lake Okeechobee. "He was looking for better grass," Pearce told me in 1975.

When that same grandfather drove cattle herds through the Florida woods to Punta Rassa on the Gulf coast, where boats loaded them up for Cuba, he came back home with his saddlebags filled with Spanish gold. Pearce himself, as late as 1947 when he was 54 years old, helped drive a herd of 2,000 cattle from Okeechobee across Florida to a range near Avon Park to escape floods caused when a hurricane crossed south Florida.

Nothing fascinates more in a study of Florida, I think, than revelations of how short the stretch has been from the frontier to the megastate, and how uneven that spread has been from coast to interior. Pierce's life put human dimension into significant patches of history. His family traditions were textbook stuff. His father was the first of nine children and at birth was granted Brand P1. The last born was P9. His own start in the cattle business began with a similar bestowal from his father. The (John) Olan Pearce herd would bear his initials, OP.

Pearce grew up to be a man in the fictional cowboy image—tall, tough, short-spoken, scornful of frills and show, devoted to the business. Even at 80, three years after he quit riding the prairies, he yearned for just one more old-time roundup. "I'd rather see them days come when we'd go out to round up the cattle than anything," he remembered. "We'd be gone about two weeks. Carry our food, homemade stuff, in a wagon with a tarpaulin cover. Sleep out. It was open range then, lots of deer and turkey, and everybody's cattle ran together. We'd ride out and put 'em in pens, sort 'em out.

"Some of those boys could learn 'em, you know, recognize 'em just like people. I never could. I got a brother-in-law who could look over 100 cows and calves belonging to 35 or 40 different people. He'd ride through 'em out there in the woods, put 'em in the pen and never count 'em. Just get in there and catch 'em and brand 'em. He'd name every one of 'em, just like that, who they belonged to. Takes a lot of know-how to do such as that."

John Olan Pearce was born at Fort Basinger in 1895. He grew up a half mile from the Kissimmee River in a seven-foot frame house, plus kitchen and dining room, with a pine log barn. "That river was a beautiful thing then," he recalled. "Meandered all around. Wonderful place to fish. But that was a long time ago. They straightened that thing out, you know, made a raceway all the way to Kissimmee. Damn, they cut her straight through. The engineers and flood control, you know, they wanted it. Now they want to put it back like it originally was. Probably cost $90 million."

Once a week a steamboat—Capt. Clay Johnson's flat-bottomed stern-wheeler from Kissimmee—would come down the old, meandering river with mail and supplies. "If you wanted a shirt, that's how you got it. If a letter came, it would have to come on that boat," he said.

Each family then had about 20 acres of its own, most of it planted in citrus. When the steamboat came, sometimes it would haul away boxes of oranges to market. Kissimmee was linked to the world by railroad. Passengers shared space with the freight. There was little overland transportation except by oxcart over dirt roads made difficult by sand in dry weather and slush in wet. To school the young ones, a handful of families in the area would get together and send for a teacher from the outside.

Even when Pearce was a boy, to get cattle to market you had to drive them across country, sometimes to Kissimmee, sometimes to the Tampa area. One dozen or fewer men would drive 1,000 or more cattle. He remembered herding cattle for 100 miles without seeing a fence. "Take us about five or six days to get over around Tampa, depending on how things went," he said. "About five days to Kissimmee, I guess. Sometimes we went to La Belle or Fort Pierce. One time I remember us driving 1,000 head to Kissimmee, all steers, two and three years old. Sold 'em for $23 a head to a man going to Texas."

Some of the food carried on those drives, as well as on roundups, was beef they themselves had dried. Pearce said he would shoot a steer in the head, skin it and then gut it. "Lots of times we'd cut a little tree, trim it all up and hang a little piece of meat on every limb where you'd cut it off. Sometimes we'd use a shed, have nails up overhead on the rafters, you know, and hang it up. We'd smoke it and dry it. Salt it first, when we could. Let it stay in that salt for a couple of days and nights and then take it out and hang it up and dry it and smoke it for three or four days, or maybe a week.

"If we hung it out on a tree, we'd throw a cloth over it to keep the flies off. When we got through, it was real good eating. You could eat it dry—little pieces where it had dried out good, you know—but it was better if you cooked it. We don't do that anymore. Now we freeze all our beef, but I'd sure like to have some of that good old smoked stuff again."

Pearce made his first trip to Okeechobee (later to be his home) in 1910. It was called Tantie then. "Came over for a visit, just to look around. Wasn't much to it. The old schoolhouse was there, and L. M. Raulerson's store was in a log building. That was about it," he said.

When the Pearce family needed a doctor—and with five children that was not an unusual occasion—one of the ladies of the family usually did the job. "We had to take care of ourselves. Not many doctors around here then. Mother could set bones, do whatever had to be done." He held up both wrists. "She set this one when I broke it. My aunt set this other one. It's a little crooked. I fell off a horse and broke this one. The bone stuck out right through the skin. I had an uncle that come to me, pulled that thing and got it back under the skin, and we put an old red bandanna handkerchief around it and tied it.

"I rode on about seven or eight miles after that to this aunt's house, and we spent the night there. She got some little pine boards, fixed splints and put 'em on, and next morning I got up and put that thing in a sling and went right on to work. But you don't find men like that this day and time. Boys, either. Nossir. They'd saddle my horse for me, and I'd mount him and we went on."

In 1917, the family sent Pearce away on a steamboat to attend Columbia College, a Baptist institution in Lake City. "That was about the only one in the state then, I think. I went one year, and then the next year the family took the measles and sent for me to come home. So I come home and didn't go back. Measles was a serious thing in those days."

The next year, the Army drafted Pearce. "Arcadia was the county seat then, and they was a boy short and it didn't look like he was gonna show up, so I went over there to replace him. After I got there, he showed up anyway and so I didn't have to go. But they told me I would have to go in a week or two anyway, and it was a long way back home, and so I just told 'em I'd go on while I was there. But that was a mistake. They never did have another draft. The war ended."

When a pretty young girl from Oklahoma came to Fort Basinger to visit her sister, Pearce found romance. After a three-week visit, she went back to Oklahoma. Olan got on a train and went after her. They were married, and the years brought three children. Only one, a son who is a cattleman in the Pearce tradition, still survived.

As a married man, Pearce moved to Okeechobee in 1925 to look for work to supplement his beginning cattle business. He divided his time between the ranch and working for the Florida East Coast

Railroad, which had built a spur line to Okeechobee city (the name by then had been changed from Tantie), shifting Fort Basinger's transportation and communication focus there.

The two big businesses for Okeechobee then were cattle and catfish, and Pearce became involved with both. "They were seining fish out of the lake [Lake Okeechobee] then and shipping 'em north on the railroad. They'd ice 'em down, put 'em in barrels and ship 'em out. While I was working for the railroad, they'd have that express car loaded down with fish pretty near every morning."

In 1934, Pearce helped organize the Florida Cattlemen's Association to promote the industry and served on its statewide board of directors (his son was later to become chairman of that board). He also had served on a long list of boards, committees and advisory councils, and as a bank director.

Among the big changes he had seen in the cattle business, in addition to the steadily improving reputation of Florida beef cattle and improved breeds (he prefers a crossbreed of whiteface, Brahma and Black Angus), was the end of the open range nearly 30 years ago. It forced the cattlemen to buy or lease land, and keep their stock under fence.

Pearce bought. "I like ownership," he said. "Then nobody can come in and say move over. You can't put your finger on it when you've got leased land."

Not all the changes in the business have pleased Pearce. He pointed out the price of beefsteak had reached nearly three dollars a pound for some cuts. He contended the rancher got little of that money. "We don't get no such price as that for it," he said. "These top steers now, we can't get 30 cents [a pound] out of 'em. All the money goes in between the producer and the consumer."

Neither did he think the modern cowboy (or cow hunter) had improved as much as the cow. "Not as good as they used to be. Used to, you could get more work and less complaints. We used to work for two or three dollars a day. What do you suppose a common cowboy gets that's not half as good as I was when I was a boy? Thirty bucks a day," he said.

Pearce feared that the traditions of independence and individualism had gone from most people, including cowboys. "Government's feeding too damn many of them," he said. "They're not dependent anymore. If a man's depending on his livelihood out of his business, he'll go ahead and work. If he's not, well, he don't care."

As a young man, Pearce knew Florida's legendary Cracker Cowboy, Bone Mizell of Arcadia. There was a man he smiled about, "a character, a drinker, but a good cowboy. Bone, he lived on his horse, in the woods, all the time. He stole a yearling for hisself one time, and old Judge King had him up, trying him. Bone said he wished the judge was settin' straddle the North Pole with nothin' in the world on but a celluloid collar and a pair of spurs.

"Bone was looking at a newspaper one day. Couldn't read, and he had it upside down. Somebody asked him what was the news and he told 'em there'd been a helluva storm at sea because there was pictures there that showed all the ships bottom-side up."

The lives of the Pearce men, from Polk County to Okeechobee, tell the story of the Florida cattle industry. John Olan Pearce, after much thought, decided that modern cattle might be better, but for him, nothing he saw in his late years matched the old days and the old cowboys. Beyond that he knew, as few others did, that much of Florida's glitz and glitter rode into being on skint knuckles and cow manure.

—April 19, 1975, and September 3, 1994

Tending to Pahokee

The lives of pioneers like Duncan Padgett illustrate the history of the small towns where they lived. Pahokee and Padgett grew up together.

Pahokee was Duncan Padgett's town, you might say. By the time I visited him in 1974, he had lived there along u.s. 441 on the southeast bank of Lake Okeechobee for 60 years. For 16 of those he had guided Pahokee's affairs as mayor and local judge. He had seen Pahokee change from a remote fishing village, which you could reach only by boat and where only a handful lived, into a winter vegetable and sugarcane center with a permanent population of 5,600.

For a half century he watched the development of farms and the seasonal labor pattern, which swelled Pahokee to a lively 24-hour town of 24,000 or more during the winter season and emptied it out again for the summer. He watched all the families grow, generation after generation, and the town build slowly around them, until for him Padgett and Pahokee became practically one.

"Being judge has been the tough part," he said. "All offenders must come before the mayor. That's where I've had a lot of problems. First, you know, you're trying to settle real offenses and then you get involved in domestic things, family arguments. In a little town, you know everybody. They come to me for everything known to mankind, I guess."

Padgett, though elected mayor for the eighth time, kept his telephone numbers listed in the public book, and at one or the other you nearly always could find him, day or night. "I accept all calls," he said. "I mean, you know, some people may not be important people

Duncan Padgett. Photo by the author, 1974.

but they have a problem they think's just as important as some important person's." He paused a moment to ponder those words and plunged on. "I listen to all of 'em. It's paid off."

The mayor learned long ago to stay off committees picking beauty queens, scholarship winners or things like that. "Everybody thinks their baby or their daughter's the prettiest," he explained, indicating the trouble that could result.

But when he went to court, he had to make decisions. There was no way around it. He indicated he prefers benevolent over the blind justice so often portrayed as the ideal. "I know that in the court I don't promise to give everybody a fair and impartial trial. I just promise to give 'em a trial," he said. "Because, you know, kids that you went to see when they were babies and then they're grown up and they're married and they've got families and then they come in your court, it's just a little bit hard to say you're going to give them a fair and impartial trial—because you might be lying about it. I might not give 'em one."

The Padgetts first tried prospecting for gold in Texas, then farming the sand around Hallandale (Broward County, where Duncan was born in 1905) before coming to Pahokee in 1914 to seek their fortunes as fishermen. After two years ("We like to have starved to death") they turned to farming the black muck around Lake Okeechobee. They knew they had found a home in 1917, after a winter freeze ruined other south Florida crops but those around the lake survived. With 65 cents' worth of cabbage seed, the Padgetts made $2,000 that winter.

For the next 44 years, during which he married and raised three children, the mayor was a farmer. Eventually he gave that up and owned a welding shop for a while, but because he was reluctant to send out bills, he finally gave that up too and concentrated on politics. In 1974 he had his hands full as mayor, judge and manager of a pumphouse for the Flood Control District.

"We gettin' a whole lot more stable town around here now," said the mayor. "Few retired people comin' in. They like to get out in these little towns. Few fishermen and tourists still comin'. Things are changin'. Along about now [May] used to be leavin' time. You'd see all those trucks and buses pullin' out, carryin' the workers north to the next crops. Don't believe 10 percent of our working class, in Pahokee at least, follow produce anymore.

"Still got seasonal labor around, of course, but it's movin' toward year-round. Sugar brings a lot of 'em in, but the mills keep a lot on in summer too, doing overhaul work. Not lookin' for any big booms around here. Never have had any, really. Might get 10,000 permanent population, but I think somewhere down the road we're gonna wind up as just a good place to live."

For Duncan Padgett and his town, who took care of each other, that was the target.

—May 26, 1974

Mr. Rawlings Remembers Mrs. Baskin

Marjorie Kinnan Rawlings, the most acclaimed writing champion that native or Cracker Florida ever had, leaned on Norton Baskin during her most productive years. She created Cracker literature, and together they enjoyed a social mix that ranged from Cross Creek neighbors, to an array of famed writers, to academics such as University of Florida president John Tigert. I wrote about Baskin several times during the 1980s. The following new essay combines those stories with previously unpublished material.

Norton Baskin, the gentlemanly Alabama Cracker who courted the writer Marjorie Kinnan Rawlings at Cross Creek, made subtle additions to Florida history. Their marriage matched near opposites: she was introspective and temperamental, he was outgoing and calm. She did her best work while married to her "hotel man," and he had his greatest successes in the hotel business while married to her.

Baskin described it as a "stormy" relationship. Nevertheless their lives together included devotion and mutual dependence as well as adventure. For years he was known publicly as "Mr. Rawlings." Rather than being offended, he thought it was funny. He loved telling stories about it. Baskin was the charming one, her protector; Rawlings was the volatile one wrestling with a peculiar genius. It was a match properly made in the legendary Cross Creek.

Before and after their marriage, things happened to him that might have sent Rawlings into a tantrum. Baskin found them amusing. Even at Marjorie's funeral, there was a mixup. By mistake, she was buried in the wrong cemetery. He took it in good humor, chuck-

Norton Baskin and Marjorie Kinnan Rawlings, about 1941. Photo courtesy of the University of Florida, Special Collections.

ling at how Marjorie might have reacted. Then, oddly, at his own funeral in 1997, there was another mixup. They misspelled his name on the tombstone. Baskin probably would have chuckled at that too.

The mistake at Rawlings' funeral was incorporated into the mystique that outgrew the facts about her life, work and love for the natural beauty of Cross Creek. It was never corrected. Baskin's friends David Nolan of St. Augustine and Phil May, Jr., of Jacksonville took it upon themselves to have the error on his tombstone corrected.

The Rawlings funeral mixup resulted in such poetic irony that many a writer dwelled on it in telling her story. She was buried in 1953 only a few yards from the grave of Zelma Cason, an old friend who had been so angered by Rawlings' description of her in the book *Cross Creek* that she sued Rawlings for invasion of privacy. But that proximity of graves was not Rawlings' idea. It was an accident.

Baskin told me the story in 1986. It began in 1950, when he and Marjorie attended the funeral of Tom Glisson at a cemetery near Citra, south of Island Grove on u.s. 301. Glisson had been their neighbor and friend, and also a character in the book *Cross Creek*. She liked the setting. "Marjorie said, 'This is where I'd like to be buried, too. I could rest here,'" Baskin recalled. Later she reaffirmed that choice.

When Rawlings died on December 14, 1953, of a cerebral hemorrhage, they were living in St. Augustine. At the time, Baskin remembered her chosen cemetery as being closer to the village Island Grove. His burial instructions were based on that. "All the preparations were made and we headed for the funeral," Baskin said. During the procession, he discovered there had been a mistake. "I didn't realize what had happened until we turned north [not south to Citra] and drove into Antioch cemetery, the wrong one," Baskin said.

"I hated to make a last-minute fuss. Didn't seem like the thing to do. She had friends buried at Antioch, too, and it seemed perfectly all right. I saw no reason to make a change. But," he added, chuckling, "instead of being buried near her friend Tom Glisson, she was buried near Zelma Cason."

On her tombstone, he dealt tenderly with the "Mr. Rawlings" business. Chiseled in granite were the dates and the name, Marjorie Kinnan Rawlings, plus one line at the bottom identifying her to his satisfaction as well: "Wife of Norton Baskin." He said, "It was the only way to state it."

Baskin died on August 15, 1997, and was buried next to Rawlings at the Antioch cemetery. David Nolan, the St. Augustine historian who was his friend and biographer, delivered the eulogy. He called Baskin a great storyteller. "Norton was our last link with the golden age of American literature," Nolan said. "He could speak of Ernest Hemingway and Scott and Zelda Fitzgerald and Maxwell Perkins, the most legendary editor in American history. He knew Margaret Mitchell, the author of *Gone with the Wind,* and the famous black novelist Zora Neale Hurston. . . . From now on, *we* will tell the stories—about you. And we will keep the flame alive, not just for Marjorie Rawlings, but for Norton Baskin as well."

The engraving on the tombstone simply listed Norton Sandford Baskin as "Beloved Husband." Later, Nolan realized the mistake. Baskin's middle name was *Sanford,* not Sandford. Baskin, the master storyteller, would have used it to regale his friends with one more bit of deprecating humor about "Mr. Rawlings."

* * *

Baskin could tell stories by the hour. During another 1986 visit with him at the house he and Rawlings once shared in St. Augustine, he spun some of his tales out in a long, tape-recorded session. He would stop now and then to ask, "Are you interested in all this?" I was.

Once, he told me, he proudly showed a stylish lady visitor his hotel, the fine old Castle Warden, a place of distinction in the St. Augustine of the 1940s. (Later it was turned into Ripley's Believe It or Not Museum. The hotel originally had been built by a partner of railroad tycoon Henry Flagler, a man with 14 children. It had no telephones in the rooms and had been vacant for 18 years when Baskin bought it in 1941.)

"Are you Mr. Rawlings?" the lady asked.

"No, ma'am. My name is Baskin," he said.

"But they told me that Marjorie Kinnan Rawlings' husband owned this place."

"Well, I am her husband, but I am just the foster father of her books," Baskin replied with gentlemanly restraint.

The old stories remained fresh to him. Since about 1960, he said, there had been a renewal of interest in Rawlings that continued to build. Following two movies (*Gal Young Un* and *Cross Creek*) based on Rawlings' work, it picked up speed. His role as Mr. Rawlings became a more intense performance than ever.

Baskin played a bit part in the movie *Cross Creek*, but the actor Peter Coyote played the Baskin role. On the set, Coyote asked Baskin how he should play it. "With charm, goddammit, with charm," Baskin replied. Later he said of Coyote's performance, "He out-charmed me, ten to one."

Baskin helped promote the movie and went to France for a film festival. With the actors, producer and director, Baskin attended a press conference while suffering from jet lag. There were several hundred newsmen and photographers present. Two interpreters translated questions and answers for all. It got interesting.

"Whenever I'm out of my element, I go Southern," Baskin explained. "It's a protective thing. I was so damned Southern over there I wasn't anything understandable."

After one question and answer, someone in the audience asked for a translation into French. A man from the *Manchester Guardian* asked a question, and afterward he raised his hand and asked that Baskin's drawling answer be translated into English.

* * *

Whatever happened to him, Baskin retained his balance. He patiently told his stories over and over, year after year, to researchers wanting to know more about Rawlings. Someone once asked him what he did for a living, and Baskin replied. "I don't do anything. Being Mr. Rawlings is a full-time job."

"I live on the people I've met," he said. "I'm the first to realize I wouldn't have met them a-tall if it hadn't been for Marjorie. But I've been Mr. Rawlings for so long that it's going to be a pleasure when I can get back to being Norton Baskin. I mean, I was never bored with

Newlyweds Norton Baskin and Marjorie Kinnan Rawlings, 1941. Photo courtesy of the University of Florida, Special Collections.

Marjorie a minute in my life, but I'm getting bored with Mr. Rawlings."

They met in 1933, he said, the day after she filed for divorce from her first husband, Charles Rawlings. She had been living at Cross Creek for five years and her first novel, *South Moon Under*, was fresh in the bookstores. Baskin was the new manager of the Marion Hotel in Ocala, 24 miles south of Cross Creek. Her lawyer's wife invited him to a party at Cross Creek to cheer up Marjorie. Baskin did not know where Cross Creek was and had never heard of Rawlings, but he went.

"I've wanted to meet you," Marjorie said when they were introduced. "Why?" he asked.

She pulled out a newspaper clipping that mentioned how attentive he had been to a bridge party of Episcopal churchwomen. "It says here," she said, reading the clipping, 'During the evening the new hotel manager, Mr. Baskin, passed water at each of the tables'." She looked at him. "I wanted to meet somebody who could do that."

On that spark of bawdy humor, a romance slowly grew between the shy, reclusive, temperamental 37-year-old writer and the gregarious, professionally charming 32-year-old hotel man.

"After that," Baskin said, "I would go out with the group. Marjorie would come over to the hotel in Ocala and leave her car and we'd go out, but always as a group. After months of that, Marjorie said to me one time, 'You know, we have a lot of fun together'. I said yes. 'But I think there is a much more decent man behind that damned hotel facade that you've got, and I don't think I'm ever going to meet him as long as we go with this group because you're always going to be putting on this show'. I said, 'Well I don't know about him, but come on'. So we had a couple of dates. Then one day I ran into her friend and she said, 'Well, what do you think of my friend Marjorie Rawlings?' I said, 'Well, I was enchanted with her. What did she think of me?' The friend said, 'You really want to know? She said, "Just one of those charm boys. Throw him away".' After that, it got to where when I was with Marjorie I became a different person.

"Then she got to where she depended on me. Anybody came, she would expect me to be there and entertain and all. I told her, 'Look, you're getting me out of my element. I never will forget the first night she wanted me to come up there that Dr. Tigert [John Tigert, then president of the University of Florida] and Mrs. Tigert and Mr. Scribner [Rawlings' publisher] and Mrs. Scribner were there for dinner. It was quite cold and 24 miles up there, so I took a pint and it was colder than I thought, and I had about three [drinks] on the way. Kept talking to myself, and drinking, trying to get ready." He arrived socially loose.

"One thing I was always conscious of was the difference in our education, but it never worried Marjorie at all. She was very close to the University of Florida, and they did a lot of things for her and she was with them all the time and she insisted that I go, too. I said, 'Marjorie, I'm allergic to academe. It just gets me down. I just can't do it'. She said, 'That's ridiculous. You're smarter than any of them'.

I get up there and meet these young professors and we're getting along fine and they say, 'Norton, where did you go to school?' I've got to say, Union Springs, Alabama."

She liked that. "She said to tell them I went to Tuskegee [Institute], which was 20 miles from Union Springs. This was before anybody ever heard of Tuskegee. So I did." Years later, two friends of Baskin's were talking and one asked the other how he thought an old Alabama boy like Norton was able to get along so well with the blacks. "The other guy said, 'Well, it was probably those four years Norton spent at Tuskegee'."

None of that mattered to Rawlings. "When I was alone with her, I became a different kind of person, the kind that she thought of as down-home. I wasn't trying to impress anybody. And yet, when she'd have me up there with any and everybody including Mr. Wyeth [N. C. Wyeth, the artist] and anybody like that, if I went in there and acted the way I did with her, she'd want me to put on my act. If I didn't put on my act, she'd say, 'Tell them about so-and-so. Tell them that story'. I asked her about that and she said, 'That's fine. That's a good way to break ground, but when you're only with me you just stick on like you are'."

One academic he enjoyed was Dr. Tigert. "He and I became good friends. He used to come to Cross Creek, and he and I'd get drunk but we'd have a good time. Even when I moved over to Castle Warden, on Sundays they would come over. He didn't frighten me because he was no more academe than I was. He was a wonderful president and administrator, but he was not the pedagogue type.

"Mrs. Tigert was one of the most wonderful ladies I've ever seen. She sat straight up and her back never touched. Marjorie said he [Dr. Tigert] would go around making messes and she would come along behind him sweeping up. We were in my hotel having drinks and telling stories and I said something to 'Mrs. Tigert'. He said, 'Hell, call her Edith. Why are you calling her Mrs. Tigert?' Before I could say anything, Mrs. Tigert said, 'If you don't mind, I shall say who calls me Edith'. I said, 'Mrs. Tigert, it would never occur to me. I wouldn't do it a-tall.' Then she turned to me and said, '*You* may call me Babe'.

"Once we were at a party at the Tigert house. Supposed to be no alcohol. Mrs. Tigert had invited somebody special, and all of us were standing around waiting for him. John Erskine was there. Tigert came around and said it looked like it was going to be a long time. 'You go back there in the kitchen and look up on the shelf behind the grits and you'll find a pint bottle. Help yourself,' he told me.

"So I excused myself and went back to the kitchen. I came back and everybody was all right. In a few minutes I excused myself and went back to the kitchen and came back again. Generally I sat around and spoke when I was spoken to, but there comes a time when you don't wait to be spoken to, so I went over near John Erskine and asked him about his books. He had written four, and one of 'em was about Eve and one of 'em was about Cleopatra—historical things like that, but very light. We got to talking, and he said it was nice of me to remember his books and then he said, 'Where have you been going?' I told him there was a bottle back in the kitchen and he said, 'Lead me to it'. So we went back there and had a good one, and he and I got along fine.

"After lunch, Marjorie wanted to know what I was talking to Erskine about. I told her we were talking about his novels. She said, 'He's not a novelist. He's a musicologist'. I told her that Erskine had written four books and if she didn't believe me to go ask him. She was a little put out. 'Well,' she said, 'why in the hell didn't you tell me?'"

After *Gone with the Wind* came out, Margaret Mitchell, the author, invited Rawlings and Baskin to the Atlanta premiere of the movie as her guests. "We had a wonderful time," Baskin said. "Marjorie was not yet well known then, and we could enjoy ourselves and nobody bothered us. We went in a parade of cars—open convertibles—over to the Georgian Terrace Hotel for a party. I had spent a number of years in Atlanta as a hotel man, remember.

"The hotel was jammed but there was an aisle opened for people to get out of their cars and go in, and people were taking their pictures and all. When Marjorie and I started in, it was all quiet, and all of a sudden one of my friends—I'm sure it was one of my taxi-driver friends, that was the kind of friends I had—all of a sudden I heard this man shout out, 'I'm a sonofabitch, it's Norton Baskin'. Marjorie turned to me, 'A friend of yours?'" Baskin rode with it. "One of the very best," he said.

*　　*　　*

Rawlings was a native of Washington, D.C., who grew up with a dislike for cities, a Phi Beta Kappa graduate of the University of Wisconsin, a newspaperwoman in Rochester, New York, who gave it up to write fiction. Baskin was a Cracker from Union Springs, Alabama, who loved bright lights, a graduate of Bullock County High School, an avid reader, a hotel man since the age of 17, polished by experiences in Atlanta and Palm Beach.

"The thing was, I was two people," he said. "I went to work in a hotel when I was 17. Three years later, Mr. Dinkler of the Dinkler Hotel chain called me in and said, 'You've got promise in this but you need some training'." Baskin went to a six-week seminar conducted by Dinkler. "He said I knew how to win friends and influence people. This was before that book was written. He said you're in this business and it must be because you like people, but the key to success is to make people like *you*. It's not enough for you to like people. They have to like you.

"Anytime I stepped off the elevator coming to work I put on this personality. So outgoing. Mr. Dinkler gave me a job at the Ansley Hotel in Atlanta as a greeter. I wasn't a desk clerk. I had a desk in the lobby. Anybody that came in, I would greet them. I entertained the wife, or anyone else that was waiting, and made plans. I mean, I was a glorified concierge. I went along with that and finally got into managing hotels.

"I really was two people. The first thing he taught was to forget about the man. Don't try to sell yourself. Find out about him and then get to talking about his interests. Read all the time. This is what got me started with books. Mother started me. By the time I was 12 I had been through Dickens and everything else. All my life I was like this. But he put me on to that again and I read technical books and everything else. You did it so you could talk. You had this surface knowledge of anything.

"After that I went to work in more or less the resort places—in

Palm Beach and Lake Worth. They were always hotels not so commercial. A lot of times people lived there and they would stay for weeks at a time. I'm not kidding you—when I came downstairs in the morning, when I stepped off that elevator, I might have had the worst hangover in the world, but I put on this hotel facade and got out there. That was the way I made my living."

Even for the hotel man, though, the relationship with Rawlings was not always smooth. He described it as stormy. "Well, let me tell you," he said. "Anything around Marjorie was stormy. We did have a rather stormy relationship before we were married. But when we got married she said you've been through enough, you *know* how I am. You've got to sign something that says no matter what happens, you're not going to get out of this. You're going to stand it, to take it.

"We were so different temperamentally. She was almost a recluse. I had this hotel personality that I could put on like a facade. She showed all her feelings. Alone, she wanted me to be the Cracker I was. But at parties, she liked to show off my hotel personality.

"She didn't care for cocktail parties at all, not these big things. She liked groups of six or seven people. Marjorie was terribly shy. We'd go to one and she'd always say, 'Don't you leave me now,' and she'd hold my hand—until we'd had one drink [usually bourbon], and then, nine times out of ten, she'd open up. She had a drinking problem, but she wasn't an alcoholic. She'd look around and spot someone and say, 'Who is that little sonofabitch?'"

The courtship lasted eight years (they married October 27, 1941), a period during which she became increasingly dependent on Baskin and that produced her greatest successes as a writer.

"Marjorie needed me to stand between her and people," Baskin said. "She was not a good judge of people. She'd get mixed up with them and misunderstand them and all of a sudden ask me, 'Please get me out of this'. So I was protective of her, but she was even more protective of me. If anybody called me 'Mr. Rawlings' around her, she'd be furious."

After *Cross Creek* came out and the Cason lawsuit resulted, Rawlings experienced some emotional depression. "This was during the trial and right before," Baskin said. "Marjorie got into this because she thought all the people at the Creek were against her. It wasn't true, but at one point she said, 'I'm going to leave the Creek. I can't stay here with these people feeling like this'. For instance, Zelma went around telling all these people that she was suing, and she said, 'Now if you are upset, all you've got to do is testify for me, and when I collect, you put in a suit and they will pay you automatically'. Not a one of them fell for it. All of them came and testified for Marjorie. And after she saw how they really felt, you couldn't have driven her away.

"Marjorie couldn't write anywhere else, at least for the first draft. I fixed the house over at Crescent Beach, where I thought she could work. She wrote one short story over there. She could rewrite and correct galley proofs there, but she couldn't do the first draft." He described her as torn between love and wanting a change. "She wanted to get away from Cross Creek but she felt so close to it. Her last book was deliberately not about Florida, *The Sojourner.* I don't think she ever actually gave the locale of it.

"There were things she didn't like. One was being called a female writer. She felt she was a writer. And she didn't like the idea that she was called a regional writer. She felt she had something to say and it was just as true in any climate or country or location.

"Early on in her letters, you notice even then she wanted to get out of the cities. She mentions going to England. This was before the Peace Corps. Her idea was to do something like that, to work with people who were close to the land, not necessarily Cross Creek people."

At one point in the letters she left, Baskin said, she made a reference to *Cross Creek* and indicated that she wanted to write another, "more honest" book about Cross Creek. It was a comment that puzzled students of her work. Baskin said he did not fully understand it either but offered his best explanation. "While everything in there [*Cross Creek*] happened, Marjorie had the knack of putting an O. Henry ending to it. It was true up to a point, but she added a little, which made it wonderful. That's where I thought she might have made it more truthful," he said. "Up to the end, they're all true, but she had that beautiful way of adding that dramatic end in the O. Henry style."

Her biographer, Gordon E. Bigelow (*Frontier Eden: The Literary*

Career of Marjorie Kinnan Rawlings), once made a similar point. "Her Cross Creek was a creation of literary art, a creation of her own," he said. "Hers was a middle ground between the ideal world and the real world, touching both, creating a new kind of reality."

Baskin liked the Bigelow book. He was less enthusiastic about one by Samuel I. Bellman (*Marjorie Kinnan Rawlings*). "I got a letter from him [Bellman] saying that he was going to write this biography. I've had such letters from a lot of other people, but they've asked for permission or help or something like that. He just told me he was doing this and said, 'Would you please sit down and send me three or four thousand words of your life with Mrs. Rawlings'. I wrote him back and said, 'Well, it's very fine that you're going to do this book, but I wasn't going to sit down and do that. If I were going to do that, I'd write the damned thing myself'. I think the book [Bellman's] is no good a-tall."

Baskin was particularly vulnerable to one comment in her letters. "There's one line in there that was devastating," he said. It was written during a disagreement. "She was saying that she didn't want to have anything to do with me, and then went on to say she couldn't be sure about me because I had this—I don't know whether she said fatal, but some kind of—charm, and that nobody knew it better than I did. That killed me."

* * *

While she was writing *Golden Apples*, Baskin said she fell off a horse and broke her neck. "She had finished the first draft, and *Cosmopolitan* magazine had bought the serial rights to it. She had to finish the book wearing a [medical] collar, and she always felt like she didn't do the book justice. She felt about that book like you would feel about a crippled child."

Baskin described *Golden Apples* as the story of an English remittance man in Rawlings' scrub country. Rawlings went over to England for two-and-a-half months doing research before finishing the first draft to send to Maxwell Perkins, the renowned Scribner's editor. Perkins replied that she had a wonderful story, but that she was using the wrong viewpoint to tell it. She had been writing it as experienced by the Englishman. Perkins wanted her to write it as the Crackers saw it, and she changed it to comply with his advice.

* * *

Baskin pointed out that Rawlings' love of nature came from her father during her time living in Washington, D.C. Her father had been a lawyer in the U.S. Patent Office. "He had a farm out in Virginia and he was crazy about it," Baskin said. "Had a cottage of some kind, and some cattle, raised things. He and Marjorie would go out there every weekend practically. In the summer, she went there and stayed two or three months. Mrs. Kinnan didn't care anything about it and neither did Arthur, the boy [Marjorie's brother]. That's where Marjorie got her love of the land and most of her information about it. Her father was the one that taught her that you owe the land, the land doesn't owe you." When her father died, her mother moved to Wisconsin so she and her brother could go to the university there.

* * *

After they were married, Baskin and Rawlings moved to St. Augustine, where he had established the Castle Warden Hotel. In her letters (*Selected Letters of Marjorie Kinnan Rawlings*), she wrote of the "strange despair" that often overcame her. Baskin helped her through those times.

"The problem was not her drinking, particularly; it was physical," he said. "She had terrible problems with blood pressure. This would build up, and, finally, she would go into a tirade of some kind. But other than that it was always up and down with her. Very little of this," he noted, gesturing to indicate a straight line. "They talk about these people who lived in their own ivory tower. I told her, 'Hell, you live in an ivory dungeon. Get up there in the tower where there's some light'. But her doctor understood; he knew that contented cows don't produce books."

Baskin did not dodge the issue of Rawlings' taste for alcohol. "The stories about her drinking weren't exaggerated. She didn't do it so bad when she was working, but there were times when she definitely had a drinking problem. When she was actually working, she stuck to it pretty good. I mean, there were a few exaggerations because the ladies of Cross Creek, most of them, didn't drink. Marjorie not only did, but with the gentlemen. That caused talk."

Baskin remembered some of the marital disagreements. "The worst fights we ever had were over the fact that I wouldn't fight. She claimed a good fight would clear the air. I'd say, 'No, a good fight makes me sick at the stomach. I can't take it. Ruins my nerves. I can't do that. I'm going to walk away and the next day we can talk. I'm not going to get into a shouting match'.

"She'd say, 'Well, why won't you fight?' I'd say, 'To begin with, you're almost as big as I am and I think you could beat hell out of me and I won't stand for that. And another thing, you've got much more control over the words. I'm not going to have you beat me down and have us saying things that neither one of us will forget'. But she never forgave me for not fighting. She thought it was a necessary thing."

During World War II, Baskin, age 42, volunteered to help. He joined the American Field Service as an ambulance driver and was shipped out to India, spending a year along the India-Burma border, attached to British troops who were opposing the Japanese. "She wrote to me about three times a week," Baskin said. "Instead of a letter saying what she had for dinner and everything like that, she would write me a little vignette, a little short story or something. Whenever she wrote me anything but her letters, she always signed them Lollie Popp Twitters. That was her nom de plume."

She was being playful. "This was one of those things. What it was, she was throwing off on herself. This woman from *The Christian Science Monitor* came down and did a beautiful interview, and it was called 'Today's Woman'—a thing about Marjorie. But it was so much sweetness and light that it would kill you. Marjorie almost threw up when she read the damned thing. Stuff like 'she saw the love that jumped between these Crackers and Marjorie' and all like that." So Rawlings invented Lollie Popp Twitters and used that to make light of what was happening to her. "She had a wonderful sense of humor," said Baskin. "This is what kept us together." Lollie Popp Twitters, he said, was a takeoff on Capt. Billy Whiz Bang, a cartoonlike character of that time. One of her vignettes featured

Lollie Popp Twitters doing a bawdy interview with Today's Woman (Rawlings), including descriptions of her as a hard-drinking, big-butted woman who might shoot unexpected visitors.

*   *   *

Baskin loved his time in India. "I was fascinated with the country, the contrasts," he said. At one point the British troops he was with became cut off, surrounded by the Japanese. He was living in his ambulance. "I decided since we couldn't do anything, I'd write a short story," he said. "I went back to when I was seven years old in Union Springs. With the censorship it was hard to get messages out of there, but I managed to send the story back to Marjorie, figuring she would know what to do with it. First letter back she said, 'My God, just because it happened to you don't think it's of interest to anyone else. Besides that, one author in the family is enough. If you come down the gangplank bearing a manuscript under your arm, I'll shoot you like a rat bearing the plague'. I was sure it was professional jealousy," he said, chuckling at the memory.

After more than a year in India, Baskin became ill. He was hospitalized two months with dysentery and returned home, weighing 102 pounds, to Marjorie's care. The doctor prescribed rest and told him to stay away from the hotel. Marjorie hid the bourbon bottles from him. After five months, his weight went back up to 133 (of a normal 155).

Baskin told me what he called one of his favorite stories, about the Sunday he was allowed his first drink, a Bloody Mary, and a visitor arrived that day with a box of candy for Marjorie. "Who are you?" the visitor asked Baskin.

"I'm Norton Baskin."

"What do you do?" the visitor asked.

At this point, Marjorie butted in. "Leave him alone. He's retired to stud," she said.

The visitor looked at Baskin again. "He looks might puny for that," she said.

Baskin went on. "One time N. C. Wyeth came down here. He was going to do illustrations for *The Yearling* when it first came out. At this time, Marjorie depended on me very much. I was happy to be depended on. People like that would come to see her, stay at my hotel, and we'd all have dinner, anything they wanted to do. She'd arrange it. She asked me if I would take Wyeth out to Silver Glen Springs [in the Ocala forest and part of *The Yearling* setting] to do sketches. He had his son, Andrew, with him. The boy was about 16 or 17, I guess. Andrew stayed at Cross Creek while we went out to the springs. While he was there he did a watercolor of Cross Creek, showing the orange grove and the lake in the distance. When we came back Marjorie asked him how much he wanted for it. He wanted to sell it for $150. Neither of us had any money then, and so she passed it up." Later, after Andrew, too, became famous, it would have been valuable.

Rawlings' publisher, Scribner's, sent 1,000 of the special, numbered N. C. Wyeth frontispieces for Marjorie to sign. Then they went back to Wyeth for him to sign, too. By the time he reached the 876th illustration, he was tired, and he found Rawlings had signed it Lollie Popp Twitters. Wyeth just wrote down, 'I always thought she did'."

*   *   *

The year 1988 brought new realities to Baskin's life. Doctors gave him a pig valve for his heart, and friends began a mission to rescue the memory of Rawlings from people who do not read. Both projects had him smiling. The valve worked fine, but he felt a bit funny about it. In the Old South where he grew up, a pig's highest calling was to be spread-eagled over the glowing red coals of a hickory fire and barbecued. The new valve prompted an adjustment to that thinking.

Another new reality was the launching in the spring of the year the Marjorie Kinnan Rawlings Society, an enterprise dedicated to renewing national literary appreciation of Rawlings. The society planned to deal in the area of one of Florida's true needs—greater knowledge of its varied heritage, the assembling of appreciations that build a special sense and love of the place. It planned to encourage study of Rawlings' life and work in their full and proper dimensions. Those were bounded by her books, letters and papers, and by the recollections of those who knew her.

This was an attempt to rescue Rawlings from myth and misinformation. The message was that if you do not read her books, you cannot have any real sense of this remarkable woman. A revival in the celebration of Rawlings the woman, a feminist long before it was fashionable, had been led popularly by nonreaders, principally because of the 1983 movie *Cross Creek.*

With wonderful pictures and appealing tales put together by imagination little hindered either by the book or the facts, it made Rawlings a cult figure. Crowds visiting the old 1890s Cracker house where she lived in Cross Creek (a place open to the public as a state historic site) in one year increased from an average 15,000 per year to 40,000 per year. The increased traffic so stressed the old house that part of it had to be replaced. Visitation had to be limited. Parking became difficult, and occasionally Cross Creek experienced the horror of a traffic jam in front of the house. That was not the only jarring change, though.

The authentic Cross Creek, which had been as real as an outhouse and as human as a smile or a tear, crossed into fantasy, into the dimension of a tourists' theme park. The movie-inspired visitors envisioned it as a backwoods Camelot, sans sandspurs and snakes and hunger and any other unpleasantness, one that substituted quaint Crackers for knights.

The new fans, most of them not Rawlings readers but moviegoers, were more interested in confirming the movie's fantasies than discovering the realities. Neither the real Rawlings' words nor the real Rawlings' vision had priority. "Before the Cross Creek movies, most who visited came on a pilgrimage," wrote Sally Morrison, Florida park ranger and curator at the site, in the Rawlings Society's newsletter. "They had read Marjorie Rawlings' books and were glad for the opportunity to spend a time here. They walked quietly through the house and garden; lingered and browsed through the scrapbooks; sat quietly in the yard absorbing the tranquil setting."

After the movie, the quiet appreciation and the unhurried pace of the house tour were gone, Morrison said. The new visitors tended to be restless and impatient. They were puzzled why the realities did not match the movie: The house looked different; the lake was not in the right place. There was a tendency to be disappointed.

On the 50th publishing anniversary of *The Yearling* in 1988, old friends and later admirers of Rawlings' literary skills and truths formed the Marjorie Kinnan Rawlings Society with Baskin's blessing. The society started in the mind of Phil May, Jr., of Jacksonville, the son of Rawlings' longtime friend and lawyer. He had visited in the Rawlings home as a boy. He belonged to the Thomas Wolfe Society, which celebrated that author, a contemporary of Rawlings' who had shared with her (as well as Hemingway and Fitzgerald) the same publisher and editor. He wanted the same kind of celebration for Rawlings.

With the support of Baskin and the University of Florida English Department, the society (with May as president) held its first meeting in the spring, a three-day affair that utilized both Cross Creek and the university campus. During that meeting, one old-timer noted that now there were three Cross Creeks—the real one, the backwoods Camelot that Rawlings wrote about and the movie version.

*   *   *

So began a turn in the Rawlings revival, again with Baskin in a supporting role. The society encouraged that revival while trying to herd it back toward reality. If you liked the movie, the society suggested, you would love the books. Baskin was around for that beginning, and he was glad. "I think Marjorie would be pleased, too," he said.

Finally, with both their deaths, the story of Mr. Rawlings and Mrs. Baskin entered Florida history, if not Cracker heaven. Theirs was a union that weathered the differences. Each borrowed from the other's differing strengths and crossed into the other's sphere. Both benefited, as did we all.

The Ferryman

Eddie Babbitt, a tobacco-chewing, 45-year-old fifth-generation Floridian, grew up right there at the Georgetown boat landing across from Drayton Island, and in 1976 he was still living under the same big live oaks that had shaded his father and grandfather. In Florida, all this—plus his job running a river ferry—made him a rare Floridian, a man who knew his past and was committed to his future.

"Only time I ever left here was to go to the army," Babbitt said. "And nobody was ever so glad to get back anywhere as I was here. I don't hardly want to go anywhere now. I won't even go to town [Palatka] if I can help it."

There may be no prettier vistas on the St. Johns River than those that stretch along the tree-lined bends and bluffs of the riverbanks near Lake George. The river splits around 1,600-acre Drayton Island at the north end of the lake and flows north to Jacksonville before it curves east to the Atlantic Ocean.

From his family and from this place, Babbitt inherited most of his life. First his grandfather tended beacon lights on the river for the Coast Guard, then his father and now Babbitt himself. His father ran the Drayton Island ferry from the time Putnam County opened it in 1939, and in 1976 Babbitt was running it. His father ran a boatyard, and Eddie was repairing boats in his spare time.

"When Granddad tended those beacon lights, he had to fill 'em with kerosene every day, and he went by sail as much as he could. I only have to catch 'em when one's reported out. Might need batteries, a new flasher, or maybe lightning hit it. I been running this ferry off and on since I was 14," he said. "I can walk from here to my house in two minutes." If a horn blows at the landing, he can hear it at home.

Indians were the first residents around Drayton, and they quarrelled over the fine hunting offered on the island. Finally, a subchief named Edelano won control, and the island took his name. Then came a procession of Europeans, and finally the first of Eddie Babbitt's family moved to the area from Marion County in 1854.

French artist Jacques Le Moyne saw the island in 1565 and called it the most delightful in the world. Within a few years, the Spaniard Pedro Menéndez explored the river and lake looking for a short route to Mexico. The name changed when William Drayton, chief justice of the British colony of East Florida, was granted ownership. His heirs lost it in a dispute with England, which granted it to slave owner Zephaniah Kingsley in 1825. Kingsley built a plantation and planted orange groves. From the Kingsley heirs, it passed to John Caldwell Calhoun, son of the famed South Carolina statesman, and then to Maj. William Rembert of Georgia. After him, it was split into parcels.

There once were grand homes on the island, and a hotel that was filled with guests. Steamboats moving up and down the river from Jacksonville stopped at both the island and at Georgetown. In 1879, Ulysses S. Grant and author George M. Barbour toured Florida, and Barbour wrote the book *Florida for Tourists, Invalids and Settlers* about it. On Lake George, he took special note of the charm of Georgetown, then a trading stop. He described the beauty of the area and the good taste of the people living near the landing. They were Eddie Babbitt's family.

When the railroads began to spread over Florida and paved highways began to appear (about 1927), the steamboat business faded and so did the glory days of Drayton Island and Georgetown. Eddie's widowed mother, Mrs. Olivette Babbitt, remembered the days of the steamboats. She lived in a two-story, tin-roofed, 13-room riverfront home next to her son and his family of three children. Her three children had grown up, and she had filled the home with a collection of 200 owls sewn into pillows, painted on porcelain or sketched in colors on canvas.

She remembered when the island's old three-story Calhoun house, built with lumber brought from South Carolina, burned. She remembered riding on the Clyde Line steamboats, the *Osceola* and the *City of Jacksonville*, to Jacksonville. "In those days, everything came by boat," she said. "Even your visitors. They would come and stay at your home. There weren't that many hotels and motels then. They would spend the winter with you. We got ice from Palatka by boat. They'd bring a 300-pound cake [of ice] once or twice a week. We didn't have electricity then. That didn't come until 1940 or 1942. We used kerosene lamps, and later we had a kerosene refrigerator. It wasn't too bad. What you don't have doesn't bother you. We never felt it was a hardship. You don't ever feel that way until you've had something and then lose it."

Babbitt's ferry was a 48-foot barge pushed by an outboard, and he operated it a short while each day except Wednesday for a $2 fare each way. He was on call at any time for emergencies, which sometimes included ferrying the Georgetown Volunteer Fire Department truck to answer a call.

"Things changed around here," Babbitt said. "When I was a kid, everybody fished or raised oranges for a living. Some still do. But fishing's not as good as it was, and lots of people have come in here to retire, living in trailers. Don't blame 'em. Georgetown [estimated population then: 1,000] and around here is one of the finest areas in Florida. I was taught to be proud of where I came from, and I am."

Down at the boat landing one day, the boys from the volunteer fire department gathered around after answering a rescue call. When a stranger arrived, some of them started telling tall tales. "Tell you about them folks over on the island," said one. "There used to be some lazy ones over there. Not too smart, either. One day one of 'em couldn't catch the ferry or a boat, and he just started swimming across here. About that time, the noon whistle blew—that's dinner-quitting time, you know—and that fella just stopped swimming and drowned."

Eddie Babbitt laughed with the rest of the boys. "They're just having fun," he said. "You're lucky. When you drove up, we thought you was a politician. We was gonna run you off, tell you to get on out. We not too big on politicians."

What Eddie Babbitt and the boys were big on around there was the river. It was their life, and if you didn't like it, they'd invite you to leave it.

—*August 4, 1976*

Florida's Soul River

Rivers and lakes and springs, each of them with special appeals, give interior Florida its special character, but the Suwannee stood out as the great soul river.

In the town of Suwannee, at the mouth of Florida's great soul river, Grannie Odlund sat in the yard of the Salt Creek Baptist Church late one cold December afternoon in 1973, enjoying a last chew of snuff before the Missionary Union met. The Suwannee was Florida's soul river, and Grannie Odlund was its soul citizen.

At age 18, she had been Luella Robinson, living at James Island on the Ochlockonee River. She met and married a roving Swedish sailor named Eric A. Odlund, and in 1910 he brought her to the mouth of the Suwannee on their honeymoon. From a lumber company, they bought a 10-acre island (then called the Big Belcher) in the mouth of the river, made it their home and stayed to become Suwannee River legends.

She had come over to church from her island in a skiff. A stiff breeze whipped across the Gulf, and Grannie wrapped a scarf under her chin and around the top of her baseball cap to keep out the chill. Occasionally, she would lean over and spit a jigger of brown juice to the ground. She voiced the classic lament of oldtime Floridians. "If we'd had any judgment," she said, "we'd of bought up a whole lot of this land around here, and we could sell it now for a good price."

Eric built the first home for his bride, one room, out of scrap wood and palmetto fronds. He would catch mullet and trout, and

Luella would help him salt and pack it so they could sell it down the coast at Cedar Key. She learned to make soap, use lanterns for light and not fight nature. They ate turtles and fish and vegetables from their garden. Nine children arrived, Grannie said that afternoon, the first eight of them girls, and none of them ever left the river to stay.

When Eric died in 1941, at age 67, he was buried on the island in the shade of cedars, near two daughters who had gone before him, beneath a Georgia granite tombstone inscribed: "King of the Suwannee." For nine years after that, Grannie lived alone on the island. Eventually, the daughters and their families gathered in the area, most of them within 30 miles.

Electricity reached Odlund Island in 1953, and in the late 1960s telephone wires stretched across the water and further diminished the isolation. Grannie would rent a cottage or rooms to fishermen, usually in the fall or the spring, and would serve them old-fashioned meals at a long table covered by a red-and-white oilcloth. A place at her table became prized among visiting fishermen. Her Suwannee chicken (cooter) stew was a favorite.

Because she learned about life the hard way, Grannie lived carefully. Her thrifty habits earned a place among the river legends. In Suwannee, they told one story about a man who became irritated with her. "You're so stingy you'd walk a rotten rail to hell to skin a flea for his hide and tallow," he complained. That story drew a cackle from Grannie. She enjoyed it. Her notion, she said, was that those who save are not necessarily bound to divide with those who waste and then come to borrow.

Grannie, her friends say, was a practical woman and saved her concern for those who deserve it. "If you're born to hang, you won't drown," was the way she put it. She had one of her practical thoughts as we talked in the churchyard. "I just wonder," she said, "how much there is in it for me to tell stories. I ain't been gettin' nothing out of it so far." Deciding that there was no prospect for profit in our chat, either, her generosity typically overcame her practical nature and she kept talking. "This here fancy rig ain't for meeting strangers," she said at one point, apologizing for the way she had wrapped up. "It's just cold."

Whatever Grannie did, you could be sure she had a reason for it. Long ago, she gave up pretense as wasteful. For her, practicality made the world go round. She believed in God and nature, and wondered about almost everything else except snuff and her baseball cap. If Eric was the King of the Suwannee, by the time she joined him she had become the commonsense Queen.

*   *   *

The Suwannee River has been worthy wine for the poet and composer, as well as the practical. Its wilds and waters have been a refuge for the outdoorsman, and its jeopardy to pollution has become a soapbox for the ecologist. Writers always seemed to raise their sights a notch when they described it.

James Craig, an editorial writer for the *New York Telegram and Mail*, wrote in 1900: "The real Suwannee does not rise in any part of Georgia. It rises in the highest mountains of the human soul and is fed by the deepest springs in the human heart. . . . It does not empty into any material sea, but into the glorious ocean of unfulfilled dreams."

*   *   *

The soul river was kept mysterious in the public mind by its remoteness. No other stream in the state imparts so many echoes and nuances and flavors of the genuine Florida. Indians, pirates and steamboats once floated down it, Stephen Foster's song gave it a measure of international fame, and nature bestowed upon it a certain mystic elegance. Yet for years it remained a river whose people took pride in being called Cracker, and whose most famous product probably was catfish.

The Suwannee curls out of a south Georgia swamp and flows a 245-mile snake's path around and through the farms and small towns of north Florida into the Gulf of Mexico, without ever wetting a major population base. Three major tributaries feed it—the Alapaha, the Withlacoochee and the Santa Fe, plus the beautiful Ichetucknee that flows into the Santa Fe—as well as an estimated one-third of all the springs in Florida.

The late Archie Carr, world-renowned herpetologist from the

University of Florida, a brilliant writer, once called the seven-mile run of the Ichetucknee from its headsprings to the Santa Fe "the most beautiful landscape in the world." Its waters bubble up out of the ground and flow like melted diamonds across a sandy bottom through a natural forest. Visitors can drop a rental inner tube in any one of a dozen individual springs—the largest, Blue Hole, issues 60 million gallons of water a minute—and drift with the current for three-and-a-half hours without leaving the 2,241-acre Ichetucknee State Park. The river widens and narrows, runs deep and shallow; trees bend tunnellike over the banks; tubers float into clearings where they can see north Florida hardwoods growing tall and fierce as spikes. They might splash up a few bream, gar, pickerel, bass, otters, turtles, even alligators. Anhingas hang in the trees, spreading their wings to dry. Startled limpkins and blue and green herons might flutter up.

The springs are located between Fort White and Branford, along the route of the old Bellamy Road between St. Augustine and Tallahassee. In the 1890s, when the phosphate boom began, hard-rock phosphate was mined in the area. County prisoners broke the rocks, and tramways hauled them out. In 1961, the state paid the Loncala Phosphate Company (which came along after the days of hardrock mining) $1.8 million for the park site and the collection of springs that produces 231 million gallons of water each day. The spring run, from the source to where the park ends, is one of Florida's most beautiful natural attractions.

*   *   *

The Suwannee begins as black water in the marshes of Sapling's Prairie in the Great Okefenokee Swamp, seeps across that vast bog and flows into a pond called Billy's Lake, ringed by cypress trees that drip with Spanish moss. Out of the lake it moves southwest, taking definition as a river while escaping the wilderness. It drops 35 feet closer to sea level by the time it reaches Florida.

Then, for about 30 miles, it flattens out and wanders through a forested plain where tupelo, ash, elm, locust, maple and birch join the cypresses. White-tailed deer and wild turkey, and occasionally panther and black bear, roam along the banks.

As the plain ends, the Suwannee begins to move in a hurry. The channel deepens and the river flows between high limestone banks and across frequent shoals. Six miles before it reaches the first Florida town, White Springs, are the biggest rapids in Florida. It drops seven feet in a short distance, and the shoals and speed are sufficient to churn up white water. From there it meanders past White Springs, under the bridge at u.s. 41, past the high banks and cypress trees of Stephen Foster Memorial Park, and begins a long curve heading first north and then back south.

In that parenthetical path between White Springs and Ellaville, the Suwannee goes by the Sheriff's Boys Ranch and the Suwannee River State Park, and joins bodies with two major tributaries—the Alapaha and the Withlacoochee (at Suwannee River State Park near Ellaville).

The river, which came out of the Okefenokee stained dark by tannic acid from the cypress trees and decaying vegetation, begins to change color. Fed by hundreds of springs that pour half a billion gallons of fresh water into it daily, it lightens, going from black to diluted bourbon. The springs bubble out of sinkholes and underground caves (engineers say that underneath a light layer of topsoil, there is a Swiss cheese-like limestone rock structure). They are a favorite gathering spot for tube floaters, canoeists and fishermen. Though the fishing improves downstream, even near the springs and in the stillwater sloughs there are catfish and redbreast.

At Ellaville, the river changes again. The Alapaha and the Withlacoochee force it to widen, and the springs become more numerous. Shortly, it turns almost directly south for 30 miles, past Dowling Park to Luraville, and southeasterly to Branford.

Another eight miles down the river, past Branford, the last major tributary—the spring-fed Santa Fe River—merges with the Suwannee. The river widens still more and follows a leisurely pace past Old Town and Suwannee River (Fannin Springs), where u.s. 19–98 crosses. Here, 30 miles from the Gulf, there are signs of tidal action, and the Suwannee becomes broad and sluggish, with stretches of high bluffs and sandy banks. Cabbage palms appear, and the fishing improves.

After a long journey through 12 Georgia and Florida counties, from 115 feet above sea level, the Suwannee streams into the Gulf of Mexico.

Periodic spring floods, some of them serious (including 1948, 1973 and 1998) have been only a mild deterrent to development. The charm of the river is such that refugees from the cities, retirees and land investors keep coming anyway, no matter what.

* * *

Without Stephen Foster, the melancholy composer from Pennsylvania, the Suwannee might never have been appreciated at all outside Florida. His song "The Old Folks at Home" gave it a mystique that has grown with the years rather than diminished. A random search of the map and a little poetic license with syllables put the Suwannee into the song. The story is an old and familiar one.

Foster, in 1851, sought a two-syllable river to use in a song about the South. On the map, he found two—the Peedee of South Carolina and the Yazoo of Mississippi. But somehow the phrasing—"Way Down Upon the Peedee" (or "the Yazoo")—just didn't fit the mood. He searched on and found the Suwannee, but it had three syllables. Foster dropped one, calling it the "Swannee," and the river became famous as the melody became popular. In 1935 Florida adopted it as the official state song. Foster, say most reports, never even saw the Suwannee.

Steamboats ran on the Suwannee until as late as 1923, though most had departed the scene by the turn of the century. Before and just after the Civil War, they were small wood-burners that carried cotton, tobacco, peanuts, naval stores and lumber from high-masted schooners that could not get past the river's mouth. They supplied the great manor houses, staffed by slaves, along the high bluffs up the river. Their steam whistles could be heard 10 miles away, and the arrival of a boat became something of a social event.

No steamboat, however, excited imaginations more than the *Belle of the Suwannee*, built in 1889. (A small replica of her operates at the Stephen Foster Memorial.) She was 111 feet long, 24 feet wide and had a special bridal suite. During the Gay '90s, a honeymoon aboard the *Belle of the Suwannee* was an event of social importance. Dan McQueen, a mulatto and former slave, became the *Belle*'s most celebrated captain.

*　*　*

Capt. Ed Ericksen might have seemed to be an unlikely successor to the historic Suwanee steamboat captains, but in his way, he did his bit. He had been a docking pilot in New York City Harbor. Upon retirement he and his wife came to Florida, finally settling in Old Town, where the Suwannee makes a last plunge of 24 miles toward the Gulf. In 1973, when I discovered him while touring the length of the river, Ericksen had found his way back to the water.

Where once he had piloted a powerful tug and docked ships up to 800 feet long and weighing as much as 80,000 tons, he then donned a sporty yachting cap each morning and tooled up and down the Suwannee in a 24-foot pontoon boat with a 60-horsepower motor. With Mrs. Ericksen as guide, Captain Ed offered visitors' tours of the Suwannee River. It was not exactly the Cunard Line, but it made them happy.

"Can you believe Mark Twain wrote that song about the Suwannee without ever seeing it?" he asked.

What the Ericksens first lacked in expertise, they made up for with enthusiasm. They learned their stretch of the river, and its people, well. If occasionally Mark Twain got a plug that should have gone to Stephen Foster, they would make it up to Foster, and Twain, later. In many ways, the Ericksens symbolized those who retired to Florida and found the Suwannee an irresistible lure.

"They didn't tell me it would be so cold down here. You know what I mean? It's the condensation. Whattaya call it—your humidity. That's what does it," he explained. Still, the Ericksens loved it. They had become converts , new Floridians, even apprentice Southerners.

"Oh, yeah. No problem there," the captain said.

*　*　*

Once, the great tourist attractions of the Suwannee were health spas, with the one at White Springs the best known. (Another spa was at Suwannee Springs, five miles down the river.) Since the days of the Indians, mineral springs along the river had been known for their medicinal qualities. The Seminoles brought sick braves there to be cured, and later White Springs—known then as White Sulphur Springs—became the place to go to "take the waters." The springs were said to cure anything from arthritis to mental disorders to dandruff. The springs bubbled up from a rock hollow near the level of the river, site of a three-story bathhouse. The top story was at street level. Admission was 25 cents and the ladies were permitted to bathe without stockings, a daring innovation as well as an attraction for oglers.

*　*　*

Aubrey Jones owned seven acres, a general store and three homes at Suwannee Springs when I talked with him in the winter of 1974. It was a town where the latest Florida boom had barely made a pop. "I wouldn't exactly call it a town," Jones said. He was 53 years old then, and sunning himself on the store porch, trying to find a spot to stay warm on a cool day. "It's more like just a community. We got maybe 15 to 20 families around here." At least three generations of the Jones family grew up along the Suwannee River from there up to White Springs.

Jones said while he was growing up, he learned the virtues of what he calls "need more" and "must have," meaning that necessity teaches a man a lot. He told stories of when he was a boy and walked four miles through the woods to catch a bus that would carry him an additional 10 miles to a school that operated only four months a year. The rest of the time he worked and learned a variety of trades. For him, the trades were like money in the bank, giving him flexibility during hard times.

In the old days, Suwannee Springs thought it had a golden future, one to be built on a large sulfur or mineral spring a few hundred yards up the river. A health spa developed around that spring, with a rock-lined bathing area, a hotel and cottages. The waters were believed to have medicinal if not magical qualities.

"Yep," Jones said. "Folks said those springs helped 'em. They thought they were powerful stuff. Because of the way they smelled, I guess. To tell ya the truth, certain times of the year you can still smell that water several miles away, the odor of it. They'd come in here and lay around bathin' and drinkin' and everything. They got up a thing here where they'd bottle up that water and ship it up north to folks."

But the business faded away. By 1974, Suwannee Springs had become one of Florida's forgotten little places, still charming and picturesque but not as compelling to visitors as Mickey Mouse or the springlike winters of south Florida. The rocked bathing area was still standing, and some of the cottages were still there, but tourists had quit coming.

Beyond that, a few years earlier a new bridge had been built over u.s. 129 and the highway rerouted several hundred yards down the river, away from the Jones store. Cars on the highway could not see Jones's store or even his community. Now he has time to go fishing, he said.

"I been accused of fishin' all my life, but it ain't so. Every fish I've actually caught has cost me $150 or better a pound. Yessir, I love those catfish. But when you get right down to it, I can find something cheaper to eat. You count up your boats and equipment and all, pretty soon that catfish might ring up like a sirloin," he said.

* * *

For at least a century, the Suwannee has been written about and sketched and photographed and exploited, yet somehow it has persisted and endured. It has managed to retain its natural beauty, its spring-fed sweet waters and its scenic variety—the high sand bluffs and rugged limestone rock banks, the rapids and stillwater sloughs, protective trees, birds and small wildlife.

Whatever the siege and however serious the wounds it suffered—whether from the damaging impact of population growth or from natural disasters—the great soul river of Florida rolled on and somehow its capacity to fascinate never seemed to diminish.

—October 29, 1974

The Bears and the Bees

Long before the movies discovered beekeeping in the Panhandle, pioneer Floridians were battling the bears in order to raise the bees and make honey. Horace Wilson talked about it in 1975.

Horace Wilson began learning about the bears and the bees when he was a boy, and at 57 he was still learning. Almost nobody around Smith Creek (population 150), where he lived, liked bears, but even after all these years bees were still mysterious and attractive. "I started working with bees before I was big enough to lift a super of honey," Wilson said. He had three children and five grandchildren. "Bears are just mean, destructive. Bees are smart. We know they do certain things, but we don't always know why, and we don't always know what to expect."

When Wilson's family moved to Smith Creek from Defuniak Springs in 1919, it was still pretty much a frontier. At the time of my visit in 1975, it had changed little. It sat on the east side of the Apalachicola River in the middle of the Apalachicola National Forest.

The first settlers came to Smith Creek from South Carolina during the 1840s, and slaves cleared the land. After they moved on, selling part of their land to Hiram Smith, the creek and the village bore his name.

In those days, even men on horseback feared attack from panthers while on the trails through the forest. Bears explored yards and gardens for food. Bobcats stalked on the edges of clearings. Families survived by farming, turpentining and beekeeping, sometimes using the honey to make moonshine. Tugboats moved up and down the river, picking up goods and leaving supplies.

The Mt. Elon Baptist Church, which has had a regular congregation since 1854, was the principal institution, one so powerful that erring men voluntarily would confess in open church to extramarital courting rather than risk the chance that gossip might cost them their membership.

Until 1950, the nearest paved road was 15 miles away. Regular telephone lines came through in 1963, bringing instant communication with such places as Sopchoppy, 20 miles south along the Ochlockonee River, and Tallahassee, about 30 miles northeast.

For Wilson, Smith Creek and beekeeping meant both a beloved home and independence. He had to work for nobody, and the forest was a pleasant though demanding little kingdom. He owned 18 acres of land and leased beekeeping rights in the national forest. There the bees could find plenty of nectar and produce plenty of honey to fill the 55-gallon drums he sold wholesale.

The bears were his nemesis and sometimes it seemed to him that the law and nature favored them.

Wilson put the hives out in the spring and tried to protect them. He put them up on platforms and behind electrified fences, but bears still got to them. Sometimes the bears crawled out on tree limbs and dropped behind the fences. Sometimes they just crashed through the charged wires. They climbed platforms. Hives were smashed, the honey and young bees eaten.

"We used to know how to deal with 'em," Smith said, "but we can't do it anymore. Haven't killed one in 14 years. The hunters' clubs don't like us messin' with 'em. The game commission won't let us."

In the spring, the white blooms of the titi flowers and highbush gallberries produced amber-colored or bakery honey. The tupelo tree and the lowbush gallberry brought lighter colored, table-grade honey. Through the summer and into the fall, when production was less certain, the bees found nectar in the yellow pollen of saw palmettos, or in tassels of corn, blooming pea patches and flowering vines.

"The main thing I've found about bees is that I don't know much about them," Wilson said. "We don't know how they communicate, how they divide up the duties and where they get the orders from."

In hot weather, bees in a hive-body would line up on either side of the tiny entrance. "On one side, the bees'll have their heads turned in and wings flopping. On the other side, they'll have their heads turned out and wings flopping. What they're doing is fanning air through the colony to keep it cool."

Certain bees scouted for honey and others stayed in the hive. All drones were killed in the winter, so they wouldn't eat honey. Drones have no stinger. The egg from a worker's (or drone's) cell will produce a queen bee if raised in the queen's cell, and vice versa.

Wilson enjoyed citing the endless mysteries of the bee, but he did not like to talk about the bears. "They're trouble," he said. "The least we talk about 'em, the better off we'll be as beekeepers."

At Smith Creek then, where it was easy to imagine what Florida was like 1,000 years ago, learning about the bears and the bees was not a matter just for children. They were a lifetime lesson.

—October 26, 1975

Conch Minister of Music

Coffee Butler was part of the Key West scene, like the palm trees and the pelicans and the Caribbean breezes. He loved the place, and it loved him. He had the bloodlines and the Key West rhythms, and the music that flowed out of his voice and fingers made it a happier place. This recalls a memorable 1985 visit with him at his home on Olivia Street and at the saloon where he performed.

Maybe nobody custom fits Key West any better, or loves it more, than Coffee Butler. He was blooded for the place. Long before he became the Conch Republic's Minister of Music, long before anyone else much was listening, he and Key West sang to each other. Forty years ago, music took him off the streets, and with it he made himself part of the Key West scene.

Visitors who first came as youths on a fling have grown older and comfortably respectable along with him. Several generations of them, some of whom later became local citizens, have made a tradition of searching out the short, happy Coffee-man and his classic one-man saloon show. He played the piano and sang in a style that seemed a little bit of Nat King Cole, a little bit of Fats Waller and a touch of Frank Sinatra, but it came out a rich blend of Coffee.

He had seen a lot of Key West come and go, but except for a stretch in the Army and a few brief musical explorations elsewhere, Coffee stayed. A young fellow named Jimmy Buffett once filled in for him during intermissions down at Howie's Lounge on Duval Street.

For Coffee, born Lofton Ambrose Butler, the streets and sounds and smells of growing up in the comfortable, multicolored family mix of Key West was how life ought to be. His parents were born in Key West. His grandparents came over from the Out Islands in the Bahamas as young people and stayed.

Coffee never could break away for long, which made it difficult to win that popular commercial success others had. He briefly tried his luck on the road, but never felt secure about his family being anyplace but Key West. So he stuck with a civil service job that made him a part-time musician but a full-time father and grandfather.

He made it in a different way. He drove a red Cadillac almost as big as his house, had a pretty wife named Martha and filled his living room with family pictures. Home was 844 Olivia Street, one block from where he was born in 1928 and about a half dozen blocks from the house where Hemingway lived. He and No. 844 had shared depressions, births, deaths, hurricanes and lots of good times.

Across the street, barely a midnight whisper away, were the white mausoleums of the Key West cemetery where a lot of the city's history has been buried, some of it to the festive sounds of New Orleans–styled marching bands that included one or two of Coffee's uncles.

Coffee grew up in a Key West where almost everybody was poor, a condition that encouraged them to share or to commiserate with their neighbors in a family way. Nobody went without food or sympathy. He remembered how, on hot nights, the men would drink beer and smoke cigars and then sleep on their porches, where they could catch the ocean breezes.

If a Conch is a Keys native of Bahamian descent, and if the mythical Conch Republic is an island nation that has seceded (as declared in 1982), Coffee Butler by birth and devotion should be rated among the Conch royalty. He was an island man as far back as he could trace his lineage. All four of his grandparents migrated to the Keys from the Bahamas Out Islands in the 19th century, from Cat Cay, Eleuthera, Harbor Island, Green Turtle Cay.

As the Keys changed—to a place where there was a wide gap between the poor and the rich, where living costs became extraordinarily high, where the pervasive drug trade warped lifestyles, where the family mix long ago ran thin—many of the old Conchs were selling out and moving away.

Coffee himself sometimes was tempted, but not for long. "I've been to New York and I loved it," he said. "I've been to California and I loved it. But I always come back to Key West. This is my place. I'm like a captain with his ship. I'm gonna stay right here with it all the way. Maybe things are a little rough now, but they're rough all over."

Almost as if these difficult times demanded it, there were three Coffee Butlers. One was the family man who got up at five each morning to go to work. Another was the Minister of Music in a loud sport shirt who played at official functions with his calypso band, the Junkanoos. Late afternoons on the docks, they bid farewell to the cruise ships and their tourists. And, finally, there was the weekend Coffee, the saloon entertainer who donned a spiffy guayabera to entertain one more generation of Key Westers and tourists.

Coffee could sit down at a piano and transform any gin joint or classy lounge into old Key West, or even old Casablanca, depending upon your imagination. He had the look and the sound of the legendary Sam, except that he was true Key West—born, bred, tuned to the island ways and the island sounds.

When Coffee played the piano and sang, you expected a world-weary Bogey to walk in, sadly shake his head, tilt a glass back and call for "As Time Goes By." When some tourist supplied the line— "Play it again, Coffee-man"—you knew that old Key West lived.

—May 26, 1985

The Father of Ruskin

How you see Florida depends a lot on when you came here, and why. Paul Dickman arrived at age 11, fresh off a Missouri farm, and he saw a piney-woods flatland that resisted settlers. The Dickmans moved to Ruskin, Florida, with two mules, a milk cow, some Berkshire hogs, plus Paul and his twin sister. They came as pioneers.

Ruskin (area population in 1975 estimated at 17,000) straddled U.S. 41 on the east side of Tampa Bay, across the water from St. Petersburg and a 20-minute drive south of Tampa. In 1908, when the Dickmans arrived, a mule or oxcart could make the trip from Tampa in eight hours. By motorboat, it took four.

Paul grew up trying to tame the land, struggling to wrestle a living out of it. At times, the issue was in doubt. But largely because of him, Ruskin became famous for his tomatoes and for winter vegetables and developed its self-applied title as the "salad bowl of America."

Not long before my visit with him in December of 1975, the town had given Dickman a plaque and dubbed him "the father of Ruskin." Few men can look back on a life more meaningful and successful. In his lifetime, he found answers that worked, but when he looked around at Florida then, the pioneer in him fretted. People were adopting different answers.

"My whole life was spent ruining the country, according to some people," Dickman said. "And I'm damned proud of it. A bunch of nuts have got hold of this country—the ecologists, the environmentalists, the conservationists. When we came here this was flatwoods country. It was worthless until we drained it, cleared it and burned off the pine and palmetto stumps. We made it attractive for people, not just raccoons and possums and snakes."

Dickman had retired a few years earlier and turned his enterprises over to his son and three grandsons. He began to spend a lot of time on his boat. "Retirement's not so easy as people think," he said. "I keep in touch but they run the business. They handle all the details. I just bother them." He has plenty of time to think, and he has come to at least one firm conclusion: "The do-gooders are going to ruin this country."

Ruskin was named indirectly for John Ruskin, British writer and social theorist, who believed that all art is based on morality and integrity. Ruskin College, following his theories, was founded in Tennessee late in the 19th century, but then moved to Missouri and later to Illinois. Dr. George Miller, married to Dickman's aunt, was president of the college.

Looking for a more benign climate and cheap land, Miller came to this wilderness on the Gulf coast. There were no roads, bridges or railroads and only a few natives. With the help of his wife's three brothers, Dr. Miller arranged to buy 12,000 acres of land. On it was only an abandoned turpentine mill and a few rough houses.

All four families moved there in 1908. The Millers first took up residence in the old mill and began work to establish not only Ruskin College but also The Communal Good Society, an attempt at practical application of Ruskin's social theories. A. P. Dickman, Paul's father, traded his Missouri farm to help stake the Millers. Young Paul's new home went up near the Little Manatee River in wilderness Florida.

Communal lots cost $10 to $20 an acre. Dickman's boat, the *Kilcare*, brought prospects in from Tampa for 50 cents each. For every one sold, another went into the "common good" to be used or sold as necessary for public improvements. There were strict rules: no booze, no smoking, no wild behavior, whites only.

World War I broke it up. The young men went away to war, and Paul was one of the few to come back and finish work for the Ruskin diploma. In 1919 Dr. Miller died, the college burned, and the original Ruskin dream was gone.

Paul Dickman first operated a sawmill, turned to real estate during Florida's boom, got rich on paper and went broke in the bust. To save his land, he and his wife operated The Coffee Cup Restaurant and began to dabble in tomato growing on one-and-a-half acres out back. From that point, the histories of Dickman and Ruskin became one.

He made agriculture big business on the Gulf coast, pioneering growing techniques, developing new equipment and new methods, organizing cooperatives and using packaging techniques that revolutionized the business of marketing vegetables to distant cities. He went into cattle, citrus and real estate; organized the first Ruskin bank; developed Bahia Beach on the Gulf; established a hunting preserve. He had been hailed nationally for his varied achievements.

Paul Dickman made Florida a better place but complained that people no longer honored the old ethics that had made it possible. "If I came along now, I couldn't do it again," he said. "The do-gooders wouldn't let me."

The change distressed him. His golden years had developed this touch of brass and he didn't understand why. The day of the pioneer had passed and he was left with both honors and burdens.

—December 28, 1975

Logarithms and a Kleagle

Invading Turks killed the first John Atanasoff in Bulgaria when he shielded his baby son. The bullets only grazed the child's forehead. At 13, the boy fled to America, made his way through public school and then Colgate University to become an engineer, and in 1912 moved to Florida to work in the booming phosphate mines.

By that time, the family included another John Atanasoff, grandson of the original. He was a precocious eight-year-old, wide-eyed at the turbulent Florida of those days, with a head full of numbers and ideas. He lived with his family in a place called Brewster in central Florida's Polk County, a few miles south of Mulberry, the phosphate center.

At 10, young Atanasoff found pleasure in studying slide rule logarithms. At 12, he decided to be a theoretical physicist. By 18 he was committed. The pattern of life had been set. By the time I talked with him in 1974, the world was honoring him as the father of the digital computer. His name was being mentioned in the company of Edison, Bell, Marconi and Whitney.

Still, on a visit to his alma mater, the University of Florida in Gainesville, Atanasoff's most vivid memories were not of mines or theory or logarithms. They were of people, and of his boyhood home in Cracker Florida. "Florida to me then was a panoply of delightful sensations," Atanasoff said. "We lived in the Old South, and we almost never saw a damn Yankee."

Atanasoff remembered kind and wonderful people, the accent he picked up without realizing it, the old-time religions, the Ku Klux Klan, the guns and the violence of those days. "In my first 10 years, there were 20 violent deaths I had some association with," he said. "I didn't see them all, but there was a degree of immediacy. There hasn't been another 20 in all my life." Under one mulberry tree, the one that gave the town its name, Atanasoff said 15 men were hanged. "One day they looked at the mulberry tree and said it wasn't safe, and they went down and hung the fellow on the bridge," he said, smiling at the irony.

The Ku Klux Klan once got after his uncle for being too tough on whiskey runners. "He got a letter from the Klan telling him to get out of town," Atanasoff said. "My uncle went to the county seat for counsel. They told him their best advice was to get out of town. For their next best advice, they pulled out a prepared sheet of instructions. They kept one on hand."

These suggestions included: never answer the front door, buy two good guns and learn how to shoot them equally well with either hand. About that time, Atanasoff said he himself began to worry about the Klan. "I was pretty broad-minded about religion and things, and my name was Atanasoff and my father was Bulgarian, and I enjoyed things like logarithms. In those days that was reason enough to worry. They ran one lawyer out of Plant City on a rail because he was Catholic."

One evening he mentioned his concerns to his girlfriend. "Stop worrying," she said. "My father's Kleagle of the Klan. You just tell me and I'll tell him and he'll tell them. Nothing more will happen." The problem was solved.

Mulberry in 1974 was not the place Atanasoff remembered, but it was still unusual. On a visit that year, the place seemed almost surreal. Railroad cars covered with whitish dust trundled in and out of town. The sky had a faint, eerie glow. Neon signs along the highway stood ready to blink their counsel: CAUTION. FOG.

Draglines crawled up and down huge, circular piles of dirt that from the outside looked like giant anthills. Inside them were gaping holes into which a football stadium might fit easily. Mulberry was not the prettiest city in Florida, but it was the phosphate capital.

Until 1890, it had been only a sawmill site. Then came the phosphate boom, and it was transformed. In the first, frenzied rush to dig wealth out of the earth, Mulberry bloomed with saloons and dance halls and all the trappings. Men carried guns and used them. Every

Monday morning there was a coroner's inquest to tote up official recognition of the weekend murders. From an old mulberry tree, at a spot where the railroads once dumped their freight, men were lynched. Against its trunk, some were shot. Law was often home-made and creative. Some leftovers from those early days were what Atanasoff had seen as a boy.

By 1974 the mulberry tree was gone. A new one had been planted at the same spot. Some of the phosphate remained. Florida produced one-third of the world's phosphate, and most of that came out of the ground in Polk County or nearby.

Years later, Atanasoff said, while sipping bourbon in an Illinois tavern one winter night in 1938 (he was on the faculty of Iowa State College at the time, and had taken a 200-mile drive "to think"), the principles of the digital computer became clear to him. It was not patented, however, and not until the fall of 1973 did full credit come to him. At that time, he said, a federal district court ruled that he was the legitimate father of that technological breakthrough rather than two other claimants who had borrowed from his research.

For Dr. Atanasoff, who then was living in New York, it was a matter of prestige, not finances. He had sold his engineering company in 1962 to Aerojet General, accepting stock and a vice presidency in the larger corporation. He also had "about 30" other patents.

"I have been very lucky," Dr. Atanasoff said. "My mother and father got me ready. They taught me at home. At Mulberry and here at the University of Florida, teachers showed an interest in me. That's all it takes."

That, plus a girlfriend whose daddy was the Kleagle and could give him shelter from the Klan.

—April 28, 1974

Bold, Brilliant, Tragic Zora

Zora Neale Hurston dazzled New York with her literary gifts during the Roaring Twenties, but in 1960 she died broke in Fort Pierce. Her story has a mythic Florida quality now celebrated each February by the Zora Neale Hurston Festival of the Arts and Humanities in Eatonville. For many years, however, her contributions were overlooked.

She was one of Florida's forgotten daughters.

A brilliant, flamboyant, stubbornly inconsistent woman, Zora Neale Hurston wrote of the neighbors in her hometown of Eatonville as lovingly and revealingly as Marjorie Kinnan Rawlings wrote of Cross Creek.

Hurston's accomplishments, balanced against the formidable restraints of her time, sex and race, were extraordinary, but the special, even peculiar, perceptions that made her a gifted artist also made her a tragic human being.

She had been born in 1901 at all-black Eatonville, just outside of Orlando. Her wit and charm carried her from a maid's job at 14 to become, only 11 years later, one of the darlings of the Harlem Renaissance literary set in New York in the Roaring Twenties.

She wrote seven books, including an autobiography, four novels and two collections of folklore, and for nearly 30 years she contributed to such national magazines as *The Saturday Evening Post* and *American Mercury*. But when she died at 59 in Fort Pierce, she was a pauper, her personality misunderstood and her work unappreciated.

Her work ranged from Uncle Remus–style tales explaining natural phenomena to novels webbed with insights into the lives of migrant laborers. Her research on workers in Florida's bean fields, turpentine camps and phosphate mines remains standard reference for other writers.

Hurston built her writing around Eatonville. She evoked a rich, distinct language and culture, and her work, like Rawlings', remains unmatched in its chosen arena. Her characters had dignity and complexity, though sometimes the words sounded strange and were often misunderstood.

She paid a high price for seeing things differently and living differently at a time when blacks—and white liberals—argued that oppressive conditions could not be changed without a lockstep challenge. She rebelled against that, and her rebellion made her an outcast. She spiraled downward almost as fast as she had risen.

Critics accused her of ignoring the serious side of black life in the United States, being entertaining and naive, and even commercially exploiting black culture. She replied that her life was not tragic, her feelings were not hurt and she was too busy contending with the world to weep about injustices. She said simply that she was puzzled that anyone would want to deny themselves the pleasure of her company.

Her literary career did not begin until 1924. Twelve years earlier her mother had died, and Hurston was passed from relative to relative until she became a housemaid. After several such jobs, she joined a traveling actors' troupe, which took her to Baltimore. She completed high school there, and friends helped her to attend Howard University in Washington, D.C., where she supported herself as a manicurist and became popular with politicians and journalists.

In 1924 and 1925 her short stories caught the attention of novelist Fannie Hurst, who hired Hurston as a secretary and arranged a scholarship for her at Barnard College. She was its first black graduate.

At Barnard she became the protégée of the renowned anthropologist Dr. Franz Boas (she called him "Papa Franz," and he joked that she was one of his "mistakes"), who steered her toward a serious study of Afro-American folklore. With Dr. Boas' help, she won two Guggenheim fellowships and one Rosenwald grant to pursue her studies in Florida and the Caribbean.

In her early days, especially, there was no one like her.

Who else, in the 1920s, would have had the temerity to prowl the streets of Harlem and carry a set of calipers to measure heads for an anthropological study?

Who else would have written Sir Winston Churchill and made a chapter-by-chapter commentary in a book about the biblical King Herod, whom she regarded as a misunderstood hero?

Who else would regularly enrage blacks by playfully calling them "Negrotarians" if they were civic-minded and "Niggerati" if they were writers?

In 1927 she married, but separated from her husband after a few months and divorced in 1931. The Depression sapped her flow of academic money and, in 1932, she turned to serious writing and began her best work.

After she wrote a short story for *Story* magazine, one of its editors helped her reach an agreement with the New York publishing firm of J. P. Lippincott to write a novel. She moved to Sanford, Florida, rented a house for $1.50 a week and finished the book *Jonah's Gourd Vine* in three months. She had to borrow $2 for postage to mail the manuscript.

Carl Sandburg called it "a bold and beautiful" book. It was the story of a minister who could not resist dabbling in the sins of the flesh. It also included an argument between two characters over whether blacks can faint.

In dialect, phonetically spelled, one predicted that blacks one day would faint just as white people did. This was another of Hurston's put-ons, her way of poking fun at the idea that blacks did not function as whites, but some black critics found the passage demeaning on the grounds that it denied that slaves ever fainted from hunger or exhaustion. Such was the burden of her time; few could laugh as she did.

A year later, Lippincott published her studies of Southern folklore, *Of Mules and Men*, with an introduction by Dr. Boas. It included explanations of "hoodoo," conjuring and even root-doctors' medicine for such ailments as gonorrhea and syphilis.

She spent 1933 to 1934 as an instructor at Bethune-Cookman College in Daytona Beach. From 1938 to 1939, she was among those who worked on the WPA (Works Progress Administration) Florida project, producing a state guidebook still unequalled for depth and detail. From 1942 to 1945, she lived on a houseboat at Daytona Beach and, with Dorothy Waring, wrote a stage comedy, *Polk County*, dealing with life in lumber and turpentine camps. (The play was never published.)

But the late 1930s were her best years. In 1937, during an intense seven weeks in Haiti, she wrote what has been called her finest novel, *Their Eyes Were Watching God*. It is a love story, with autobiographical touches, that begins with a flashback in Eatonville and carries the principal characters to the migrant worker camps around Belle Glade. A great hurricane hits, and tragedy follows.

In this book, her rarely noticed feminism surfaces. Hurston wrote that the white man passed his burdens on to the black man, who put them on his woman. She described the black woman as the mule of the world.

Her autobiography, *Dust Tracks on a Road* (Lippincott, 1942), was written in California, where she was briefly employed by Paramount Pictures as a screenwriter. Her last book, *Seraph on the Suwannee*, published by Scribner's in 1948, was her only novel whose central characters were white. It was dedicated to Rawlings and to Mrs. Spessard L. Holland, whose husband was a U.S. senator from Florida.

That same year, Hurston was indicted on a morals charge. All evidence indicated that it was false, but she was hurt irreparably by the scandal. The white press in general gave little coverage to the incident but the black press, in Hurston's view, sensationalized it.

The heart seemed to go out of her. She gave up the black folklore themes that had given her work its greatest significance. She lost faith that others would recognize and appreciate, as she did, the values that resided in the simple lives of her Eatonville characters. She noted that the damage to her had been done not in the South but in the North.

For two years, she virtually dropped out of sight. Then she appeared again—working for Mrs. Kenneth Burritt on Rivo Alto Island (Miami Beach) as a maid. Burritt said Hurston told her that she had sold her houseboat to finance a year-long folk expedition to

Honduras, that she had been back only a few months and that she wanted to return.

Burritt, who still lived on the island in 1976, remembered Hurston fondly. "She was down on her luck," Burritt said. "She had been planning another trip, using her own money, to study more about voodoo. As best I can remember, two white men had conned Zora into letting them handle her money, pay all the bills and arrange everything. They lost it at the racetrack."

Hurston supported George Smathers in his attempt to unseat liberal U.S. senator Claude Pepper (D., Fla.) in the Democratic primary in May 1950, and Burritt remembered that Hurston, after canvassing in Miami's black districts, laughed and said, "Oh, Mrs. Burritt, I done promised all them colored men I'd sleep with 'em if they'd just vote for George Smathers. They over there now waiting for me to come back."

Later, however, Hurston told Burritt she really hadn't done that. "I don't dare," Hurston said. "Just ain't no way for a prominent lady like me to have a private diddle. Those men would be goin' all around braggin' about it the next day."

Smathers won the statewide primary but lost the local black vote by a wide margin. The following October, an article by Hurston alleging that black votes were bought for $2 each in Miami was published in *American Legion* magazine. Blacks nationwide expressed outrage at the charges, and Bill Baggs, the *Miami News* editor, interpreting the article as critical of Pepper, labeled it "a slander against the community." Hurston ignored it all.

But Hurston was unable to ignore her other problems. She had nearly always been broke, because of her own improvidence and because she had the misfortune of having been most prolific during the Depression. Her books were successful but not best-sellers.

Her papers, collected in the Rare Books Department at the University of Florida, indicate that she tried again to sell her fiction but could not. She sold a few more magazine articles, but they increasingly dwelled on her alienation from her race.

In 1951 her article endorsing Sen. Robert Taft, who would battle Gen. Dwight D. Eisenhower in 1952 for the Republican presidential nomination, appeared in *The Saturday Evening Post*. She predicted that Taft would carry the Negro vote; later, she tried unsuccessfully to get a job with the Taft campaign.

She wrote a letter to the editor of the *Orlando Sentinel* to criticize the 1954 U.S. Supreme Court decision calling for public school desegregation. Hurston called the ruling an insult, especially to black teachers. "The whole matter revolves around the self-respect of my people," she wrote. "How much satisfaction can I get from a court order for somebody to associate with me who does not wish me to be near them?"

She had difficulty finding and holding jobs. She was fired as technical librarian at Patrick Air Force Base near Cocoa, then worked briefly as editor of the *Chronicle* in Fort Pierce, a newspaper tailored for black readers. She left to be a substitute English teacher at Fort Pierce's Lincoln Park Academy, a black institution. That job, too, lasted a short time; she left in a dispute over whether she had to have state certification to be a teacher. She complained to the Florida State Department of Education that the requirement was an excuse to get rid of her.

"My name as an author is too big to be tolerated," she wrote, "lest it gather to itself the 'glory' of the school here. . . . But perhaps it is natural. The mediocre have no importance except through appointment. They feel invaded and defeated by the presence of creative folk among them."

Those for whom and with whom she worked remember her with respect. "Whatever she wrote, that's what she thought," said C. E. Bolen, who established the *Chronicle* and hired Hurston. "She could cuss you out in a nice way, and you never would know what she was talking about. She was something with those words, I'm telling you."

But he also noticed what he regarded as her loss of pride. "Everybody appreciated her, but Zora looked like she came from a trashpile, really," he said. "She was a good-looking, handsome woman but she paid little attention to how she dressed."

Mrs. Margaret Paige, an administrative assistant at Lincoln Park when Hurston taught there, said, "I liked her. Everybody did. She lived a different life than a lot of people, so far as personal pride is concerned. She just didn't seem to care about things the way the rest of us did—about a comfortable place to live, nice clothes, that kind of thing. She was just different," Paige said.

Hurston's closest friend in Fort Pierce probably was Marjorie Silver Alder, whose husband was a *Miami Herald* correspondent there. A freelance writer then, Alder was asked by an unemployment office representative to help "a black woman in town who needed a friend, a remarkable person who had written books."

"Zora and another woman came across town to see me," Alder recalled. "I knew immediately which was her. She had a real presence; there was instant compatibility. She was different, but she was proud. I asked her to come to dinner, and we had a congenial group. Zora was an entertainer, a good storyteller. She became one of the regulars.

"She had enormous feet, and could slap them down for comedy effect. She would do a kind of Uncle Tom act. Nothing bothered her. She had a depth of perception second to none. She liked to 'put on' people."

By 1958 the end was nearing. Friends, black and white, found Hurston a rent-free house near Lincoln Park and furnished it with items from their own homes. On a trip to New York, Alder tried to interest publishers in Hurston's book on King Herod.

"They gave excuses," she remembered, "but I knew. I had read the first three chapters, and Zora was just not Zora. The writing was muddled and unclear. When I came back from New York, Zora was feeling grim. She didn't want to go on welfare. She was too proud. She didn't want to do anything but research that book and sit out in the yard and tell stories to the neighborhood children."

Early in 1959, Hurston had a stroke. Finally, she was forced to go to a welfare home, where friends brought her books and magazines to read. On January 28, 1960, she died in Fort Pierce Memorial Hospital of another stroke.

The funeral was delayed while Paige, Alder and others raised money to pay for it. On February 7, 1960, Hurston was buried in an unmarked grave at the Garden of Heavenly Rest Cemetery. Lincoln Park students gave a short memorial program, and faculty members were pallbearers. In 1975 a marker was erected hailing her as "a genius of the South." It was the only stone standing in the weed-overgrown field near her last home.

Few knew Hurston well. She was an extravagant and sometimes illogical wanderer who shed charm wherever she went but took no root. Perhaps the best assessment of Hurston is to be found in words that she wrote. She could have been explaining the unusual paths of her own life as she had the character Janie describe love in the closing passages of *Their Eyes Were Watching God.* Janie said love was a fluid thing, like the sea, taking the shape of whatever it embraced, something made different with each encounter.

—*August 22, 1976*

Bending and Winning

Virgil Hawkins applied for admission to the University of Florida law school in 1949, the first black ever to do so. He was denied, and so began a crusade for admission to the Florida bar that achieved success only after his death. The University of Florida has commemorated that historic quest with a bronze plaque posted outside Bryan Hall, former site of the law school. In 1977, then still in the midst of the tortured journey, Hawkins talked about his unusual view of it.

In his 70 years, Virgil D. Hawkins learned something about the ways to fight and to survive and sometimes to succeed, but he wondered whether he could explain those hard lessons to the young. "The young ones," he said, shaking his head. "They think if you've got gray hair, you're a head-bower—that you went along with everything. You weren't violent, they say. They think they know everything.

"My daddy showed me how the pines and the oaks were the first to get blown down in the hurricanes, but the palms had a chance because they bent with the winds. The young don't understand that. They have the idea of throwing bricks and retaliation and things of that type. They think that when you're born, you're born in a posture of instant success. Don't have to do anything, don't have to try anything, don't have to suffer anything. They think they can get on a show and answer a few questions and win a million dollars. They think they can touch the right fellow and get a job. They don't care anything about being fit for the job. Being prepared for it don't make any difference. Just want the job.

"Black youth has too far to go. He is behind, way behind. He don't have time for pointing fingers and that stuff. When O. J. Simpson gets the football, he don't stop to find fault with the men trying to tackle him. He just outruns 'em.

"All the things they said and did to me in my day, if I paid attention to them, if I stopped to hate, I never would have done anything." Hawkins, a stocky, gray-haired man who wore gold-rimmed glasses, then worked in a second-story office above a shoe store in Eustis. He was director of the Lake County Community Action Agency in central Florida.

Not many could speak so bluntly and expect to retain stature in their community. Hawkins could, because he had been through the fire, even though it was the fire of another time and he did it his own way.

He had contended before the Florida Supreme Court that in effect the state had barred him from being a practicing attorney for purely racial reasons. He argued that same court in the late 1950s had refused to admit him to the University of Florida law school, even though the U.S. Supreme Court had ordered that it be done promptly. The Florida court had argued at the time that to desegregate the University of Florida would cause "great public mischief."

Hawkins finally won agreement that he would be admitted to the Florida bar within a year provided that he served a six-month internship before taking cases. At the time we talked, he was working that out. Nights and Saturdays, after he finished work at the agency, he interned in a Leesburg law office.

All that was an old and long story, but an important one. The manner and length of Hawkins' struggle to practice law was one of the things that made him special, but also a reason many of the young did not understand him.

He was born in Okahumpka, a small town southwest of Eustis in north-central Florida. It was then a kaolin mining town. He was the son of a laborer who preached each Sunday in the African Methodist Episcopal Church. He had seven brothers and sisters. He attended the first six grades in an all-black elementary school where one teacher in one room taught 60 children of all grades.

"It was tough in those days. Most counties in Florida were tough then," he said. "Blacks didn't have much chance. It was generally conceded you didn't do certain things, like go to town at night. There were separate restrooms, separate waiting rooms, separate fountains. Everything was separate.

"A black man was not thought of as an individual, unless he had a particular white friend. Then they might say, 'Old Virgil, he's all right. We'll do this for him'. A black man had no rights, no rights whatsoever. He just bowed and took whatever the white man gave him. He could be satisfied or be shot."

After the sixth grade, he went to Edward Waters College in Jacksonville, where he cut and split and stacked furnace firewood to pay his way. "A black man paid as much to go to high school as the white man did to go to college. We had to go away somewhere." Only one of his brothers and sisters made it as far as Edward Waters College with him.

Briefly, he attended Lincoln University in Chester, Pennsylvania, and then came back to Bethune-Cookman College in Daytona Beach, where he worked and went to school part-time until he got a bachelor's degree.

In 1949, married, 42 years old and living in Ocala, he applied for admission to the University of Florida law school. He got a letter from the Board of Control (now the Board of Regents), saying the law forebade his enrollment.

A legal battle kept Hawkins in the courts (three times in the U.S. Supreme Court) for nine years. At the time he applied for admission, University of Florida law graduates automatically were admitted to the bar when they received their diplomas. Later, that diploma privilege was eliminated.

In 1958 a federal district court ruled that the University of Florida had to admit Hawkins. Then he changed his mind and decided not to go. "I wanted to, but I couldn't do it," he said. "I knew they were settin' for me, ready for me. I would have been the whipping boy. I didn't want to do that anymore." But because of the fight he had waged, blacks were admitted to the law school from then on.

Hawkins, then 52, instead enrolled at Boston University, where he earned a master's degree in public relations, and then at the New England School of Law, where he finally got the law degree. He took and passed the bar examination and was eligible to practice in Massachusetts.

"But I didn't like the North," he said. "I never did like the North. I never could understand anybody volunteering to live there. I could understand it if you were sent there as a punishment, like a sentence, but not volunteering."

He found the difference in Southern racism and Northern racism to be one of subtlety. "There was just as much but they wouldn't show it openly," he said. "I didn't like that. I never knew where I was. In the South, you always knew. It's just like walking on a carpet with a snake in it. I'd rather see the snake out here so I can hit him than to have him hiding in the carpet and I don't know when he's going to bite me.

"You know, that's why we've been able to break down a lot of this feeling in the South quicker. When a thing's out in the open, you can hit it. Be a long time before we get everything straightened out in the North."

Hawkins returned to Leesburg and went to work. "I wanted to make some money. It'd been a long time. I owed it to my wife. I got a job. I thought I'd get around to that bar exam later."

But Hawkins never took the Florida bar exam. His own explanation is that he got involved in making a living and kept putting it off, and that he found it hard after all the years to buckle down again to studying. Maybe he feared that "the politicians" were still waiting for him, or that he might fail it. He didn't make it clear.

Whatever the reason, he petitioned the courts for permission to practice law on grounds that had he been admitted to law school in 1949; upon graduation his membership in the bar would have been automatic. That year, 1977, he was looking forward to July and the promise of being a full-fledged attorney. (Note: The bar, however, found cause to suspend Hawkins before he qualified. Not until after his death, on February 11, 1988, did he reach his goal. The bar then admitted him posthumously.)

Hawkins declared himself to be a happy man, not bitter. He thought bitterness was a distraction from the goal—"We've got to put on the whole armor of citizenship"—and a waste of effort. He kept looking for a way to make the young realize that in other times and other circumstances there could be something heroic even in the heritage from "Uncle Tom" and the "Handkerchief Heads."

"They were fighting but at the same time bowing and accommodating to the situation so that when the sun started shining, the black man could stand up like a palm tree. They were taking all that for their ancestry," Hawkins said. "If they could take those lashes on the back, I could take the verbal lashes. Each of us has to do the best we can in our time."

Virgil Hawkins, a patient warrior, warned of snakes in the carpet almost in the same breath that he praised Uncle Tom and the Handkerchief Heads. Some didn't understand that, but it was his way.

—April 3, 1977

The Dean of Death Row

*R. P. McLendon in his day never doubted that death could be a just pun-
ishment, and he had more personal knowledge of administering it than
anyone else. In 1978 he was concerned that the death penalty would not
be enforced.*

R. P. McLendon has retired. The lawn at his fine home in Starke has
been clipped to the perfection of a golf green. Vines cling with discipline, just so, to the carport. Nothing needs painting. All is trim,
neat, in order. He demands that it be that way.

Mr. Mac sits inside in a big living-room chair, rocking and stew-
ing. "I'm a gray-haired old bastard," he said. "And I'm pissed off.
We got all these guys over there on Death Row, and we got these
candidates for governor running around here trying to get votes,
and not a damned one of 'em's got the guts to sign a death warrant.
Just wait. They say they will, but they won't."

He ranked as an authority on capital punishment in Florida. During a lifetime spent in the prison system, working his way up at Florida State Prison in nearby Raiford from tower guard to senior
official with statewide responsibilities, he took part in 114 of the 196
legal executions (132 of the condemned were black) that Florida carried out from 1924 to 1964. There may have been no other man
alive then (1978) more personally knowledgeable about the process.

"I believe in it," he said. "I believe in it one hundred percent. It
may not be a deterrent to crime—I think it is, but we've got a bunch
of do-gooders that say no—but whenever you execute one, you

damn sure ain't bothered with him anymore. You may have to get on to something else, but that one problem's been eliminated."

Although Florida at the time had not held an execution since 1964, it was willing. There were candidates aplenty, and one execution was scheduled to take place before the end of the year. In 1972, after the U.S. Supreme Court ruled all existing death penalty statutes unconstitutional, Florida quickly passed another. It passed one test of constitutionality in 1976.

Death Row at Raiford held 115 persons. That number, higher than in any other state and more than one-fourth of all persons under sentence to die in the United States, included John Spenkelink, convicted of first-degree murder in 1973. Gov. Reubin Askew signed the death warrant, but Spenkelink's scheduled execution in September 1977 was stayed by an appeal that went to the U.S. Supreme Court. The next governor faced a probability of having to sign—or refuse to sign—many death warrants.

McLendon, born on an Alabama farm, got his first job at the Raiford prison in 1933, at age 24. State Road 16 from Starke to Raiford was not yet paved. "They paved it in 1936," he said, "but management didn't want it paved even then. They liked being iso-

R. P. McLendon. Photo by the author, 1978.

lated and not bothered with all that traffic." In those days, prisoners wore striped uniforms known as "coontail stripes."

McLendon married, raised two sons and maintained his home at Raiford for 39 years. In 1971, a year before his retirement, he moved 15 miles southeast to Starke.

A rifle leaned handily against the wall just inside the back door. He had turned the garage into a photo studio (he developed his photographic skills working in the identification section of the prison) and kept busy doing commercial work, weddings and portraits. "Did a hippie wedding the other day." he said. "Got my money in advance, though."

He was a tall, friendly, talkative man with thinning hair who wore glasses and saw a world gone flabby, unable to make hard but necessary decisions, unwilling to acknowledge that crime deserves punishment. "I'm a strict law and order man," he said. "If I tell you to walk that line, by damn you better be walking it. I believe the best way to get somebody's attention is to take him to the woodpile and take a strap or a gallberry bush and give him a good tanning. That's the way my daddy did me.

"Prison's a punishment. It should be. But everybody's got away from the word *punishment* and they've gone to the word *rehabilitation*. That's a word in the dictionary, *rehabilitation*, but I have no respect, no regard for it. You've got to put fear in your prison operation. I don't mean necessarily to take a lightwood knot out and beat on a fellow. There's other physical punishment. Put him on useful work. Convicts used to maintain the highways. But you need fear. A prison runs on fear.

"Certain people just can't be rehabilitated," he continued. "They just can't. It's not there. Maybe 10 or 15 percent of the people who go to prison can be rehabilitated. People make a mistake thinking everybody can. There are professional criminals, just like there are doctor and lawyer professionals. That's how they make their living. That's all they plan to do. They got to be punished. Prison's the place."

Until 1924, executions in Florida were performed by counties. The function then shifted to Raiford, and the sheriff of the involved county went there and carried out the death order. The sheriffs did not like being publicly identified as executioners, and the legislature enacted a law in 1941 passing the chore to the state, creating the post of paid executioner (up to $300, if he was an electrician) with a guarantee of anonymity.

The first electric chair was built in the carpenter shop at the prison. The wood was cut from a white oak that grew near the New River, cured, sawed in the prison sawmill and fashioned into a chair. McLendon said it was still being used. In October 1924 the first execution was held in a storage room of the prison's hospital wing.

McLendon said he remembered helping to investigate one case involving prisoners in special confinement where two of them killed a third in order to be put on Death Row, where they could get off restricted diets, smoke cigarettes and obtain television privileges. "Came out at the trial," he said.

Though bizarre things sometimes happened, McLendon said the execution itself never disturbed him. "Never bothered me a bit in the world," he said. He experienced no religious conflict, no doubts. "I never saw a man go to the electric chair in my life that I thought was innocent," he explained. "You've got to remember what these fellows did to get there.

"The only thing that ever bothered me was the last visit that the family had with the condemned. Now that bothered me. Sometimes he'd be a kid and he would hang on to the screen, to the cell, and you'd have to pull him away. He'd be crying and his mama'd be crying. That was tough."

Executions then took place on Monday mornings at eight o'clock. The executioner wore a black hood and robe and drew public focus, but his role was symbolic. He was like a mayor cutting a ribbon on a new highway and then saying he had opened the highway. In reality, execution was a team job.

The governor signed the death warrant, the superintendent officiated and gave the order, an assistant supervised and a six-man Death Strap Squad went to the cell and brought out the condemned. The squad strapped his legs, arms, waist, chest and chin to the wooden chair. Sometimes the condemned came easily; sometimes he screamed and fought; sometimes he blubbered. An electrician, whose job was to guarantee the efficiency of the chair, applied an electrical pad on the right leg just above the ankle and attached the death cap with a mask that dropped over the face.

When the superintendent nodded, the electrician passed word to the hooded and robed executioner, who then performed his only duty. He pulled a switch sending 2,250 volts through the condemned. Within five minutes, a doctor pronounced death. Official witnesses, including the press, attested to the legal procedures.

McLendon always had an assignment. "I never was the executioner," he said. "No, I never did that." He served on the Death Strap Squad, or as official in charge if the superintendent and his assistant were absent, or as supervising official, or as sergeant-at-arms and information officer for the witnesses.

McLendon outlined the death-day routine. "The man eats his breakfast at six o'clock before the execution at eight. The Death Strap Squad takes him from his cell to a nearby bathroom, and they clip his hair and shave a spot on his head, and if his face needs shaving they do that. Then he's privileged to bathe. Then he puts on his civilian clothes, but no shoes. By that time it's roughly around seven," he said.

"You take him back to his cell and this is where the preacher really works on him. At eight the superintendent comes, and the doctor, and they are ready. The superintendent, a very kind fellow, says to him, 'John, are you ready?' 'Yessir,' John says. 'Can you go unassisted or do you need some help?' 'Nossir, I don't need any help,' John says.

"Of course, if he needs a hypodermic they'll give him one. If he needs a drink of booze, they'll give him a drink of booze. Because they want this person to go in as calm and as cool and as collected as he can, without creating any excitement in there. We know all these things, see."

Sometimes, one of the participants would balk. Once, a prisoner had the job of helping the electrician, and the men became friends. He got out of prison, got drunk and killed two detectives in Jacksonville, and was sent back to Raiford's Death Row. "When the electrician saw he was going to have to kill his old buddy, he quit," said McLendon. "He came over here to Starke and went into the appliance business. They damn sure executed the fellow, but his old bossman wouldn't do it."

The most famous incident occurred in 1927, before McLendon arrived. As McLendon reconstructs the story, a man named Jim Williams was to be executed. His home county sheriff begged off sick and sent two deputies. After Williams was strapped in, the chief deputy told the other deputy, "Go ahead." The fellow declined. "You the chief deputy," he said. "You do it." They argued for four or five minutes. The warden came in and said somebody had to pull the switch. Neither would do it. The warden called the governor, who ordered that Williams be put back in his cell. Three months later he was returned to county jail. An appeal to the state cabinet changed his sentence to life, and in 1936 McLendon was the officer who discharged Williams for good behavior.

A radio show, *Ripley's Believe It or Not*, called and sought McLendon's help. The show would pay Williams $1,000 for his story. McLendon found him in Louisiana and a tape-recorded version of the affair was broadcast nationally. "But I never did find out whether he got that $1,000," McLendon said.

Once, McLendon carried a father to see his son on Death Row the morning before execution. "He told the boy good-bye, and as we started to leave the boy said, 'Daddy, I've got a request.' 'What is it, Son?' 'I want you to stay and see my execution.' The man said he was not prepared for anything like that. 'Daddy. It's important to me,' the boy said. The man looked at me and said, 'Mr. Mac, is that permitted?' We arranged it. Next morning, neither the boy nor his daddy said anything. All the boy did was just give a little motion of his hand. That kind of got me."

Perhaps the most grotesque execution day involved three young men from west Florida accused of rape. One Panhandle trial had been postponed because of a possible lynch mob. With a tank escort from the military, trial finally was held in central Florida with conviction and death sentences. All three were to be executed the same morning.

"We looked out the main gate and there were 300 damn people to see these three guys go," McLendon said. "And all of them were mad. The superintendent didn't know what to do. I had a suggestion. I told him we had three men, so let's divide these people in three groups. If we took the chairs out, we could get 75 to 100 people in for each one. He said all right. We stretched a rope across 10 feet from the electric chair, and brought 'em in one group at a time.

"They'd make a big deal out of something like that now, but what we did over the years, we never turned nobody down. Now, looks like they're going to give out numbers, limit the passes to an execution. I think that is wrong.

"Anyway, things went along that day, till we got to the third one. He was a little fellow. Looked like he was about 16. After the second one, I noticed the electrician talking to the superintendent and I knew damn well something went wrong. I later found out that part of the death cap had burned up. The electrician told the superintendent, 'We're in a mess.' The superintendent said, 'Well, what in the world can we do? We got this last man and people out there waiting to see him.' The electrician said, 'I'll take care of it.' He put on leather gloves, and a brand-new pair of rubber gloves, got that little old boy in there and he stood there and held that [death] cap in place on his head while the executioner pulled the switch. The last group got to see it. So you see, anything happens."

McLendon once wanted to be a mortician. "When I was a boy back home, any number of people, elderly people, would die in the community and I'd help bathe 'em, plug 'em, shave 'em. Fix the gals as best I could, the old women. Back in those days we didn't have any embalming, so to speak. We'd go downtown and buy a casket from a general mercantile store, dress 'em up and put 'em in that. We'd usually set the casket on two straight-backed chairs while people in the community sat up with it around the clock. I don't know, I got interested in that kind of work. I just liked it."

After the 1942 law passed creating a state executioner, McLendon said there were three applicants for the job. "We decided on this elderly man in Tampa. He was a little bitty fellow. He'd always come on a bus and we'd send him out on a different bus. Sometimes we'd meet him in Gainesville, and when he got through we'd take him to a bus in Ocala. We'd just move him about like that so nobody'd know. He spent the night in some of our homes. We'd slip him into the prison in a van, and he'd work in that black robe.

"I had some doubts about that first fellow. The first execution for him was the first time we'd ever electrocuted four people in one morning. I said to myself, that old man ain't gonna stand up under this. But he went right through it. Died four, five years later.

"The second time around we got five applications for the job and one of 'em was a woman. Married but separated. Four, five kids. Had a lot of domestic troubles. Her husband was a drunk, a wife beater. She'd had a helluva time with him. We interviewed her, and I got the impression she wanted the executioner's job hoping that her husband would take a fall and come to be executed and she'd get to do the job. But we took an older man from Jacksonville. He's dead now, too. I believe the two of them executed 141 people."

From his earliest days, Mr. Mac kept records about legalized death and looked up statistics. He became such an expert that even then, six years after retirement, the state referred some questions on the subject to him.

"I always thought there'd be a good book in it," he said. "Didn't know who would write it, but looked like it was something people ought to know about." His son, James McLendon, wrote his first novel, and Lippincott published it under the title *Deathwork*. Bantam issued it in paperback.

The book was a hypnotizing, grisly account of Florida resuming capital punishment after a lapse of many years, of three men and a woman dying in Raiford's electric chair under the supervision of a tough old prison official named John McPeters. James McLendon described McPeters as a brutal, repressive, semiliterate Cracker, a man with no questions and all answers, who looked on prison rehabilitation as a joke and on every prisoner as a low form of humanity.

James dedicated *Deathwork* to his wife and to his father, "who, in his time, knew death-work as well as any prison man in America."

The book was compelling but curious in that it made an argument on an intellectual level for capital punishment, yet on emotional and human levels it amounted to a powerful indictment of it. The details provoked near nausea. *Deathwork* also portrayed the struggle within the prison between men of the old school, like McPeters, and the less resolute but more sensitive prison officials of the new school who flinched at McPeters' methods and capital punishment.

"Am I McPeters?" Mr. Mac asked. "People ask me that, but McPeters is not one person. He represents all of us, all of us old-timers. When the chips are down, it's the old-timers who do the fighting for you, not the new crowd. That's what it's all about."

"Did I like the book?" Mr. Mac could not believe the question. "Hell, yes," he said.

—*October 15, 1978*

The Happy Cemetery

Not everyone considered a cemetery a happy place, but Elmer Turner did. He had special reasons. All that was left of the place where he grew up, a community called Gaitor, was the cemetery. For him, that made it a happy, important place.

The Turners represented a significant stage in the evolution of Florida from a wilderness into an urban state. The first of them came in three covered wagons more than 100 years ago. Their little wagon train did not experience the high adventure, perhaps, that those Western pioneers knew in crossing mountains and plains and hostile Indian territories, but there was drama.

All of that seemed fresh and real one Saturday each fall when the families who had helped fill the cemetery came to renew their ties and pay homage to a time when families were tight units permanently bonded together by love and mutual interest. I joined them one fall morning in 1981.

On that day, all of them who were alive and able had come back to Gaitor, a small enclave among fenced lumber company woods not far from the Withlacoochee River in Marion County. They gathered in the morning under the oaks and tall pines and thick cedars, near a little white church, and spent the first hour identifying each other—not only by names, usually, for that was not enough. Each person was somebody's son or daughter, or brother or sister, and each was the one who had lived in a certain house, or the one who had done a certain thing long ago that then seemed to have been typical and funny.

Once the memories were renewed, the visitors cleaned up the cemetery. They pulled the weeds from graves, cut the grass, planted flowers. The work satisfied a need in them. Later, at midday, the ladies spread cloths across the tables under the trees and piled an old-fashioned king's banquet upon it, the kind of food their mamas cooked. There was a feast and a celebration of the past.

The old folk hugged and kissed and laughed. The young ones skipped about the cemetery as though it were a park, and nobody considered it disrespectful, for it was not. This cemetery was a place for being happy.

Elmer Turner, 85, who once had four brothers and five sisters, sat in a folding chair next to his little brother, Burke, only 71, and talked about the family. All the brothers were still alive, but he had only one sister, Grace Pringle, left. Seeing them again, being with them, stimulated this kinship that went beyond blood, which was thick enough. They reinforced and reassured each other.

Elmer was putting together the family history. His grandfather and father arrived in the 1870s from Tennessee, when Ocala (16 miles to the northeast, a day's wagon ride across sandy roads and watery prairies) had a population of less than 1,000. The land was open and free to homesteaders. They staked a claim, built a log house and went back to get the family.

Elmer's grandparents and their clan (including Elmer's father, newly married) piled into the covered wagons and headed south. Going down a hill at Americus, Georgia, the horses spooked and ran. Elmer's grandfather fell under the wagon wheels and was killed. They buried him in Americus, pushed on and arrived at their new home in 1878, just two years after federal troops—a hangover from the Civil War and Reconstruction—had been withdrawn from Florida.

Elmer's father farmed. He also was an exhorter, an unpaid lay preacher, at the little Methodist church. After phosphate was discovered in nearby Dunnellon in 1889, turning that little village into a boomtown, he peddled garden vegetables there.

Those were the memories. Sawmills dotted the woods, and turpentiners soon came in, but the Turners remained farmers. They moved out of the log cabin into a two-story frame house their father built. He planted a grove of Parson Brown oranges. Four years later, when the trees were heavy with their first good crop, the historic 1895 freeze ruined every tree and every orange.

When Elmer was six, while his father was away peddling collard greens to the miners for five cents a bunch, a spark from Mother Turner's woodstove caught in the shingle roof. Their house and all its belongings burned. They moved into a log barn.

Elmer completed the growing-up process early. "During hog-killing, Mama and Papa had fried out some lard. The handle on a five-gallon pot melted off and spilled hot lard on her and burned her feet and shoes. They got bad and gangrene set in. A doctor from Martel [an area village] saved her feet but she could not walk for months. Burke was three months old then," Elmer said. At 14, Elmer, the second oldest of the brothers, quit his classes at the one-room schoolhouse and did the housework, cooked, washed, filled the kerosene lamps and diapered the babies.

That was how the Turners grew up. In a day when there were no instant solutions to anything, they improvised. There were no answers except hard-earned ones. "I guess it was worth it," Elmer said, smiling at the memories. "We lived through it."

He managed to go back to school and finish the 10th grade, join the Marines, return home and become a traveling salesman, eventually working as a regional representative for Quaker Oats and making his home for many years in Coral Gables. Retired, he lived in Palmetto with his wife, Lois, a native of Cotton Plant, a Marion County village with a history somewhat like Gaitor's.

On that special day the oldest Turner brother, 91-year-old Charles, said grace before dinner. He thanked God for his family, friends and the privilege one more time of having them all gather together in a happy place.

—*November 16, 1981*

Professor Pork Chop

In the University of Florida's old Peabody Hall, where the stairs creaked and the gothic arches looked tired, a 67-year-old Prussian-like professor pursued the ragged science of politics as though it were a 100-yard dash. Dr. Manning J. Dauer, a tall, gruff-voiced man who wore thick glasses, had been associated with the university in Gainesville as a student and teacher for half a century.

His work altered the course of Florida history, and he earned the right to sit back among his books and play the role of the kind old white-haired professor. Yet he still was more inclined to spit out opinions that pierced like bullets than to put old victories on a shelf and try to preserve them.

His greatest achievement probably came when he devised the legislative reapportionment formula of 1967, which broke up Pork Chop rule, a system by which rural lawmakers representing a small minority of the state's population were able to control the legislature. The legislature had been so unrepresentative that 12.3 percent of the population had votes enough to control the senate and 14.7 percent enough to control the house.

The name Pork Chopper originated in a 1955 *Tampa Tribune* editorial charging that opponents of reapportionment—most of them rural legislators—were more interested in pork (self-interest) than principle. The editorial dubbed them "Pork Choppers," and the rural legislators became so known popularly.

"Some of them were highly skilled politicians, but they also thought that they were sort of chosen people to govern and that Florida was a frontier. It was a matter of outlook. They were not too concerned with things like environment. Filling up the marshes and the land meant development to them," Dr. Dauer said.

Old-line lobbyists, he continued, knew the legislature and where to place the grease that would influence the Pork Choppers. "For example, Gulfstream or Hialeah Race Track might take their insurance from somebody up here in one of our Panhandle counties."

Florida had been under court order in 1965 to adjust its legislative apportionment to population patterns. When the legislature failed to reform itself, the court in 1967 accepted a formula offered by Dr. Dauer. He already was an acknowledged expert. As early as 1955, his opinions had been cited by the U.S. Supreme Court. Dr. Dauer later had a hand in the 1972 reapportionment that reinforced the 1967 victory. "Reapportionment broke up a lot of those old combinations, and it brought in a lot of very able people, but many of them have dropped out now," he said.

Reviewing that work now with the eye of a critic, he pronounced that a new gang had replaced the old. "The lobbyists have regained their empire by shifting favors to the urban legislators," he said. "The lobbies which had contacts with the old Pork Choppers initially had some difficulty adjusting to the change, but they're back.

"By and large, I would say the economic interests—the lobbyists—have resumed the power they had in the early days through the Pork Choppers. It was not just campaign contributions, then or now. It was and is giving business to the firm of the legislator. That's more significant in my judgment than just campaign contributions. It used to go to the rural legislators, and now it goes to the urban districts.

"We're back to a legislature which is more influenced than it was five years ago by a number of well-organized lobby groups such as the cigarette people, the liquor people, the associated industries. Gov. [Reubin] Askew's fiscal disclosure law would help. It would let people see where the person in the legislature or the executive branch has his investments and who he does business with, but there's not any great race to implement that by funding a proper ethics commission."

Dr. Dauer gave up chairmanship of the university's political science department in 1975 but remained fully active with the title of

Distinguished Service Professor. He contributed to a book, *The Changing Politics of the South*, published by Louisiana State University and edited by W. C. Havard, in which he said that Florida had the makings of a two-party state but abortive Republican leadership (he cited former governor Claude Kirk and former U.S. senator Ed Gurney) arrested that trend.

He recently had argued against a movement toward single-member districts, through an analysis offered to the Supreme Court, on grounds that it would be of little help to minorities and would encourage legislators to cultivate their district through favors rather than issues. But perhaps he had his critical eyes fixed most on the return to power of the lobbyists, and this time there was no formula to bring down their empire. "We're back to where we were," he said. "It depends now on whether the electorate is alert."

Reapportionment brought in urban legislators who made Florida more sensitive to the issues of environment and growth; that was good for the state, but those city boys developed a taste for pork too. To Manning Dauer, it looked like the old gang had simply gone to town.

—March 20, 1977

Cracker from Cincinnati

John Pennekamp, for many years the hard-charging editorial voice of The Miami Herald, *was a converted Cracker from Cincinnati who learned to love mullet and grits. He became known as the "father of the Everglades," and a world-famous undersea coral reef park in Key Largo bears his name. His accomplishments already had made history by the time of his 50th anniversary as a Floridian, when he reviewed with me his unusual life.*

At age 14, when John Pennekamp began looking for a job, all he could find open was a spot as office boy on the *Cincinnati Post*. The pay was $4 a week. Newspapering did not impress young Pennekamp, but he tried it anyway. In a few weeks he was even less impressed. Not only did the salary vanish into lunches and carfare (a nickel each way). He didn't like the tightwad news editor, a fellow named O. O. McIntyre.

"He would see an ad for coffee at a penny discount, buy it and send me hiking 10 blocks to deliver it to his wife," Pennekamp said. Trudging down Fourth Street in Cincinnati with a can of bargain coffee under his arm, Pennekamp doubted the wisdom of a newspaper career. Once, when McIntyre asked him to work overtime, Pennekamp refused. "To hell with it," he said, and walked out. But, typically, he came back and stuck with the job.

Pennekamp was born New Year's Day 1897, in an old German community halfway up Cincinnati's Vine Street hill. His grandparents came over from Germany, and his father was a shoe salesman.

The stubbornness of McIntyre, the Scot, and Pennekamp, the German, was a match. McIntyre later moved to New York and became known as the father of the signed newspaper commentary (column).

Pennekamp in 14 years rose from office boy to news editor, McIntyre's old job. Then in 1925, he chased a dream and the lady of his choice to Miami, where be became city editor of *The Miami Herald* in September, married Irene McQuillan on New Year's Eve and began fashioning a distinct place in Florida history.

One week in August 1975 marked his 50th year at the *Herald*, a half century as an editor, daily columnist and civic pillar. History will show that he was involved in, and sometimes directly responsible for, virtually every significant development in Dade County during these years. Pennekamp grew with the *Herald* to become an important voice in Florida affairs as well, distinguishing himself for courage and independence.

He joined the *Herald* in the chaotic boom days, served through great hurricanes, the Depression and the difficult days of World War II and its aftermath. He helped found the Orange Bowl Pageant (first known as the Palm Festival) and editorialized to consolidate county health and school services and then to establish the concept of consolidated county government.

Pennekamp played a major part in the development of Florida's parks system (he was the first chairman of the state parks board), became known as the "father" of Everglades National Park, and secured the land adjoining an undersea coral reef park in the Florida Keys that now bears his name.

His angry, blunt editorials criticizing judges for permitting technicalities to thwart justice led to one of the most famous freedom-of-the-press cases ever heard by the U.S. Supreme Court.

As a conservationist, he received numerous national and state awards. He was a consultant for the U.S. Fish and Wildlife Service. He served on state commissions under five Florida governors, including those overseeing policies toward the Seminole Indians and on state prison paroles. He was a member of many local boards.

Pennekamp looked back upon it all with some wonder, as though surprised to see how impressive the accomplishments appear in total. "I just did my job," he said. "There wasn't anything special about it. I was lucky to be here and to be working for this newspaper."

If his record of civic involvement seemed at odds with a statement he once made about how an editor should conduct himself in his community, he did not see it so. "I believe an editor's independence is on the line when he is a joiner," he had said. He distinguished between being a "joiner" and being "involved." He was involved.

"An editor has to be a part of his community," he explained, "but he also must be a strong enough individual to stand apart when the time comes for criticism. It can be very difficult at times. I often found that I could be more effective if I stayed in the background. I would get things started and let somebody else take over. We needed everybody in those days, and it was easier to get help if there was a broad range of commitment."

Pennekamp never left any doubts about where he stood on issues. One Dade County politician, remembering Pennekamp in his prime, said officeholders went to see him with "hat in hand." His editorials could be excoriating, and not just for politicians.

Once, after World War II, when Miami was in the doldrums, Pennekamp became incensed because the area did not have enough telephones. He estimated it was 25,000 short. He filled the entire editorial page with a demand that went directly to the point: "Get us some telephones."

Shortly, he had a visit from the president of the American Telephone and Telegraph Co., who, as Pennekamp remembers it, was equally direct. "What the hell's this all about?" the man wanted to know.

Pennekamp then proceeded to read off the accomplishments and potential of Miami, arguing that scarcity of telephones was holding the city back. As was often the case with Pennekamp, facts and plain talk won the point. "After that, we had telephones," he said. "In those days we had to convince people that we were a big city and would be getting bigger."

Pennekamp came to Miami in 1925 for two reasons—a series of stories for the *Cincinnati Post* on Cincinnati money invested in the

Florida boom, and because the McQuillan family had moved here from Cincinnati and brought his girl, Irene, with them. Since she was going to stay, he did, too.

"There were about 100,000 people here then," Pennekamp said, "but not all of them were going to stay. Hard times were beginning.

"Florida really had three depressions, you know, not one. First there was the end of the boom, which began to decline in 1925, and then there were a couple of acts of fate in 1926, and the big depression that ran along from 1932 until 1937."

The boom was ending by the time Pennekamp arrived, but not everyone knew it. Transportation services had begun to break down. The Florida East Coast Railroad was so overloaded it put an embargo on freight, and the port of Miami was clogged.

In January, that grew worse when the 240-foot converted hotel ship, the *Prins Valdemar,* sank in the harbor, blocking it.

It has been estimated that during this period nearly 1,000 carloads of freight for Miami were sidetracked, and that some 45 million feet of lumber floated aboard ships just outside the blocked harbor. Business halted for a month.

When a hurricane hit the following September, devastating the Miami area and taking 200 lives, the second depression was under way and the third was not far behind.

During the crisis days of 1926 after the hurricane, power wires were down for 10 days. Florida Power and Light Co. ran a line from its nearest power plant to the *Herald.* "The *Herald* was important in the function of the city. There was no other way to get news out. I don't think we missed one edition," said Pennekamp. "Later, we let the *Miami News* start printing in our building until they could get power. Rival reporters would use the same desks, in shifts.

"The city was run then by people who came here with Henry Flagler. Community leaders were real patriots where Miami was concerned. The *Herald* had been a leader, but this experience after the hurricane established us."

In 1932, with the nation as well as Florida suffering from the Depression, Pennekamp got involved in the beginning of the Orange

Bowl. At the time, California's Rose Bowl was the only postseason college football game in operation.

At a party there was discussion of an old subject: How could Miami extend its winter season to keep tourists here for longer periods of time?

"George Hussey, a flamboyant Irishman from New York who was the Florida Power and Light Co.'s recreation director, said he didn't like the idea of California getting all that Rose Bowl publicity," Pennekamp said. "We thought of starting something like that here, but at first we decided not to call it a bowl. It would be the Palm Festival. Hussey said he could get Chick Meehan, a friend of his, to bring his Manhattan University team down here to play if I could get Henry L. Doherty, owner of the Miami Biltmore and Roney Plaza Hotels, to support the thing and the University of Miami as the other team."

With Pennekamp working in the background, the community got behind the idea, brought nationally known Bob Zuppke of Illinois to coach the UM team for two weeks, and the game was on. The first Palm Festival drew 2,200 spectators to local Moore Park, where UM surprised everyone by winning the game, 7–0.

The U.S. Supreme Court case was far more dramatic. On November 13, 1944, a Dade County grand jury issued a report citing breakdown in law enforcement and criticizing agencies charged with the administration of justice. It offered supporting statistics.

Eleven days earlier, however, Pennekamp already had gone into action. He editorially attacked what he felt were technicalities being used to impede justice.

On November 2, 1944, in an editorial accompanied by a cartoon, the *Herald* said: "The seeming ease and pat facility with which the criminally charged have been given technical safeguard have set people to wondering whether their courts are being subverted into refuges for lawbreakers."

Five days after that, another editorial followed, citing two examples "of why people wonder about the law's delays and obstructing technicalities."

Three days later, Pennekamp met Judge Paul D. Barns on the

street in front of the Urmey Hotel. "I'm just going to Rotary Club. Come have lunch with us," Pennekamp said Barns told him. Later that day, a deputy sheriff served a contempt citation on Pennekamp and the *Herald* signed by two judges, one of them Paul D. Barns.

At a hearing November 28, the *Herald*'s attorneys tried to remove the citation, and on December 9 their plea was denied. On December 15, the judges handed down something called "findings of fact," introducing new charges the *Herald* regarded as false.

In response the next day Pennekamp fired another blast, this time on the front page. "The judges are giving the public in their handling of this case an illustration of what we criticized," the editorial said. "In meeting their accusations fully and on time we kept the faith with our own publicly expressed opinion. Where is their decision?"

It came quickly. On December 18, a guilty judgment was handed down. The *Herald* was fined $1,000 and Pennekamp $250. The *Herald* appealed to the Florida Supreme Court and lost again.

The *Herald* then took the case to the U.S. Supreme Court and won a unanimous decision handed down June 3, 1946. Justice Frankfurter's concurring opinion noted: "A free press is not to be preferred to an independent judiciary, nor an independent judiciary to a free press. Neither has primacy over the other; both are indispensable to a free society. . . . And one of the potent means for assuring judges their independence is a free press. . . . Weak characters ought not to be judges"

In all his newspaper career, Pennekamp thought, that verdict might have been the greatest thing that ever happened to him.

The other most publicly well-known accomplishment was the founding of Everglades National Park. The suggestion had lain more or less dormant until, in 1944, Spessard L. Holland, then a U.S. senator, came to John S. Knight, the *Herald*'s editor and publisher. Knight asked Pennekamp for a report and then suggested he attempt to get the park established. "I wasn't an environmentalist," Pennekamp said. "I was just doing my job." His efforts led directly to the acquiring of 1.4 million acres of the Everglades, and when it was dedicated in 1947, he shared the platform with President Harry Truman.

Pennekamp's favorite story about acquiring the park involved a social outing, at which he won a "$2 million poker hand" from a party of Pork Chop Gang legislators at an Orange Springs, Florida, camp near the Ocala National Forest. The event entered Florida legend, and it went this way:

After a meal of fried chicken, collard greens and cornbread, nickel-and-dime poker started. Pennekamp had been asking the Florida legislature for $400,000 for the Everglades National Park Commission. That was the amount needed to start acquiring the necessary park lands.

Pennekamp had a run of good luck—"I couldn't lose," he said—and finally came to a confrontation with the chairman of the Senate Finance Committee, Bill Pearce of Palatka. Pearce laid down a good hand, muttering about Pennekamp's luck, and Pennekamp topped him with three kings.

"Just how much money do you need for that goddam park of yours?" Pearce asked. Pennekamp replied, "Two million dollars." (On impulse, he decided to ride his luck and ask for all the money.)

"Why don't you come over to the legislature and get it instead of taking it out of our pockets," Pearce suggested. To the Pork Choppers (rural legislators) of that day, such a suggestion was a contract. Pennekamp liked and understood men who knew what they wanted, for that was his way too. The park commission got the money.

The idea for John Pennekamp Coral Reef Park at Key Largo began with a biological conference in 1957, which passed a resolution calling on the U.S. Department of the Interior to save the coral reefs.

Pennekamp picked it up. With state and federal help, plus donations of land by Radford Crane of LaGorce Island and Herb Shaw of Key Largo, the nation's first underwater park was created. At its dedication in 1963, Gov. LeRoy Collins paid unusual tribute to Pennekamp, calling him "the father of our great Everglades National Park."

Collins added, "There may be those who have loved Miami and Florida more, but none have I known who has proved it through service more dedicated. We owe him—and future generations will always owe him—a great debt." Pennekamp was flabbergasted that the underwater park would be named for him, and upset that it might jeopardize the financing. "I thought it was a mistake," he said. "I thought, who the hell's Pennekamp? The legislature won't put up any money for it now."

During World War II, the military all but took over Miami. The port was closed. Miami and Miami Beach hotels were occupied for military purposes. "There was a lot of military brass here," Pennekamp remembered. "The younger guys were out fighting, and the older ones were around here running things.

"After the war, when they all moved out, everybody thought that would be the finish of Miami. We were looking for things we could do to improve the economic situation. I thought consolidating all the political agencies was a good idea, making one town of the county. We already had done some of that with health services and schools. Paul Scott, Dan Mahoney and George Whitten supported it. After several community meetings we came up with the idea of a uniform government. "The city of Miami put up $50,000 for a study by the University of Miami, and the metropolitan government charter for Dade County was written as a result of that." Dade County voters approved the charter in 1957.

Pennekamp's 50 years at the *Herald* were hectic, involved ones, and that's the way he liked it. "When I was editor," he said, "I did whatever I pleased. John S. Knight was free with his editors, and I liked that. We had disagreements frequently, but only once do I remember him changing my mind. That was back about 1946 when George Smathers was running for the U.S. House of Representatives against Pat Cannon. Pat was a friend of mine, but JSK thought Smathers would be the better man. We endorsed Smathers, but I didn't write the editorial. I assigned somebody else."

Pennekamp started at the *Herald* as city editor, became managing editor in 1937 and associate editor (directing editorial policy) and daily columnist in 1941.

His wife, Irene, had died several years earlier, and Pennekamp in 1975 worked in semiretirement, but still produced five columns a week. He had two sons, nine grandchildren, too many friends and accomplishments to count and more memories than most men ever have a chance to accumulate.

The years had left him a little grayer and a little heavier, and perhaps had softened a little that Germanic delight in being forceful and decisive.

He had traveled over all of Florida, and still enjoyed seeing the backwoods and partying outdoors. At a woodsy gathering upstate at my home near Melrose, at which his cheese-onion recipe for grits was being served with fried mullet, he was opening doors for the ladies, offering them chairs, helping them with picnic plates and making Cracker small talk as though he were born to it. "Now that," said one decidedly Southern lady, "is my idea of a Southern gentleman."

John Pennekamp, the German from Cincinnati, the scourge of politicians and the civic Lone Ranger coming unmasked, would have liked that. For 50 years, he and Florida had been a perfect fit.

—August 31, 1975

Cracker Brilliance

Harry Crews, the novelist, knew the dark side of Cracker fact and mythology. He was brilliant, productive and excessive in whatever he chose to do. When he hitched his mind to the task of writing, book after book rolled out. His 16th novel, Celebration, *was published late in 1997. Crews, the man, charmed and puzzled and sometimes alarmed. In what most consider his best book,* A Childhood, *a nonfiction work he called the biography of a place, he wrote movingly, precisely and wisely of his own life and the human condition. It was a classic.*

Talking with him, reading his work, I came to believe that Crews was tortured as only a sensitive man can be, one who had seen and felt a lot of pain. If he occasionally exploded in behavior that made the rest of us pale, it only seemed to prove that along with his giant talent, he also had fire and steel of unusual magnitude.

I first met him in 1974, when he was living in a cabin on Lake Swan, near Melrose. Over the years I talked with him several times, and several times wrote about him. He always said things that contributed to my understanding of both writing and humanity. Following are two stories I wrote about Crews, one that was published in 1974, in which he talks about writing and explains how he geared himself up to break away from the novels and write A Childhood. *His words would be instructive and useful for any writer. The other story, written in 1978, illustrates the evolving preoccupations and directions of his life.*

Working the Kinks Out

Harry Crews decided maybe he would get off the freaks for a while. Maybe it was time to try something else. He was getting a reputation as a kinky guy. In his first seven novels, a fascinating menagerie of freaks crept out of his typewriter. Inside their heads, they had some normal ideas, but they were trapped by their outsides.

There were freaks of beautiful bodies and freaks of incredibly misshaped bodies, but either way the burdens were too heavy. There were midgets and fat men and cripples mixed in with go-go dancers and sideshow entertainers and evangelists and physical culturists. They intertwined through a bizarre kind of counterpoint that produced unusual appetites and enterprising means of satisfying them.

In one book, for example, Crews' hero was a deaf mute whose legs were so useless that he tied them under the seat of his trousers. The young man lived in a gymnasium with an elderly weight lifter and two wasted boxers, and made a living with a sensational hand-balancing act. Marvin might have been the world's greatest hand-balancer. He could pirouette slowly on one finger, holding it for applause. But he was too grotesque to make the big time. Ed Sullivan could not use him because his head was too big and square, and his body was too ugly with his legs all tied up like that.

Crews called this parable *The Gypsy's Curse*, and it was a gem. Underneath the sex and hairy language, there were the anguish and pain of the freak who could live only by exploiting his freakishness. The Curse, for Marvin, was finding the perfect sexual partner in Hester, a blonde beach beauty looking for someone who would love her enough to kill her for being faithless. Even in perfection, Marvin lost. Again, a theme of unbearable cost in perfection and unbearable burden in imperfection. It was all very kinky.

"Not long ago," said Crews, "*Playboy* magazine sent word they wanted me to do something for them. The guy said they had a very kinky idea they thought I would like. Cocaine. They wanted me to write something about cocaine. I said, 'Aw, no, man. Do you know where I live? Not that. Maybe something else'."

Crews paused for a moment, making his point. "Yeah. Oh, yeah. No question about it. I got a reputation as the guy who writes the kinky stuff. Somebody pretty soon's gonna call me up, and when they do I'm gon' say, 'Yeah, but I want you to come down here and talk to me about it first,' and then I'm gon' beat the shit out of him. Somebody's gon' ask me if I won't want to go somewhere in a cover-up in a carnival of freaks, you know, and watch a guy eat a live chicken or something." He laughed.

Crews, 39 at the time [1974], looked a little like a primitive who has tried civilization and was unimpressed. He lounged about his lakeside cypress cabin (near Melrose, which is about 20 miles east of Gainesville and next door to a church camp locally famous because Billy Graham once had a religious experience there) in faded jeans and wrinkled shirt and tennis shoes without socks. Out of respect for the neighbors, he tried to keep the volume down on his parties and always asked the girls not to go skinny-dipping during daylight hours. His hair was long. He had the expressive face of an actor, and his hands leaped about in emphatic gestures. He was a remarkable man who seemed to speak several English languages, in addition to the one he wrote so beautifully. He shifted roles, going from the Georgia farm boy to the boisterous ex-Marine to the philosophical recluse to the college professor. His ex-wife and their son lived in Gainesville.

Crews taught a course in writing two nights a week at the University of Florida and helped conduct a writer's conference once a year. But he lived and worked in this cabin, which had a fireplace, a couple of beds, a kitchen and a table in the back where sat the old Underwood standard typewriter on which he had written his first seven novels, plus numerous short stories and essays. He had no telephone, either here or in his university office, and he took down the mailbox out on the road so that the postman could not possibly deliver him a distracting letter. Strangers could reach him by writing to the university. Those who knew him better always called and left a message at Chiappini's, a Melrose service station and general store, a very understanding place. "Sometimes we won't see him for two or three weeks, and then he'll pop in and collect his messages and stay on the phone for two or three hours," said Dave Chiappini. Sometimes Harry just dropped in, flipped the top off a beer and settled in for a chat with the boys who often gathered there to consider the state of the world.

Harry Crews. Photo by the author, 1974.

"One doesn't mind the fact of the matter," said Crews, getting back to the business of freaks. "It's just the harping on it. All fiction is about the same thing. It's about a man doing the best he can with what he's got to do with. That's how I feel about it.

"I have to insist when somebody starts talking to me about freaks. That's not my word. We're all freaks, but just in different ways, most of us. To dwell on this business of the freaks and to dwell on what they call the gothic novel offends me, yeah. I hadn't even heard of one until everybody told me I was writing 'em.

"Another thing, they talk about me being a Southern novelist. It's true I write in the South, and it's true that's where my sense of place is and sense of people is and sense of language is. But hell, every writer has to have that. You know, some guys are in the Midwest, some guys . . . Norman Mailer's a New York Jew, you know, and he knows about that. John Updike knows about Pennsylvania, and he's got that little town there.

"But even if those things are true, it seems to me sort of beside the point to harp on them. It doesn't demonstrate anything, it doesn't prove anything, it doesn't open anything up, illuminate anything. You know, I'm just not particularly fond of that. But I tell you, I have the feeling in me, and maybe it's just a feeling, I've had wrong feelings before, but I have the feeling that there is going to be some sort of departure in my work, that I'm going to do something else. I mean, I'm going to still write novels. Man, I started out to be a novelist. That's what I want to be. That's what I care about.

"I also like to write short stories but, unfortunately, what you gonna do with them? Yeah, you can publish them in literary magazines, which is where all mine have been published, and they've been anthologized. You can publish them. But man, it gets back to audience and the rest of it. Short stories are hard to write. Hard to write as anything else. So what've you got? If you're lucky, you've got 1,900 or 2,000 readers. Shit, man.

"What I'm trying to say is, I think either the subject matter is going to change—and I don't know what I mean by subject matter because you know I got novels about boxers and sponge fishermen divers—I guess it's not subject. I guess it's more the form of the thing. Maybe that's what's going to change. I don't know. But I just have this feeling in me. Maybe I'll do two or three books of nonfiction."

The National Endowment for the Arts, a federal project based in Washington, D.C., awarded Crews $5,000 to use professionally as he pleased. Two years earlier, the American Academy of Arts and Letters gave him a grant of $3,000. "I like those grants, man," he said, smiling. "Yeah."

Crews decided to use the money for an exploration of his own life as a boy in Bacon County in Alma, Georgia. "It will be biography of place. The focus will be me, autobiographical. It will be about those people up there and that time." It also would be his first book-length nonfiction. Whether it would be a conventional narrative, he did not know. "Something in my head resists that. But it can be nice, if it's done right."

The idea began the previous summer, when Crews spent seven weeks walking the Appalachian Trail from Georgia to Maryland, carrying along a photographer and a tape recorder, collecting information and anecdotes. "I talked to people all along. You'd be dumbfounded at the stories that I got off that trail, things that people told me and I heard and I saw. Really kinky, great things, right?" Part of that time, the description might have fit Crews himself. His hair grew down over his shoulders and he wore one golden earring.

Crews tried to splice together his experiences on the trail with memories of his boyhood in Bacon County. But later, he decided that wouldn't work. He planned to separate the two. The trail hike would be one story, and Bacon County another. He liked this better. The last couple of years, he has had this feeling that he needs to know more about himself and his beginnings. Going back to Bacon County would satisfy that urge.

"I think so. I think so," he said. He speaks rapidly, often in broken sentences, but the communication remains clear. "Yeah. For a long time I didn't know that. I grew to manhood without . . . some of the language, you know. Some of the things we said. Things like, 'He's so stingy he wouldn't give you the steam off his shit'. A beautiful line, 'the steam off his shit'. But the kids that always had bathrooms and things, they didn't . . . that must be a mystery to them when they heard it. Be out in the woods, or out on the ground, or even the outhouse. Hell, when it's freezing, it steams. You know, the ground's frozen. Very colorful, immediate, graphic, concrete language, and those people, you know . . ."

The University of Florida gave Crews an indefinite leave of absence, and he will go up to an uncle's farm in Bacon County and get reacquainted. "I want to talk to guys that knew my daddy," Crews said. "My daddy died when I was 18 months old. I never knew him. I grew up on faded photographs and, really, kind of legends. He was really a good man, but a strange man, a mean man, a lot of kinds of man. He died on the farm in the wintertime, of a heart attack. It's all kind of kinky.

"I mean, the whole family was in bed with him at the time. My mother and my brother and I were in the bed with him. Wintertime. It was cold. That's why we were in bed with him. No heat. Fireplace goes out, it's cold as a bitch.

"Ma woke up and, always before, he was in the field when she woke up, and she cooked breakfast and rang the bell. Well, this morning she woke up and he was still in the bed, his head kind of turned off to the side like this. And she figured well, he's been working hard, they just got through butchering stock and putting it in the smokehouse and stuff, so she went on in the kitchen and made breakfast. The only time he ever slept that late was on Sunday, and then she'd send in my brother—he was five—and get him to wake up Daddy. He would always wake him up by twisting his nose. A little game they had, right? So after a while my brother comes in and he said, 'Daddy won't wake up and his nose is cold.' She went back in there. He's dead.

"She's about 20; she's 16 miles from the nearest farmhouse. There's no car on the place. The only means of transportation is a mare in the lot that nobody can put a bridle on except the guy that's dead in the bed. You know, all that kind of thing. I mean, that was a weird time. That kind of back-against-the-wall shit that those people had to deal with day in and day out. I mean, they just never got free. Boy, we shelled corn and took it 15 miles in a mule and wagon to get it ground. You know?"

Although the language and the themes of his novels were not exactly what the rural folk in Georgia might find pleasant reading, Crews thought the state had treated him well. In Bacon County or over near his mother's present farm closer to Tifton, Georgia, he had celebrity status. One reason for that, he said, might be that more have heard he is a writer than have read his writing. "There's a paper up there, been there since 1887 or something, called the *Wiregrass Farmer*, a marvelous little paper. In Ashburn. You know, I publish a book and they put my picture on the fucking front page.

"My mother only went to the second grade, and they just insisted she be on the board of the little library. Ma's never read a book, except the ones I've written. Only ones she's ever read. Takes her about six months to get through one of my books, but she's one of the best readers I ever had. People find that strange. I mean, I've got a Baptist mother that's lived in the country all her life, one of those good women, and I don't mean that pejoratively, I mean that straight out, good women. She never blinks at anything I've written. She's been around the block. She knows what's in the world. Doesn't bother her. She knows a word's a word, that it's not the deed or the fact, you know. No. Ma at one time is primitive and sophisticated enough to know that it's all magic anyway, and that's the way she feels about it.

"She's dumbfounded, for instance, that anybody would pay you money to write something that wasn't true. That really amazes her. When I wrote *The Gospel Singer* [the first novel], when I finished it, I called her up and said I sold it, I got this much advance, and so on. Later on when I saw her, she said, 'Son, you didn't pass that off as the truth, did you? You didn't tell 'em that?' I told her, 'No, Ma, that's not the gig'."

Everything started for Crews in Bacon County: his love for the physical side of life, storytelling, his awareness of the perfections and imperfections of people, an annoying conscience, an insatiable curiosity, absorption with the unusual, a boiling kind of drive inside him to try new things, a battle with self-doubt, a compulsion to illuminate the whole thing. "I got started in all this long, long before I ever had any notion. . . . I was writing stories when I was just a little kid. I wrote 'em for my family and told 'em. I started telling 'em before I started writing 'em, for my friends. Mostly, with the exception of my brother, my playmates were black. You know, we were out on this farm. We used to get together and . . . I can tell you exactly how it started.

"The way it happened, it started with the Sears, Roebuck catalogue. We used to spend a lot of time looking at the thing and, among other things, here were all these perfect people. All these perfect people. Everybody we knew was damaged, had sores on their legs and their fingers cut off, but here were all these beautiful, perfect people in this book, and they were so well dressed and they were obviously human. I would make up stories to account for the things they were doing. You know, 'See this man in the red coat, well this girl here's his daughter and she's gonna marry him on this page back here and he don't like him because he don't make his money just by standing there in that red coat. He's the deputy sheriff on the side'. So, anyway, I got into that."

Crews joined the Marine Corps at 17, served four years, and enrolled at the University of Florida. Predictably, he became restless and left for 18 months, but the burden of writing ambition brought him back in 1958. Andrew Lytle was a writer-in-residence at the University of Florida, and Crews became first his student and then his disciple. "The only reason I've never dedicated a book to him is that I've never written anything I thought he'd want his name on. He's a demanding man," Crews said. The Lytle encounter was important to him.

One year of teaching junior high school English in Jacksonville, after graduation, sent Crews scrambling back to Gainesville for a master's degree. With that in hand, in 1962, he shifted to Broward Junior College in Fort Lauderdale, again to teach English. The year *The Gospel Singer* was published (1968) he returned to the University of Florida, where he remained. Since then, a new Crews novel has been published each year. The others, *Naked in Garden Hills* (which he thinks was his best), *This Don't Lead to Heaven, Car, The Hawk Is Dying, Karate Is a Thing of the Spirit* and, this year, *The Gypsy's Curse.*

"I wrote another book called *The Enthusiast*, which I really liked a lot, at least I liked it a lot while I was writing it. I suppose it came out of my life in a way. It was about a guy that just everything he got into, he made a passion of. I got into karate and I did *Karate Is a Thing of the Spirit*. I got into hawks, I trapped and trained hawks and wrote *The Hawk Is Dying*. The books are somehow always after the fact. But anyway, I wrote this book and it felt good the whole time I was writing it. But I never sent the damned thing off. Put it in a drawer. It just didn't work, finally. You know, you try to lie to yourself at first. It'll come back another time. The work is never wasted. Ten years from now, all that'll come back," he said.

Sometimes, something just works. The first time he drove to the farm near Tifton he got lost. He was working on *The Gospel Singer* then. He wandered into a town called Enigma, Georgia. "I said, 'God, that's where it happened. It's gotta be it'. But I changed a lot of things around, like the highway and the swamp. You know, I didn't want to piss off the people in the town. I got nothing against them. But I did manage to do it."

Naked in Garden Hills found its way into a phosphate excavation because Crews was driving from Vero Beach to Tampa, and wandered through Mulberry, the phosphate capital. *This Don't Lead to Heaven* came after a visit to a nursing home, during which he feigned sickness in order to leave quickly.

"I don't believe anything's ever created whole. For instance, my brother was a professional boxer for a while when he was about 18 years old. He fought out of Jacksonville. He used to train in a gymnasium that was called the Fireman's Gymnasium. It was at Bay and Catherine Streets and it was run by an old guy who was an ex-strongman in the Navy, and his name was Al. There was a kid there who had polio and was a deaf-mute and performed where he could. He had a balancing act. A great performer. That sounds like, if you've read *The Gypsy's Curse*, well hell you just ripped that off your own experience. But, no. No, no, no. The black dude was not there. The kid there from Georgia—my brother would be pissed off to hear me say it, but some of that probably was patterned after him—but there was no Hester, no murder, and it was not in Tarpon Springs and Clearwater. Not the same. No."

Despite the pace at which he drove himself and his expanding interests (he has written and sold screenplays of two of his books and sold a third to the movies with the script to be done by someone else), teaching never seemed a burden to Crews. He not only liked it but even in a way depended upon it to bring order to his life.

"No, it's not a burden. I'll tell you why. I guess the biggest reason is this: You get stuck when you're writing. Everybody knows that. You get stuck and you just don't know what to do, and it looks like the thing's gonna die on you. Maybe you've got three or four months in it. So you sit down. . . . I work every day. I don't give a shit whether I know what's coming next or not. I work. At least I sit at the typewriter. I tell myself, 'You go sit there three hours. You don't have to write anything. Just sit there'. So pretty soon you write something, just try something, and you find you a way out. But sometimes it's bad, and you know it's bad. When that happens, at least me, I get really down on myself. I begin to doubt everything. I think, 'Hell, you weren't a writer to start with. Now you've got this charade'. I just say terrible things to myself. Then voilà, I go to school.

"I like to teach, see. That's the weird thing about it. I really do. The students, they're honest, they'll run you up a tree. They won't take much phony stuff. I go in there and teach a sensational class. Just get in there and just wing and talk and get 'em excited. When I come out of the class, I think, 'Well, buddy, you might can't write, but goddam, you sure can teach'.

"I've got a sort of theory in my head about that. I think every man ought to have more than one thing he does well. He doesn't have to get his bread by it, but if he's just a good, competent, fine amateur butterfly preserver or coin collector or Sunday painter or bicycle rider or anything, so he can go out there and get his head clean.

"You see, I don't think of writing as a job. I think of it almost like an avocation. I would be writing novels if nobody was publishing them. I'd write novels if I had to send them out to sea in a bottle. I just know I would. So I really don't think of it as a job. At school, that's a job and it kind of gives direction to my life and, you know, I'm pretty bad to drink. As a matter of fact, I will stay drunk on you for a while, from time to time. All things being equal, I would rather not disappear into a bottle. It seems to me that's a cheap way to go. Having a job, having to go to the university, having students I'm responsible for, keeps me straighter than I otherwise would be. The hardest thing for me is to control my personal life so I can do the amount of work I want to do. I need to work. I have guilt feelings if I don't work, sourceless anxiety.

"So I teach, and as long as I teach, I'm gonna teach here at this school. I've been offered other jobs. But I like the weather, the people and the university. The university's just been tremendously decent to me. I'm in their debt, really. I feel an obligation, a commitment to this school."

When writing first-draft material, Crews forced himself to sit at the typewriter three hours a day. Three hours at that stage exhausted him. Later, rewriting or revising, he might stay with it 18 hours. When he started writing *Naked in Garden Hills*, he had an idea and one line, "Wherever he was, it looked like he had been there forever." That started as the first line in the book, describing the fat man, but at the end could be found 200 or so pages back.

*   *   *

"When you've got that first page in the typewriter, of course, you been thinking about something for a long time, but you don't quite know what it means. There's a little bit of an idea in there. I start with a place and somebody and then I just try to discover the story. Robert Penn Warren said a writer doesn't need to know the story.

All he needs to know is to be able to trust in his knowledge of craft and technique to discover the story.

"Robert Frost said all his poems end in surprise and discovery—discovery for himself. You know, when he started out with a poem he really didn't have much at all. He talked about that little poem 'Stopping by Woods.' He said, 'When I started that poem all I had was the first line, and so then I proceeded to try to write a second line in which I was consistent with the commitments made in the first. Then I wrote a third'.

"Well, that's the way I work with fiction. What apprentices don't understand is the important thing is not the fucking story. It's not any of that. The important thing is the artist whose perceptions all of this is being filtered through. The writer's vision of the world. It doesn't matter what he writes about. My writing will have a certain taste and a certain smell and a certain sound. Nobody's going to confuse Faulkner and Hemingway, no matter the story. I go on feeling when writing fiction. I don't give a rat's ass where the novel's going."

Crews said he has learned more from reading Graham Greene, the British author, than anyone else. *The Power and the Glory* was his favorite. "It's not so much the subject matter as the consummate skill. He's as accomplished a writer as I know, and both a popular and a critical success." He noted that Greene suffered the blackest kind of melancholy and depression. Both Greene and Crews have been accused of sacrilege in their books, a charge that bothers Crews. "I wouldn't do that," he said. "I take all my books to be about the nature of faith. How does a man come to believe what he believes? How do you get to belief and how do you hold on to it? God, wife, job, whatever, I feel a sense of responsibility.

"Greene always insisted upon the right to portray the unbeliever as powerfully as the believer, the crippled and halt as powerfully as he portrays the perfect. What most people want, out there in the suburb, is a papier-mâché villain. A guy really powerful and really bad at the same time scares them. The devil in Milton's *Paradise Lost* came out heroic, saying it was better to rule in hell—a ballsy son of a bitch."

Romantic, sentimentalized writing angers Crews. "Chekhov said learning to write is learning to murder your darlings. We've all got this kind of mushy thing in us. We can't write about that. We've got to write about it the way it works."

The way it worked, for Crews, was parable and metaphor. His darlings came out of the Sears, Roebuck catalogue and he murdered them long ago. He trotted them out and brutalized them with truths that made people squirm. He planned to go back to Bacon County, where it all began, and turn that withering vision upon himself and his people.

Meanwhile, another novel percolated. "I'm going to call it *The Feast of Snakes*," he said. "It's about these snake roundups. I went to one up in south Georgia not long ago. What's got me wanting to write the thing is the fact that here are these people catching these goddam rattlesnakes and they're eating them and they've got a beauty contest. . . . People hanging on the wire and looking at the snakes. Lester Maddox was there and led us in a little hymn while he played his mouth harp and all this shit.

"Now, I want to find out what that means. Your ordinary asshole on the street will say it don't mean anything. Folks get together and they just eat the snakes. No, no, no, you can't shit me. I watched those ladies. They want to eat some of that rattlesnake, and they just been hanging on the pen looking at 'em where they're all writhing in there, and they get over there and the husband says, 'Aw, come on, Dolores, just put it in your mouth, honey. It's just like fried chicken'. I don't know what all that is, but I want to know. That's the kind of thing . . ."

—June 30, 1974

*   *   *

The Troubles with Harry

Violence follows Harry Crews around like an oversized lapdog, eager to spring upon him with bone-crunching love. "I don't know why I attract it," Crews said, shaking his head, making the gold earring on his left lobe jiggle and gleam. "But I do."

He kept rubbing his right eye, still blurry from a recent concussion. The doctor has told him it will be all right. The razor cuts across his body are healing nicely, too. The knees are still a mess, though. "I can go upstairs, but going down, I have trouble with that," he said.

He mused. "Maybe it's the way I talk. Abrupt, ragged sometimes, you know. But I don't mean it that way. Maybe it's how I walk. Sort of out front. I don't know what it is, but something I do gnaws at people.

"My reputation is not good. That's part of it. The things I get into are highly suspect. Send me to Alaska and what do I write about? Whores getting tattooed on their ass while they're blowing cocaine up their noses. What is that? But it's what was up there."

He got the concussion and razor cuts and fresh damage to battered knees while researching a story on dogfighting. "Making the connection was like a dope buy," he said. "I followed instructions. Flew to Miami, flew to the west coast, drove to Boca Raton, on and on. No names. Louisiana rules. The dog don't have to take his killing. All he has to do is 'cur' out."

Pit bulls fought in an old barn. "It was madness, man," Crews said, lighting up at the memory. "The whiskey's out, the money's out. Lot of guys holding heat, lot of guys holding knives, lot of bullshit coming down. Two or three fights and the crowd's in a frenzy. Just madness."

Crews went near the pit, leaning to see better. "I just asked this guy, who was really a big guy, I would never have thought to fuck with him, I said, 'Hey man, you got a good shot of the pit. You can see. Just move over a little bit because you're in my way'." Crews put pleading into his voice, to show how reasonable he had been.

He shook his head, bewildered. "Maybe it was the tone of my voice, but that was all it took, man. Before I knew it, I was on the ground and he was on the ground with me. He had three guys with him and they started coming. I had one guy and he told 'em, 'If you're gonna get in this you gotta come by me'. Which they did, just like that. Really big guys. Nobody tried to separate us 'cause it was all just madness." One guy worked him over with a contrivance that let the edge of a straight razor fit around his hand like brass knuckles. The four left him bloody and broken.

Crews had no hard feelings. "They were pretty decent guys," he said. "They didn't want to kill anybody." He recalled it with satisfaction, like a man cataloguing his pain following a day of manual labor on his dream house. "After the fight, my guy gave his dog a shot of Demerol and cortisone," Crews said. He smiled. "Hell, he gave me a shot of Demerol, too."

Legends already have begun to build around Harry Crews, novelist and University of Florida English professor. At 43 [in 1978], his long hair and heavy mustache graying slightly, his tall athlete's body beginning to puff, he has had 10 books—eight of them novels—published, and lifted himself to the upper levels of American letters. He portrays evil so powerfully and naturally and empathetically, extending in his own way the tradition of Graham Greene and Flannery O'Connor and the young Erskine Caldwell, that he disturbs people who cling to fashion and convention for sanctuary. He makes a roller-coaster ride of the bizarre twists and violent lurches that people take when struggling to free themselves of cursed lives.

Yet more than that distinguishes him. His own life had such unusual dimension that it threatened to compete with his work for attention. In that respect, he was the Ernest Hemingway of his day, buoyed by myth-making, distracted by it, becoming one of his own best characters, though Hemingway alongside the earthy Crews might have seemed a pompous straight arrow.

Not long ago, with a pocketful of money from one of his journalistic exercises for *Playboy* or *Esquire*, Crews and a buddy went to St. Augustine to play. "Expressly to spend that money" was the way Crews put it. For the occasion, he shaved his head, setting off a full beard nicely and complementing the single earring.

A discotheque became headquarters. After three days of drinking and dancing and romancing, the inevitable occurred. He returned from a momentary diversion to find a sailor with his girl. "He knew damned well I was with the girl," Crews said, explaining the provocation. "I'd been dancing with her, buying her drinks and everything. But he was talking to her and he had his back to me."

First thing the sailor knew, a warm stream of water came coursing down his pants leg. Honor demanded, and got, a fight. "Cops came out of the woodwork, six carloads of 'em," Crews said. "They got me and the girl in the backseat of a car. She was beating at them and yelling, 'You can't do this to us'. And I'm trying to calm her down and telling her, 'Yes they can, darling, yes they can'." Crews' attorney, checking the shaved head and earring, advised him not to contest the misdemeanor in court. He left his bond, if not his heart, in St. Augustine.

Things like that just happened to him, out of nowhere. Once he was in Encino, California, with actor Vic Morrow. They had been talking about making a movie from one his books. They had a few drinks, naturally, and Morrow decided to drive Crews to his Pasadena hotel. They got lost. About 5 A.M., somewhere in Pasadena, Crews announced he felt like walking. Morrow reluctantly agreed.

Crews explained that something Morrow had said "just turned my head around. I wanted to walk awhile and think." It was a story about a woman who had a flower bloom in her mouth when she had an orgasm. "I was taken with that image," Crews said.

Preoccupied with that, he turned a corner and discovered he had gone into a dead-end alley, and two guys had walked in behind him. "I caught it," he said. "I got hurt bad." Another misfortune.

Through other misfortunes, as well as automobile and motorcycle wrecks and a tour of duty with the Marines, Crews has had his neck broken, ribs on both sides broken, sternum broken, both knees and both feet broken, his entire body bruised and sliced. Still, he remained a man passionate about all things, unslowed. "I have an incredible recovery rate," he explained.

Not long ago, Crews walked into a Gainesville bar and saw a guy and a girl sitting there. The girl spoke. "She looked vaguely familiar to me and so I said, 'Hey, how are you? You're lookin' good'. Then I walked over to the bar and ordered a draft. I had that glass almost up to my mouth when I caught this shot on the side of the head."

The punch wiped out a row of teeth and cost Crews $700 in dental work. He was mystified. "Never saw the guy before. It was between him and her. He had his balls up because he thought I'd been fooling with his girl or something. I swear to God, three weeks later I was in Atlanta and the same thing happened.

"Man, listen, it's like a snowball. I go in a bar somewhere and some jackass walks up to me and tells me a long story about something I did somewhere, some outrageous thing, and I wasn't there and I've never been there. I used to try to correct all that. I used to say, 'Wait a minute, man. You got that wrong'. But now I just shrug."

One misfortune he did not plan to risk was old age. One of his books, *This Thing Don't Lead to Heaven*, dealt with the horrors of an old folks' home. "I forgot who it was, but somebody said when you die you ought to be just a little puff of dust, that somebody could put in their hand and go *poof!* and blow away, all used up, nothing left. I don't plan to get old; I plan to wear out.

"I am 43 years old, but I don't have any friends 43 years old," Crews said. "People 43 years old usually are worried about their annuities, life-insurance policies and the mortgage on the house, and all that shit does not interest me.

"It's damned near against the law to be vulnerable anymore, but that's my whole gig. I want to be vulnerable. I want to be naked. I want to be right out there and just let it all hang out."

Never doubt that Crews does exactly that. In his latest book, *A Childhood*, his story of growing up in Bacon County, he lets so much hang out that he engages the sensitive reader with a familial concern. Crews grew up among a loving, tragedy-prone family in an atmosphere that accepted the maimed and deformed as commonplace. He narrowly escaped crippling polio and death by being boiled alive in a vat prepared for scalding a hog. It was a physical, back-against-the-wall world.

The book even told how his father, while still a bachelor, got "the clap" and feared sterility, of Crews' loss of his father as an infant and the succession of a drunken stepfather, and of the local code of conduct in which a man settled his own grievances and considered it a dangerous revelation of weakness to call in the law.

A Childhood was a beautifully written book, a Southern classic really, and it explained a lot about Crews. He dedicated it to his only child, Byron (whose mother he married and divorced three times and still spoke of lovingly), and said it was written so that Byron would know who he was by knowing who his father was, a circumstance denied to Harry. Harry searched out that father by talking with Bacon County families and old-timers. At one point he wrote disquietingly, "For half of my life I have been in the university, but never of it. Never of anywhere, really. Except the place I left."

Curiously, he felt alienated from the two places to which he was most attached, the University of Florida and Bacon County. Within the family, his mother was an exception. "I asked her if she wanted to read the book before I published it, and she said no. She said if it's the truth, write it. She has never objected to any of it."

His other kinfolk were decent to him but he felt alienated. "They act like I'm a goddam leper," he said. "My brother thinks I should write stomped-down, hard-core pornography. I'm welcome in my uncles' and aunts' houses, and my nephews', or at least they make me think so. But it's different. If I go to their house and it's cold or there's something there they think's not quite right, they apologize to me in a way they would not apologize to their other blood kin. It doesn't make you feel good. It makes you feel bad.

"I don't know what it is, exactly. I talk differently, dress differently, eat different food. And there's the notion of a man making a living without sweating, without calluses on his hands, without the use of his physical self. Something seems slightly askew about that, too."

Crews believed the university and his kin saw him in exactly oppo-site ways, producing the same result. At the university, he appeared the primitive. "See, I just don't do anything the way they do it much. I don't go to all those stand-up tea parties. Me and a couple of black cats are the only ones that's got an earring in our ear. I don't own a pair of trousers that aren't Levi's. I wear whatever comes to hand, and back when I was drinking bad I'd go three or four days without shaving, and I'd go to class just looking bad.

"I'm quick to speak my mind, too, at faculty meetings and other places. They are used to people who are much more careful than I am. If they want to tell you you're not doing your job right, they don't say, 'Hey, you're not doing your job right'. They come at it this way and then this way and over the hill and everything and finally they get down to it.

"Whenever we get a new department chairman—and we've had four or five since I've been here—I always go in and tell him, if I don't hear from you I will assume I'm doing my job well. If for some reason something begins to eat on you, don't let it nag you for three weeks before you tell me. Just say, 'Crews, you've got to change'. And if I can't change, I'll walk.

"The university has been good to me. I'm not sure what they think of me, but they treat me fine. When I was up for full professor, I remember what one sponsor said in a letter. Something like, 'Harry Crews was not to the manner born, but the university not only can stand him, it ought to stand him. He might not do things just the way we would have him do them, but it'll be all right'." He thought that sounded fine.

Crews' eight novels have dealt with the theme of the ugly being beautiful, and vice versa. Curses were blessings, and blessings were curses. Most of his characters live on the edge of violence, and often fall in. His reputation soared on grotesque comedy, beginning with *The Gospel Singer*, which depicted a golden-boy singer whose extraordinary gift led him into scenes of seduction, rape and righteous murder. The other books followed, one a year. *Naked in Garden Hills* (a fat man gets fatter on Metracal, and go-go dances in a phosphate pit); *This Thing Don't Lead to Heaven*; *Karate Is a Thing of the Spirit* (again, the study of a troubled mind, for which he became a karate expert); *Car* (a man eats a car, bite by bite); *The Hawk Is Dying* (a man tries to save his sanity through the discipline of training a hawk); *The Gypsy's Curse* (a crippled deaf-mute finds the perfect mate, a blonde looking for someone who loves her enough to kill her for being faithless, and obliges her with a hatchet); *A Feast of Snakes* (a football hero goes mad at a snake festival, commits multiple shotgun murders and leaps into a pit of rattlesnakes). His book *Blood and Grits* was a collection of essays.

Two scenes from the last novel, *A Feast of Snakes*, typify the Crews commitment to scenes of shock and violence. In the first, a woman repeatedly runs away from her husband and each time he finds her and drags her back. She gives up. The daughter finds her one day, slumped in a rocking chair, a plastic bag over her head and a one-sentence note pinned to her dress: "Bring me back now, you son of a bitch." The daughter goes mad.

The other scene involves a young girl pushed to the brink of insanity during a rattlesnake festival by a deputy sheriff who keeps forcing his passion upon her. Sitting in his squad car, she goes over the edge. She sees a snake in his lap and with a swift slap of a straight razor she severs its head. The deputy, transformed into a fountain of blood, bleeds to death.

Despite an uninterrupted string of successful novels, Crews lived with the fear that one day the magic would be gone, that he would not be able to write another book. He calls it the "dark twirlies . . . that awful, cosmic anxiety." In a strange city, overcome by twirlies, he sometimes goes to the library and looks himself up in the card catalogue for reassurance.

"Writing gets harder, not easier, as you go on," he said. "You can write 15 books, and then if you blow the 16th and you try the 17th and it dies, too, then you know. Then it's the hell with the 15. They don't even count anymore. I'm always scared I ain't gonna be able to do it again." He might be a professor, but he still loved to roll the language of south Georgia off his tongue.

Crews had just come through a critical period in his life. The crisis came when he stepped on a stage to speak to 700 university freshmen. "I was standing there, and I thought to myself, 'If I don't get out of here in about four minutes I'm going to start crying', so I just said, 'I'm sorry', and went to my chairman. I was straight with him. I said, 'Whatever's gotta come down has gotta come down'. He was great. We worked out some time and hell, I've taught a better quarter this year than I've taught in 10 years." The doctor called it nervous exhaustion, but Crews said he was on the edge.

"I had stayed drunk for about three years. I'd get up in the morning and drink half a quart of vodka while I shaved and took a shower and then I'd just ride it. I can ride on whiskey because I can control how high I am. You start to go down, and you just take little bit, don't let it get away from you. I could drink a quart of vodka and go to a dinner party and be perfectly civil and talk and everything. Of course, if I drank bad enough, I'd get so I'd be out of control. But I've beat that shit. I've been off everything, except a little beer, for eight months now. Beginning to feel good again."

The legends of Harry Crews go on. They build and build. There was the story, for example, of the time he and a buddy were out bicycling before sunrise on a country road. A young man in a car ran them into the ditch. Harry got the license number, traced it, and bicycled over to the fellow's house. An older man came to the door. "Whoever was in that car, I want him out here on the grass," Crews demanded. The man said it was his son and asked Crews not to curse. It was stalemate. The boy would not come out.

"What we oughta do," Harry called to the younger man, "what we oughta do is get down right here in the door, but because your daddy's here and your mama's inside and I don't want them to get all upset, we'll just forget it." He started to turn away and thought better of it. "Let me say one more thing," Crews added. "If you get to thinking about this and change your mind, here's my name and where I live. And if you ever do this again, like we say in Bacon County, I'll see whose ass is the blackest."

Crews has a good heart, in his way, whatever the legend. He is generous with time and gentle of manner with those he perceives to be handicapped or innocent. He had a chance, several times, to turn that withering writer's vision of his on fellow south Georgian Jimmy Carter. Magazines wanted him to do a hatchet job. Crews went over to Plains, but he never would write about the Carters or about their hometown. "I just didn't want to," he said. He did not explain further, but to me, at least, it seemed he thought that Carter had earned grace by being able to spring, unscarred, from the harsh home country of his and to bring it high honor. He wants no part of sullying that kind of miracle.

"I'm from Bacon County, Georgia," Crews said, defining himself. "Everything about me starts there. I spring from those people. Wherever I go and whatever I do, I'm one of them." Writing *A Childhood*, dredging up all those truths about himself, the kind many people would lie about, meant risk and pain. The writing was difficult and the research did violence to his already precarious peace of mind. Ordinarily, he would not mind a little violence, of course. But he prefers the conventional kind.

—*December 31, 1978*

PART 3 HANGING ON

Catfishermen: A Breed Apart

As Florida evolved toward a megastate, smoothing out all its wrinkles and uncurling all the interesting old kinks, among the last of the free-spirited independents were the catfishermen of Lake Okeechobee.

When Austin Selph was 14, his daddy taught him how to bait, rack and run a trotline on the St. Johns River in north Florida. That was enough. Selph quit school and became a catfisherman for life. It was not a job, but a world. A catfisherman had his boat, hooks and lines, and he bet his life that the water would always hold fish. If the catches grew slim one place, he went somewhere else. During the Depression, the Selphs followed the prospects south to Lake Okeechobee, the big league of catfishing, where the fish and the men who caught them had been legendary for nearly two decades.

Some of the catfish weighed as much as the boys who baited the trotlines, 60 pounds and more according to the tales. The lure of the lake had merged not only men trailing the big catch, but also some determined to escape the bridle of working for wages, and yet others simply fleeing trouble.

In his book about the early fishermen, *Okeechobee Catfishing*, Lawrence Will described the catfishermen as frontier mavericks, self-reliant and self-sufficient, hard-drinking, hardworking, hard-fighting men with a code of their own.

On such descriptions of their tradition the catfishermen—trotliners, seiners and trappers joined in later years by trawlers—have became renowned. Their work, in many ways, represented one of the last means of livelihood left for a man who followed the now faint call of the wild and preferred to set his own rules. The tradition erodes, but slowly, keeping bright a fine thread of scarlet in the fabric of Florida.

"We come down in a Model T Ford in '35," said Selph. He sat cross-legged in the doorstep of his rustic cabin on the north shore of the lake near Buckhead Ridge. "All this was water around here then. Water come up to the headlights. We drove right here to this high ground. There was frogs, snakes, coons, otters, gators, ducks, everything you could imagine. One place we had, I could sit on my porch with a rifle and shoot bass, seven- and eight-pounders. Right from the porch."

Selph, 69, a man with intense blue eyes, has health problems and does not fish anymore. But he still tutors his son, Leland, 24, who started fishing at age nine. Leland lives nearly 200 miles north in the Ocala National Forest and divides his time between fishing the lake and the St. Johns River. While Selph asked questions and offered advice, suggesting a switch from baiting with grubs to maggots, Leland listened. Selph finally said, "I love the lake, but my fishing days are over."

Sportsmen came from all over the country, or from just down the road, to part the Okeechobee waters with anything from a cane pole to a luxury cruiser. The 730-square-mile wilderness of water, shaped into a saucer by a levee, draws them all. But the commercial fishermen were a breed apart, just as the lake itself has been a thing apart in Florida history.

R. M. Dupree, probably the oldest active commercial fisherman on the lake, sat on a sofa in a little frame house in Clewiston and sighed. "Tired," he said. He began the day before light, haul seined past high sun and delivered his catch to Nesbitt's Fish House, and was taking his shirtless ease in the cool, watching television. "My daddy was a seiner," Dupree said. "Brought me to the lake when I was three years old. Come over from Fort Myers. He moved down here from Iowa to fish. When I was 11, he taught me. I quit school and I been fishing ever since."

Dupree has tried other work, but only when seining was outlawed. The haul seiner uses six boats in combination to pull, stake and haul a seine (a large fishing net with floats on the top edge and weights on

The Dupree family, Lake Okeechobee catfishermen. *Left to right:* R. M., Richard, Jr., and Billy. Photo by the author, 1979.

the bottom) nearly a mile long. His catch usually runs larger than the others, but he must divide it. There are few haul seiners left on the lake. In the year ending last June, the state issued only five permits for haul seining.

"You get out there at three, four, five o'clock in the morning, and you might hit something and you might not. But that's just part of it. I love it," Dupree said. "It's not like saltwater fishing. In saltwater, you find the fish and strike. Out here you strike blind and see what you come up with. Sometimes you make money and sometimes you don't. I caught 30,000 pounds of mullet one time, and turned loose 20,000 pounds because I didn't know whether we could sell 'em. They don't care too much about mullet. But I found out later if I'd brought 'em in, we coulda sold 'em all. Made me feel pretty bad." He puffed a cigarette and smiled. "But they still out there. We'll run into 'em again."

Dupree made a fisherman of his son, Richard, Jr., but the boy turned from the haul seine to trawling. "More money in it," Richard said, as he and teenage brother Billy joined their dad in the cool. "You can beat wages all year round. Billy helps me but it can be a one-man operation if you want it to be."

The trawler uses a 20- to 30-foot boat that pulls a baglike net, or trawl, along the bottom of the lake. They and the haul seiners by law must fish a mile off the grass line. The year before, the state had issued 127 trawl permits for the lake.

"The fish are all the time moving, migrating around the lake. You got to find them. I can be anywhere on the lake in an hour. You put in a lot more hours but you ain't got to punch no time clock. If I don't want to go fishing, I ain't got to. I banged nails last winter, but no more. I'm a fisherman," he said.

Billy hoped to graduate one day to his own rig, and by then Richard's preteen sons will be ready to learn the trade. "I'll teach 'em. Most assuredly," Richard said. "Everybody needs to know how to work."

Lake Okeechobee has been called the liquid heart of south Florida, but if so it has a separate soul. The distance from Palm Beach is but 40 miles, from Miami 70 miles and from Fort Myers 60, but the kinship is remote—like tinsel to barbed wire. Established lake dwellers, or at least many of them, were proud Crackers holding on to their customs a little tighter because of the steady dilution from cross-country retirees with divergent fancies.

"It's a kind of hard life," said Robert Fountain, Jr., 57, a trotliner. A trotline is a long line, anchored and buoyed, with hundreds of short lines bearing hooks hanging off it. It is baited with anything from pieces of soap to golden grubs to grasshoppers. A commercial trotliner's license on the lake permits a total of 1,500 hooks. "I pulled four lines this morning and didn't get but 88 pounds. Not much—they pay 37 cents a pound for catfish in the rough [not cleaned]—but I hate to work for somebody else. When you go out there you either hit 'em or you don't, but you feel like you got a hand in what happens to you."

Fountain was born near Okeechobee. His dad moved west to here from Sebastian on the Atlantic coast to be a haul seiner. At 14, Robert learned the trade. Both his own sons followed him into fishing, and his grandchildren are almost ready to hit the water. "I don't know how many trotliners there are on the lake. Plenty. I'd hate to guess."

Fountain had lived all around the lake, in Canal Point, South Bay, Pahokee, Clewiston. Since last spring, he has parked his trailer behind the Lightsey Fish Company (where he peddles his catch) on State Road 78 near Okeechobee. His son, Dean, 20, lives in a trailer nearby and their two boats—called skipjacks—are parked in the yard. "We just follow the fish where we catch 'em," Fountain said. "Whichever way your line catches the best, you just log on out that way and keep following. Sometimes we fish right on the hill [levee] and again we have to go 10, 12 miles out."

Okeechobee means "big water." The lake, with a mean diameter of 31 miles, is the second largest freshwater lake (Lake Michigan is No. 1) lying wholly within U.S. boundaries. The area did not manage really to become part of the U.S. scene until dredgers opened up navigable waterways north to Kissimmee and west to Fort Myers during the 1880s. The first railroad reached the lake in 1915 and the first paved highway in 1924. After hurricanes in 1926 and 1928 caused great flood destruction, a levee was completed in 1937, and the area was reined if not tamed.

T. D. (Buddy) Stokeld, a Texan, came to the lake in 1946. He was a trapper; he caught catfish in a baited wire basket. He retired because of his health but his skill is remembered around the lake. "I had four lines and 70 traps a line. You were only allowed 40 traps on a permit then, but I guess everybody fished more than they were supposed to," he said.

Stokeld introduced offshore trap fishing and a trap with two doors instead of just one. He baited with pressed cakes of soybean and cottonseed. "You'd take your traps and set 'em out there and leave 'em. When you take the fish out, you throw bait in. When I was fishing for Lightsey, they told me I was catching more fish than anybody. Sometimes I'd nearly starve to death and sometimes I'd catch a lot— maybe 700 to 1,000 pounds on the good days. That was dressed, too.

"Nobody traps for catfish much around here anymore. After all the trotliners came in around here, it got so bad they just about put me out of business. They'd run my traps, get my fish before I could get to 'em. They just about starved me out. It happens to trotliners too, though. Somebody'll run their lines on 'em. But trapping's more expensive than trotlining, and most of 'em just quit it. Scale-fish trapping, which involves a different kind of basket, continues on a large scale."

Commercial fishing on the lake began about 1900. Most of it was by haul seine, and the catch was shipped on the dredged-out water routes to Fort Myers, Kissimmee and Fort Lauderdale. When the railroad came to Okeechobee in 1915, catfish reached an annual gross of $1 million. Iced barrels of catfish were loaded into railroad cars and shipped north at the rate of up to 10 railroad cars a week. In 1924, an estimated 6.5 million pounds of catfish were shipped from the lake. About that time, Okeechobee had visions of becoming another Chicago, and it even offered land to induce the state capitol to be moved there.

There seemed no limit to the market then, even though the white meat of the catfish rarely has been regarded as a delicacy except by Southerners. One possible explanation was revealed when U.S. senator Duncan Fletcher (D., Fla.) testified at congressional hearings in 1929 that catfish "passes as salmon" when it reached Northern markets. Others said that a catfish fillet magically turned into fillet of sole when it crossed the Mason-Dixon line and, even today, the fillet you eat that bears a fancy name on the menu might in truth be catfish, that old Cracker delight.

During those glory years, after the railroad opened, Okeechobee was like the old Wild West. On weekends, the cowboys from the ranches north of the lake would gather in one part of town and the catfishermen off the lake would gather in another. Inevitably, blood flowed.

"They were both rough. Yessir," said Dupree. "You might not believe this, but I've seen as many as 15 fights going on at one time around the old Bell house in Okeechobee. Fishermen and them cow hunters, they'd just gather up.

"They used to have what they call uptown and downtown. Fishermen hung around downtown. That was Taylor's Creek. The cowboys stayed uptown. They'd get to drinking and you'd hear one holler after a while, and then they'd all get to hollering and first thing you knew they'd meet and go at it. Once they got to drinking that moonshine, they'd just fight for the fun of it."

The most famous catfisherman of them all, William (Pogy Bill) Collins, who became sheriff of Okeechobee, was Dupree's brother-in-law. "A fella came into Okeechobee one time there at the barber shop. He said, 'Pull your gun off and I'll whip ya'. Pogy just laid that gun off to one side, and they went to fighting and fought for two hours. Then Pogy took him off to jail. He was a mighty fine man."

There was one catfisherman who loved to get a shoeshine every Saturday night—it somehow nursed his ego—but he could not bear to wear shoes, and he would lose them when the fight started. He solved the problem by getting his bare feet shined.

By 1916 sports fishermen were complaining that the commercial men were ruining the fishing. The state closed the lake four months that summer and began to impose net limits. In 1925 a state law declared all seining in freshwater to be illegal. The pros countered by having Lake Okeechobee declared "not freshwater" and continued seining.

The dispute has not let up since. Commercial fishing was on-again, off-again until the early 1950s, when it was banned for nearly a quarter century. It resumed in October 1976, when the Florida Game and Fresh Water Fish Commission began the Okeechobee Fisheries Utilization and Management Program, which permitted commercial fishing for all but the largemouth bass and the redfin pickerel.

Sport fishermen and commercial fishermen still differ on whether it has helped or hurt, and the experiment continues with undiminished controversy. The game commission monitors the harvest and tries to balance the two in the overall best interests of the lake.

The commission enforced a 45-day closed season last winter and in late summer proposed a 90-day closed season for the coming winter. At public hearings on the proposal in Clewiston and Okeechobee during August, the commercial fishermen were outraged at the prospect. Some said it would force them out of business. Although the restrictions were directed only at the taking of scalefish, since haul seiners and trawlers take both scalefish and catfish, if enforced it would affect them as well as scalefish trappers. Many of the seiners and trawlers employ scalefish traps, too.

For 1978, the game commission reported a total catch of 3.32 million pounds of catfish (no scales) and 2.8 million pounds of scalefish (crappie, bluegill, etc.) taken commercially. Each scalefish must be tagged at one of the fish house designated around the lake. Tags cost 3½ cents each, and the money supports the management program. "Catfish make up about half our business," said Jerry Metz, 32-year-old manager of Nesbitt's Fish House in Clewiston, the biggest wholesale outlet for fishermen on the lake. "And trawlers probably bring in 70 percent of our catfish."

Metz grew up near Lake Apopka in central Florida, where his father, Moses Metz, was a trotliner. "In a trotline family, you start out young," he said, "maybe at five or six years old. Trotliners had large families because they needed the help. People don't have big families anymore, and a lot of them have to hire it out.

"They can bring in up to 800 pounds on a good day. A lot of these guys trotlining quit jobs in industry paying $15,000 and $20,000 a year to do it. It's the kind of people they are. Independent. Don't want to work for anybody else. They don't have much invested, like the trawlers and seiners do, and they can do as they please."

The old catfishermen, like Selph and Dupree, were not just representatives of the rugged past, not around Lake Okeechobee. Among their sons and grandsons and among those who trawled and trotlined and said to hell with the time clock, the strain survived. When that country singer wails about telling the boss to take his job and shove it, it is a message they understand. Some have done just that.

Maybe the computers and the bureaucrats and all the constraints of a security-desperate society have drawn the fire from the rest of us, but not them, not the catfishermen.

—*September 22, 1979*

An Old Crank

When a boat whistled, Tennie Steele put down her crocheting and went to work. She walked out to the middle of Starkes Ferry Bridge, inserted a long handle into a slot and began cranking. "Hard?" she said. "You ought to try it. Sometimes that thing is impossible." But the short, trim grandmother leaned into the job, and slowly the bridge swung open and cleared the channel.

The widow Steele, when I talked with her in 1978, had been a bridgetender for 18 years on one of the relics of Florida's transportation system—a manually operated swing bridge across the Ocklawaha River where it met State Road 42 in Marion County. All that time she had lived in a white frame bridgetender's house that perched behind the guardrails on what amounted to an island. She could fish off the back porch.

Her best memories were made right there at this site of an old ferry-crossing that served Confederate major Thomas Starke's plantation in the 1880s. As permanently as a human can, she built her life around the river. Her husband, who died in 1969, planted lemon and tangerine trees along the banks, and each year they were full of fruit. She planted roses. Her children grew up in this tiny six-room house where she finally lived alone.

"Lord, I love this river, and I hate to leave it," she said. "But they're going to tear down my house."

Mrs. Steele knew the old hand-cranked bridge could not last forever. Nevertheless, she had been stunned the previous spring when state officials said she could stay no longer than six months more, perhaps less. Plans called for a high-level bridge that would not need a tender, and until that got built the state would depend on non-resident tenders working reduced hours.

In a nation of easy-riding nomads, where people regularly move from job to job and city to city and mate to mate, she believed in the old rule that a person should make lasting commitments to achieve the sense of direction that makes life bearable. "There'll always be changes," she said, mentally picking her path into the future. "Life changes whether you want it to or not. But you can find a way and a reason. One thing leads out of another. I'm thankful I could carry on as long as I did. I was 65 this year, and I can get retirement. They offered to move the house for me but I told them no. The place is full of termites. I'll miss the fishing, but it seemed like they were always biting best when I had to work and couldn't take out the boat.

"Besides, that old crank is so hard to turn. I don't dread leaving as bad because of that. I'll just move on up to Anthony [also in Marion County], where my son lives, and I'll be fine. I can sew and raise flowers and maybe go fishing occasionally. I'll have plenty to do, just like I always have."

The Steeles made their way to Starkes Ferry from Alabama in 1953. "We were farmers," she said. "We never did public work." In 1960 a friend recommended her, and she readily took the job and the little state-owned house that went with it. "Made $65 a week to start. Paid $25 a month rent and they furnished utilities," she said. "It was six days a week and 24 hours a day then. Couldn't even get away to go to school meetings. But I loved it. Just suited me fine. Sometimes a month would pass without having to open the bridge—has to be a houseboat or something like that. But sometimes two or three'd come in one weekend. It wasn't too difficult, but you had to be alert."

Starkes Ferry, a rural community between Umatilla and Weirsdale, changed little in Mrs. Steele's 18 years there. The same two fish camps sat on either side of the river, but they got a little busier and a little fancier. There were fewer campsites and trailers in the early days, but even in 1978 there were not so many. Her salary rose to $600 a month and work time fell to three-and-a-half days a week (42 hours), with a relief bridgetender (also a woman) handling an equal shift from a small office next door.

Most of the boat traffic could go under the bridge without her services, but the highway traffic had increased. Barely a yard from her front door the autos whizzed by in two opposite-bound lanes closely bordered by heavy guardrails which she could reach from her front door. "The traffic gets to be a problem," she said. "Once, a truck loaded with oranges hit the house. Cleaned out all but the top and bottom of two rooms, furniture and all. Scattered oranges all over the house. I was outside fishing.

"Another time my grandson was here and we had been fishing. I was out on the back porch cleaning the fish when he came back and said, 'Granny, a box of corn fell off a truck on the road'. I looked out there, and a trailer had hit one of the guardrails and scattered corn all over everywhere. All that went with the job. I had to keep the road clear. You'd be surprised how many people stopped their cars right on the bridge to look at the alligators—we've got a 14-footer that hangs around out there—or to climb down that fence and pick some of my tangerines. Had to keep 'em moving."

She sat quietly in her living room, listening to the pendulum clock ticking, looking at a mounted bass on the kitchen wall, the framed pictures of her grandchildren and the curtains standing out in the river breeze, and sighed. "It wasn't perfect but Lord knows I'm going to miss it," she said. "If I didn't have another place to go, I'd put me a trailer down there on the river and stay right on."

One of Florida's last hand-cranked bridges was passing into history. Tennie Steele followed reluctantly, for she was leaving a life behind.

—May 21, 1978

The Alligator Man's Last Stand

Looking back now, it seemed quixotic: Ross Allen, the old alligator man, aging but world famous and still widely admired, would make one last stand at Lake City. That was 1981. In 1998 a woman at the Chamber of Commerce there barely remembered. "That never got off the ground," she said of Allen's last dream. "He died."

Think of Ross Allen as a sort of dinosaur, like the alligator, a species that flourished long after it was expected to vanish. Instinct made him a legendary name in Florida. At 16, to save an alligator from being shot, he leaped on it and wrestled it. They called him "The Boy Who Catches 'Em Alive," and he became a showman, the alligators' Buffalo Bill.

When I last talked with him in 1981, he was 73, a bit mature for gator wrestling. By then he was internationally renowned, decorated with scars made by alligator teeth, survivor of 12 rattlesnake bites, veteran of 37 expeditions to South America and historian of both the Florida frontier and the tourist trail.

Once he had taken Marjorie Kinnan Rawlings, the Pulitzer Prize–winning novelist, on a snake-hunting trip at Big Prairie near the Everglades, to help her overcome a fear of snakes. Rawlings recounted the story in *Cross Creek*. They netted 32 rattlesnakes in two days. In the movie made from her most famous novel, *The Yearling*, Allen was the expert consulted about the scene in which a rattlesnake struck Penny Baxter, the boy Jody's father.

"I'm so enthusiastic about wildlife I can't stop talking about it," Allen said. "I say, 'Don't step on a cockroach. It's somebody's breakfast.' Balance is the secret. We've got to keep the balance in nature."

Much of his reputation was built during the 46 years he spent at the Silver Springs attraction near Ocala, most of that time running the Ross Allen Reptile Institute. He ended his association there in 1975, taught wilderness survival, built shows in Sarasota and Fort Myers, and spent another three and one-half years with an attraction in St. Augustine. Everybody in Florida, it seemed, knew or had heard of Ross Allen, and in 1981 he had staked out Lake City as the place where he would make his last stand.

Allen stood in the unfinished yard of his new home, a double-wide near a fine cypress swamp, showing his 12-year-old son Sidney the long neck and tiny bottlenose of a soft-shelled turtle. Alligators love to eat turtles.

Allen, in short sleeves, ignored a windchill near freezing until Sidney, wearing Miami Dolphins jersey No. 25, shivered. Allen hugged him close, compressing the 61 years between. "He's got it in his blood. He's a natural naturalist," Allen said. "He will be 'The Alligator Boy'."

That February day Allen said he was planning to open a new alligator tourist attraction in two months—Alligator Town, U.S.A.—and said that two days a week Sidney would be one of his stars. Sidney would dive into a pool covered by hyacinths and water lettuce and containing 20 alligators. He would stay down long enough to make the tourists nervous, and then he would pop up with a splash and hand his dad a small alligator to use in a lecture. That was the plan.

"Yeah, sometimes I'm afraid," Sidney said. "But I've been practicing. They try to bite but they haven't gotten me yet." Sidney was Allen's seventh and last child. "That's okay," Allen assured him. "Sometimes it's good to be afraid."

Allen knew the feeling. A lot of people felt he was making a mistake with this venture. They questioned his timing, his location and the attraction itself. Who cared about alligators and snakes anymore? On instinct, Allen persisted. He had been lucky or right many times when it did not seem probable, including when he jumped that first alligator.

He was born in Pennsylvania, captured fishing worms at age three, dug crayfish out of Lake Michigan at age four, became so entranced with the natural processes that by age five he sat on some chicken eggs in imitation of a mother hen, moved with his family to Winter Haven at 16. Like Buffalo Bill, who was born in Iowa and turned showman at age 26 after a brief career as a hunter, Allen was not born into his life but discovered it and made the most of it.

He was an environmentalist in the 1930s, opposing draining and ditching at a time when that was considered a civic contribution. "The Everglades were fascinating to me. I studied it. I was an ecologist before I knew it was a word. I knew about wild things. Deer lived where there were wax myrtles; kept the mosquitoes off. Horses could die from mosquito bite.

"People thought gators and snakes were the enemy in those days. I told 'em if they didn't stop draining every frog swamp they could get their hands on, we'd look like Georgia. I was against ditching and draining, against those muckland farms. The water will produce more food than dry land. Wetlands are more beneficial," he said.

In addition to his time at Silver Springs, he had advised or consulted for natural attractions all over the state, and had seen many of them fade before the competition of expensive tourist complexes whose themes had little relation to Florida. "Us little guys could build an attraction for $5,000, but we got smothered out. The big boys came in and spent millions. It was less of Florida and more of big business.

"Some of it's very sad," he said, speaking of what's happened to the state. "We have gotten too fancy, too expensive, too extravagant. I want to get back down to earth again," he said. "Have an attraction that doesn't cost so much."

He said the pattern of Florida tourism changed about 1960, or with the coming of Disney World. "When I started out in 1927, we only had tourists in the winter. Summer? That's when we skinned gators. We skinned the tourists in the winter. We gave shows for a quarter. We would take people out all day hunting gators or snakes for $25. It was fun and it was educational. They learned. You never have to rake or sweep a wilderness."

For his new attraction he wanted something that would focus on what he called the "worthwhile Florida." At first it would depend upon the people who lived within 100 miles, but he also was thinking of the people who came to Florida from places like Ohio or Kentucky. "Florida's different for them, subtropical, adventurous. The climate, fishing, boating, outdoors stuff they couldn't do back home. That's what we need to give them. The ocean is a big attraction. They never see it until they come down here. I never did, either. I saw the ocean for the first time at Melbourne. Attractions should be unique to Florida, not something that could just as well be in Michigan or Montana," he said.

He believed, especially, that the tourist's enduring fascination with alligators and other reptiles represented a natural theme that never would lose its appeal. In that, he knew he was bucking a trend but he was going with his instinct. He planned to open his Alligator Town, U.S.A., with authoritative, educational reptile shows, and was even planning to expand the next year with a water-oriented theme park that would include an amphitheater for country music festivals and Florida crafts.

Allen was the kind of man who was proud of being a Distinguished Eagle Scout (awarded for 25 years' service to Scouting), a teetotaler and a nonsmoker. He had been a stuntman in the old Tarzan movies and once turned down a movie contract because he felt uncomfortable with the Hollywood lifestyle. He was a naturalist, a teacher, a scientist, an author and an individualist with a sense of tradition.

The joining of Lake City (population then estimated at 11,000) and Allen seemed natural, too. The city was once the site of a Seminole village ruled by a chief named Alligator, and originally was called Alligator Town. Five major highways crossed there (I-10, I-75, U.S. 90, U.S. 441 and U.S. 41), and Lake City had long sought a way to persuade tourists and other nomads to stop for more than a euphemistic "rest."

At a time when exotics appeared destined to take over Florida— the melaleuca tree multiplying across the Everglades, drinking up the wetlands, and Mickey Mouse sitting athwart central Florida, sucking all the tourists toward it in a festive vacuum—old Ross Allen, the old alligator man himself, had plunged in once more and was swimming upstream like Tarzan late to the rescue.

The years had been long and the changes many, and he realized it.

He looked at his young son Sidney, from a time distance that a grandfather feels, yet he also knew the immediacy of a father's role. All of it was underlined by a certain obvious sadness that he felt Sidney's Florida would be a different one. "It's a toughie," Ross Allen said, speaking of his last stand. "But we know what to do and we're going to try hard." His eyes had the slight squint of a man studying something in the distance, as he hugged Sidney again. "Anyway," he said, "I love having my boy with me."

Going against the trend of history, what passed for progress, did not matter. He was following his heart and his instinct.

—February 8, 1981

Leaving the Rock: A One-Way Trip

There was a time when the only conchs in north Florida were the colorful, spiraling mollusk shells piled up in front of tacky little roadside shops and peddled to tourists as doorstops, but those developed substantial company. The human contours of Florida changed. The natives scattered. Even some of the old-line Key Westers—called Conchs (by classic definition, Keys natives of Bahamian ancestry) because they too had protective shells, tough meat and rarely moved off The Rock (Key West)—relocated.

The Conchs were not the only example of Florida's redefinition, but their celebrated devotion to the ocean-beaten Rock made them the most compelling one. It takes a real wrench to move a Conch.

Yet even they broke loose, uprooting and settling among green hills and pastures, adjusting to landlocked habitat where the only salt came out of shakers and where the winters got colder than their Key West refrigerators did.

Along all the coasts, and across south Florida, the demands of survival stepped up. Some people were puzzled and discouraged by the change. Their answer was to move, even when moving hurt a great deal.

When a Conch abandoned The Rock and oriented himself from open ocean to sunshine bass, it compared roughly to a barnacle deciding to become a rabbit. But that was the kind of thing that was happening.

For a decade or more, there had been a gathering stream of migration within the state. Most of it appeared as a surge away from the problems of the urban Gold Coast, but the causes were more significant than simple discontent. They were as much economic as escapist, and involved way of life as much as quality of life. The migration was not just a force moving south to north; it also moved from the coasts, north or south, toward the interior.

The impetus came from out-of-state migration to Florida. Newcomers clustered first to the coasts and to the fabled climate of the South, and their lifestyle became more cosmopolitan, more urbanly troubled, more expensive. So the South began to eject a stream of people whose incomes and inclinations no longer fit their homes.

Less noticeable was the minor replay being forced upstate and inland. The pressure built first on the inland waterfront, on the rivers and lakes, and then around existing cities where employment and convenience were available. It collected around Orlando, the only inland Florida city of size, and then around places like Gainesville, Tallahassee, Ocala and Lakeland. The pressure was passed on, displacing others as it moved up the line.

Demographers were burning out their computers trying to reduce all this to scientific verity, with little luck. They could see the process, but it was too elusive to capture in precise statistics. Assessments depended upon judgment.

Richard Feger, a 34-year-old third-generation Conch, would understand their confusion. He thought what was happening in Key West was crazy. He did not see it in the perspective of a social movement, but in personal terms. What mattered to him was that he felt as though he were being forced off The Rock.

He grew up in Key West, went to school there and loved it. "The Key West of 10, 15 years ago was the kind of place nobody ever would leave," he said in 1981. "It's changed." That kind of pronouncement was being heard a lot in Florida then.

When Feger returned from service in Vietnam, he married Kathy and bounced around in a few jobs. The only thing he ever really liked was fishing, being out on the ocean. His life goals were two: to be his own boss and to own his home.

In 1978 he bought a bait-and-tackle and seafood business where he had worked. He loved it. Part-time, he fished commercially. They bought a mobile home, but planned for the day when they could buy a conventional one.

As he looked back now, he focused on cost of living as the thing that wrenched his life apart. But there were other things. On weekends, he and Kathy liked to camp out with friends on the uninhabited offshore islands, but they had to quit. "Too risky," Feger said. Drug smugglers used the islands.

Different kinds of people moved to Key West, different kinds of tourists came. Electric bills and housing costs brought the final defeat. His first month in business the power bill was $94.80. Two years later it had quintupled. His dream of owning a home receded. He could not foresee ever making enough money to buy one.

"My lease was $571 a month," he said. "We got worried. I had told Kathy that if the electric bill got higher than the lease, we'd have to get out." In 1980 it reached $590.53. They took two trips north, looking for a freshwater fishing camp to buy, finally compromised and bought the Silver Oaks Campground, five-and-a-half high and dry acres south of Ocala on u.s. 301 in north central Florida.

In 1981 Feger still missed the old Key West, but not the new one. He spoke of an easier, friendlier, more inexpensive lifestyle. He had discovered a colony of at least 15 other Key Westers who had moved to the Ocala area. "I would never go back, but I couldn't even if I wanted to. You have to face reality," Feger said. "When you sell out in Key West, there's no way you could ever afford to go back. It's a one-way road off The Rock."

He looked into the future and imagined Key West as an expensive resort owned by conglomerates, envisioning legalized gambling casinos and a return to the old days when there was free exchange with Cuba. Places like Key West focused the pressures first, but their experiences posted early warnings on which way the future was blowing, especially along the coasts and across the south. Florida was redefining itself, and a lot of people were beginning to look into the future and wonder, as Feger did, where the average folk will live—and how.

—October 18, 1981

Farming: Not a Business but a Life

In Florida, most farming is either big business or a hobby. An independent small farmer does it for the love of the land and the life. Mark Brown in 1986 was an example.

Little patches of fog still clouded the pastures, the morning was cool and the rising sun had just begun to hit the pecan and oak trees around the Brown farm. A rooster crowed, a dog barked and a tan Limousin steer refused to leave his pen. Mark Brown, 33, got behind it and pushed, while his father, Dan Brown, stood in front and beckoned.

The steer, wide-eyed and nervous, took a few steps and Dan Brown neatly shot it with a .22 caliber rifle. "Had a little curl right there on his forehead. That's where I got him," Dan said. The steer, suddenly dead weight, dropped to its knees and rolled over on its side, tongue lolling out. Its last gasps made puffs of smoke in the cool air.

Mark slit the steer's throat on each side, shoveled out a depression in the dirt where the blood could pool and, in 20 minutes, the dying beats of the steer's heart pumped its blood vessels clean.

Danny Brown, Mark's older brother, joined them. With a tractor and a winch, they hoisted the steer on the limb of a pecan tree, took out their short skinning knives and went to work. The hide peeled off. They sawed off the steer's legs at the knees. They slit the belly, and an enormous pile of guts fell out.

The smell, the grease, the blood and the primitive nastiness of slaughter gave the morning an earthy reality, beside which the headlines of the day seemed remote.

Within an hour, what had been a 1,300-pound steer was converted into 840 pounds of beef for the three Brown families—split down the middle, quartered and piled onto plastic sheets in the back of a pickup truck.

The process was not as neat and pretty as plucking steaks out of a cooler at a supermarket, but it offered graphic example of how men like Mark Brown harvest a living from small farms.

He has 120 acres at Orange Heights in north central Florida, east of Gainesville. The land and the house, where his father grew up, have been in his family since 1917. They came to him from an uncle, the purchase cost defrayed by inheritance.

In Florida, economic pressures squeeze all farms, but especially small ones. Federal officials estimated this year that 40 percent of Florida's farmers are in serious financial trouble. The marketplace is not geared for small independents, and the peculiar rewards of true farm life are not widely appreciated anymore.

Few young men are willing to do the work and take the gambles that farming demands. Even fewer have the capital to get started or the character necessary to sustain a personal commitment that involves sacrifice. That makes Mark Brown, a third-generation Floridian, exceptional. Sometimes the finances get tight, but he makes it work.

After the slaughter of the steer, one Sunday morning while his wife, Debbie, and their three girls were at church, Mark interrupted his work to talk about farm life. "In the winter, when you try to figure out what's going wrong, you get frustrated," he said. "But when springtime comes, which is February here, and things begin growing, you get charged up and ready to go. That's part of the problem. Instead of going at it as a business, you do it because you love the life, whether the figures add up just like you want them to or not."

Mark's oldest daughter, Kelly, was in the first grade this year. His wife works part-time at the post office. He works every day, at any hour that something needs to be done.

"The land is worth so much money," continued Mark, who studied agriculture at the University of Florida. For him, it becomes a tormenting luxury. "If you operate strictly on a business basis, you fold up right now. You can't make as much on the farm as you could draw in interest on the sale price. But this is what we want to do. This is how I want to live. Debbie loves it, and it's a great place for the girls to grow up."

Like most small farmers, Mark employs variety. He has a small cattle herd, both purebred and crossbred, that supplies beef to the family and breed stock for sale. His gardens provide most of the vegetables they eat. He raises feed for the cattle. He sells pecans from the huge grove that his grandfather planted. He does the work himself.

Grandfather Brown started it all. He worked as a carpenter in Miami during the 1890s, later owned orange groves on Merritt Island (an area to become famous for its Indian River citrus) but moved north to Orange Heights when the United States entered World War I. He wanted land where he could be self-sufficient in case the war lasted.

Now Mark is the last of the Browns to farm full-time, and there may not be any more who follow him. "This kind of farm is not for farmers anymore. It has turned into a hobby for people who need tax write-offs. That's not farming. I get bitter about it sometimes," he said.

"The future's kinda scary to me. By the time my kids grow up, I don't think anybody will be able to afford to live this way."

Knowledge that he follows an endangered way of life increases his attachment to it. Slaughtering a steer might be messy work but, for him, there is a kind of clean joy in it, as there is in all farm work.

He doubts whether anyone else fully understands, but he feels privileged to be a farmer.

—August 3, 1986

Hog-killing for Fun and Savings

The Flach family moved out of crowded south Florida with a plan. They would live simply and cheaply on a Panhandle farm. In 1981, as part of their experiment in life, they held a festive hog-killing.

One bright winter morning in the Florida hills, cold enough to make Rudolf Flach's breath fog, he knelt in the dirt beneath his backyard live oak tree and shot a frightened, squealing hog named Wilbur in the forehead with a .22 caliber rifle.

Wilbur fell over on his side, convulsing, kicking up little puffs of dust. Flach and his wife, Carol, dragged the carcass to a hoist hanging off an oak limb, hauled it up by the heels until it swung free in air that smelled of wood smoke.

With a long butcher knife, Rudy slit Wilbur's throat and, as the blood poured out, Carol thrust a tin kitchen pot underneath and caught six pounds of it. She handed the warm blood to a neighbor, who carried it to the kitchen.

The hog-killing, a nasty affair that must be done swiftly, started that way. When you try to squeeze a living from 30 acres of hard ground, as the city-bred Flachs do, hoping to be self-sufficient, you can waste nothing, flinch at nothing.

Yet, the Flachs managed to turn slaughter into a celebration. They invited the neighbors over, made it a party. For two south Floridians and their two school-age children, survival for one more year on this Panhandle farm was motive aplenty.

Within minutes after Rudy shot and bled Wilbur, he dipped the carcass into a tub of scalding water, loosening the reddish brown

Carol and Rudolf Flach at "Thorneycroft." Photos by the author, 1981.

Hog's head in bucket, after hog-killing.

Carol Flach cleaning hog intestines to make chitterlings.

hair, and shifted it to a worktable. Working fiercely, the Flachs and friends slowly, messily, scraped it clean.

"I've got this hair all over my mouth," Carol complained, puffing to blow it away.

"Now you know how I feel," the bearded Rudy said. The spectacle cheered Rudy. "Scraping a hog is like painting a picture," he added. "You can keep on forever. You have to just pick a time and stop."

Once Wilbur had been scraped white and naked, he was hoisted again, his belly sliced open and his guts pulled out. "When we get to this point, we usually have a big discussion about anatomy," Rudy said, still merry. "Like, what's this thing?"

Carol pulled out the heavily laden intestines, squeezed them empty and rinsed them in the hot water. "There is a joke they tell about this," she said. "But I can't repeat it. It's about slinging these things around your head to get this stuff out."

Jake, the dog, pulled at scraps and fallen mess, tried to nip at the hanging carcass. The chickens pressed in, clucking excitedly, scavenging. The scene was enough to gag an urban guest. Rudy shooed the animals away.

Carol, in a bright-red sweater, tried to ignore the blood and excrement. "I always wear red, so at least the blood won't show," she said. She talked fast about the hams and pork chops and other good things to eat that would come out of all this. Clearly, it was an effort to concentrate on something else.

"When I get through with these, you'll be able to read a newspaper through them," she said, holding up the intestines to the light. "Baking soda will take out the odors." The Flachs stuff these natural casings with sausage and liverwurst.

Rudy, wielding a saw, severed Wilbur's head and handed it to Carol. Using the butcher knife again, he split the carcass down the middle so that it began to resemble something that you might see in a butcher shop. That was the last step for this day. It had taken about two hours. He hoisted the meat out of reach of the dogs and left it hanging overnight. Next day he would carve out the hams for smoking and curing, trim out the chops, grind the sausage parts and package some into meal-size portions.

The symbolic touch came at lunch. Andre LaCroix, one of the neighbors, had mixed Wilbur's blood with bread crumbs and spices to make blood cheese, which had the consistency of a scarlet pudding. He served it with Carol's home-baked bread and home-canned beef stew on a long wooden table that Rudy had made. They swore it was delicious.

Nothing in the Flachs' background prepared them for this thorny struggle to achieve self-sufficiency on a farm. Ten years ago, they would have been shocked by a hog-killing and the daily chores they routinely do. They would have been horrified if anyone had told them they could subsist on $3,000 a year, as they did in 1981. They had never grown a garden, but all their vegetables come out of one. Carol had never home-canned, but this winter she canned 726 jars of meat and vegetables, a year's supply.

Money has become a bad word in the house. Carol spends only $20 a month on groceries, and wonders whether it is too much. They grow corn to feed the livestock, and slaughter hogs and cows to put meat on the table. They grind wheat into flour, corn into meal, always bake their own bread.

Rudy rebuilt a damaged windmill to pump water from a well into a 100-gallon storage tank that supplies the house. He rigged a solar panel to heat it. Their cows furnish milk, and Carol churns the over-supply into butter. They substitute honey from their beehives for sugar. They heat with firewood from trees on their own land. Carol makes soap from animal fat and hardwood ashes, sews on a treadle machine, makes herb tea as a coffee substitute. Rudy and their son, Jeff, 14, hunt and fish. Raccoon has become one of Rudy's favorite dishes. When they bag one, Carol and their daughter, Dory, 9, make a hash out of it.

The Flachs have learned to treat hardships as stimulating experience, but an adventure in primitivism was not what they had in mind 10 years ago in Broward County when they first began talking whimsically about moving to a farm. It began with the conventional idle fantasy of city folk about getting away to the country, buying some acreage, living pleasantly among good neighbors, being independent and safe and content, taking time in a quiet spot to do the things that make life something to savor. There was no reason then for them to believe that their life could pirouette and race away toward that dream.

It was a fantasy that usually appears about the sophomore year in college, but usually recedes into the lower consciousness until either opportunity or desperation calls it up again, often during the dangerous crosscurrents of midlife. For many it is the last ideal, the secret, impractical one kept faintly alive by illusions about retirement. The dream blames urban irritations for withdrawn lives, blindly persists in the belief that rural hardships will affect them differently.

Ironically, as the structure of society increasingly specializes, making each segment more vulnerable and dependent, more anxious for the security represented by pensions and insurance, chances for realizing the dream become more remote. But the dream itself becomes more intense.

Before families became enveloped by compulsions to wipe out every risk and ache, before they knew the appetites for push-button cooling and warmth and sanitation, before their delights became needs, the dream was within reach of many. Now, except for the talented and extraordinarily determined few, hardly any realistically can hope for it.

When their dream first began to ferment, Rudy and Carol did not appear to be exceptions. Neither had ever lived on a farm. Rudy's parents migrated to the United States from Germany in the 1930s, and he was born in New Jersey. At age 10, he moved with his parents to Broward County. Carol, born in New York, moved with her family to south Florida at age 11. After their marriage, the second for both, they bought a home in Pompano Beach. He was an electrician.

In 1970, Rudy, a thoughtful and sensitive man, began reassessing his life. He was only 35 but he had high blood pressure, high cholesterol and backaches so severe that some days he needed the assistance of a walking cane. He blamed it on stress. A vague, uneasy fear kept growing in him that city life was unhealthy.

"I became concerned about the way our lives were structured, the way we were forced to live," Rudy said. "We are not antisocial, but we began to believe that wherever there are great numbers of people, there are more and more problems. It was that simple. More people, more crime, more traffic, more stress, more sickness and on and on."

Commuting to jobs through Broward County's traffic regularly required an hour and a half each way. The jobs themselves involved a demand to rush, but carried technicalities that forced delay. "It got where I hated to see him come home," Carol said. She was 28, unhappy only because he was. "He'd come in mad." Evenings, she tried to greet him with a party atmosphere, but it was not enough.

In time Rudy's fear enlarged to something more than personal. He began to wonder whether the urban tangle itself might not break down in disaster. "We were so dependent. We had so little influence on the things of our lives," he said. "What if the water became contaminated? What if the food became scarce? What if the air got polluted? What if the power went off? Can you imagine what it would be like in south Florida if the power went off for two weeks?"

These impressions did not develop suddenly. Over a period of years, Rudy became aware of them. He followed the news, read a lot and noted this same malaise among others. He believed that it would reflect politically, perhaps worldwide. With so much reckless anxiety loose, how long before one of the many international crises ended with The Bomb?

Rudy began to dream about getting away, not knowing where or how, just focusing dim hope on the future. The dream and the uneasiness fed on each other. A conviction began to build that if his life were going to have meaning, he would have to wrestle out of it some more specific hope, some potential change of direction that had realistic dimensions. Only retirement, though, seemed to offer any possibility and that was years away.

Despite that, the feeling grew so intense that he began watching "for sale" ads about farms in rural Florida. He saw one that advertised 100 acres and a house in Chipley, a small town in the Panhandle. It sounded far off and nice. There were several others that interested him. "We talked about buying a place and preparing it for our retirement home," Carol said.

In 1971 he and Carol took a vacation to investigate. They first drove up the east coast to agricultural Flagler County, liked it, but changed their minds when they discovered the mammoth Palm Coast development scheduled there. They moved on to look at a place in Madison County and then west toward the Panhandle.

The Chipley property proved to be too expensive, but in Bonifay (population 2,700), a town almost halfway between Tallahassee and Pensacola along I-10, a real-estate agent offered something else they liked: 30 rural acres one mile down a dirt road in Holmes County (population 14,000) near the Alabama line, at the right price, with a creek running through the property. "It had nothing but a cornfield and woods, but it got us excited," said Rudy. They bought it, and on the way home mentally remodeled the dream.

"In an offhand way, the Realtor told us we probably could plant 100 pecan trees and make enough money selling pecans to retire," Carol said. "It was a little thing, but it stuck in our minds."

With the property in hand, Rudy's discontent heightened to urgency. "Pretty soon he started talking about not waiting until retirement, maybe moving up there in 10 years," Carol said. "We decided we could spend those years getting ready. We would learn how to do things that would save money. We would go up there and plant those pecan trees, and do other things with the land, maybe get a house started."

They launched themselves into an apprenticeship for country living. Carol studied organic gardening. They tore up the Broward backyard and planted vegetables. She bought a pressure cooker, began to home-can things she grew or bought at the market. She learned how to bake bread.

Rudy collected books about farming and do-it-yourself projects. "I was always mechanically inclined, but I never really had any experience at it," he said. He subscribed to *Mother Earth News*, bought the Foxfire books about old-time Appalachian survivalists. They toured flea markets, gathering ideas and tools and gadgets. Each step led to a discovery, and each discovery to another step.

Every chance, they drove up to their land, planted things, refined plans, introduced themselves to new neighbors and became more enchanted by what seemed to them an exotic lifestyle. "We ate food we hardly ever heard of before," Carol said. "Turnip greens, cornbread, black-eyed peas, biscuits, squirrels, raccoons, possums. It was so wonderful, so fresh. The people were so warm and good-hearted."

Pretty soon, it became obvious to both of them that they simply did not want to wait 10 years. "We never really sat down and decided," Carol said. "It just happened. One day Rudy said something about five years instead of 10, but by then we really didn't want to wait at all. It was something we wanted too much. We were convinced we could make it work."

Their excitement overcame any qualms about the gamble involved. By that time, we really couldn't have done anything else," Carol said. "We both felt it. We would have been too miserable." In September 1973 they sold their Broward County home for a handsome profit, moved into a trailer on the Panhandle farm and began to test their fantasies against reality.

For a year, uncertain of what to expect, they lived closer to the bone than they have since. To earn money, Rudy and Carol took any jobs available. He did small electrical chores, repaired automobiles, cut firewood. Together they picked pecans, painted houses, put roofs on barns, raked trash. Their greatest earnings that year, however, were in respect.

The neighbors, always hospitable, nevertheless did not commit themselves to close friendships with a family they expected to give up and go back to Broward County. By their sweat and determination, the Flachs began to earn a commitment. "It still took us about two more years to really feel like we belonged, though," Carol said. "There is a thing about these country people. They are very friendly and good-hearted, but there's sort of a wall there until they decide that you are as down-to-earth and hardworking and sincere as they are."

In a little more than a year, bringing in professionals at critical points, they built a four-bedroom, two-bath brick house, not air-conditioned, heated by wood. They put in twice the insulation they had been advised was necessary. "I kept the lines simple, did it the easiest way possible," Rudy said. The two of them laid cement blocks, put up the roof, did the wiring, installed the plumbing. "I had trouble with the plumbing," Rudy admitted. "I'd read a book at night on how it should be done, and the next day I would do it. Then, sometimes, I'd have to redo it."

Moving from south Florida's expensive Gold Coast housing market to the Panhandle's relatively inexpensive one was important. It made a lot of things possible. The sale of their Broward County home paid for their land and the house and gave them a comfortable cushion while getting the farm established.

In October 1974 they sold the trailer and moved into their new home. As a name for it, they chose Thorneycroft—"thorny" for the rough nature of the place when they found it, "croft" from the British term for a small farm.

As their plans took on reality, turning into sprouting leaves and fruit and eggs and milk and meat, life took on an unexpected sweetness. After that first year, Rudy realized one day that his back hardly ever hurt anymore. His blood pressure went down, and his cholesterol became normal. Carol detected new vitality in all of them. None has been to a doctor for illness in more than five years. "I can explain it very easily," said Carol. "No stress. Stress will kill you." Though it was Rudy's unease that led them to the farm, Carol's enthusiasm and enterprise may exceed his now. Rudy has worked at taking the regimentation out of his life. "It's my German blood," he said. "I tend to want everything organized, on time, efficient. The harder I work, the better I feel, but I coach myself to work when it seems natural to do it, not on some fixed schedule. I haven't felt this good since I was a kid."

As Rudy has relaxed, Carol has accelerated. She has become a fanatic about natural foods and health, an expert at improvisation who can cook anything she tastes, sew anything someone else has sewn. She takes special pride in her ability to adapt. She believes firmly that eating organically grown vegetables from their garden, eating meat fattened by natural foods only and without the use of chemical growth stimulants makes a significant difference. Except for grocery staples for which they can invent no substitutes, store-bought food is regarded as a liability both in taste and health.

In some areas, the Flachs' enchantment may lean them toward superstition. They have begun to pick up and believe in home remedies heard from old-timers or taken out of farmers' almanacs.

Some medical experts doubt that garlic, for example, will lower blood pressure and keep off fleas and ticks, but the Flachs suspect that it will. Whatever the facts on this and other remedies, there can be no doubt that the Flachs benefit by drawing psychological well-being from them.

With their plan set to fashion their lives on the farm to be as nearly self-sufficient as possible, they began early to devise backup systems and alternative procedures for producing food, power, water, fuel for working vehicles, heat, income. Their approach to farm life became a flexible thing that permitted them to roll with the setbacks, take advantages of the bonuses. They denied themselves nothing that did not detract from their commitment.

They planted black walnut trees, chestnuts, pears, apples, figs, peaches, grapes, blueberries, 500 red cedars, plus a corn crop for feed, vegetables in a garden solidly mulched by literally tons of rotting peanut hulls picked up at an area peanut mill. The cedars later could be sold as Christmas trees. The grapes and other fruit could be made into wine. The vegetables could be eaten fresh and the surplus canned. All of it was a diversified investment.

From an uncle who died, they inherited a few antiques. They had been collectors before, but this spurred them to pick up other pieces in the area. Rudy bought an old house for $50, moved it to his place and put the antiques in it. In a pinch, these would be for sale.

The Flachs assembled a variety of farm animals and finally arrived at these numbers as appropriate: three or four dozen chickens, a dozen turkeys, two milk cows, one steer (slaughtered for beef every other year), several hogs (two of which are killed each year), a few goats, one or two horses, one to two dozen flocks of geese, guineas and ducks, a few pigeons, four beehives and two or three dogs. All these represented responsibilities, as well as benefits, that demanded Rudy and Carol spend most of their time on the farm.

Rudy set up job alternatives that he could turn to for income as needed. He takes small electrical assignments—once, the possibilities became so good that he talked to Carol about getting a helper, buying a new truck and setting up a business; she pointedly asked if he wanted to bring the rat race with him to their new life, and he dropped the idea—works about 40 days a year as a substitute rural mail carrier, makes himself available for mechanical repairs and odd jobs if he needs money.

If an emergency creates a need for money, Rudy either does extra work off the farm or they turn to what they call their material bank account: they cut and sell firewood (17 acres of the farm are wooded) or sell eggs, meat, antiques or produce. "Last season we got 28 pecans off those 100 trees the Realtor told us we could retire on," said Carol. "But they're coming." The cedar Christmas trees also are still on deposit.

The horse serves as a backup system for their old tractor; the windmill (bought when another farmer gave up on it after a 1975 hurricane blew it down) is backed up by a hand pump, an electrical generator and a gas generator. Rudy converted the farm vehicles, including the tractor and an old Chevy used as a family car, to propane gas, which he can more easily store on the farm. When Rudy and Jeff hunt, Jeff cleans the game. The boy also catches fish out of their creek and makes his own fishing flies out of hair from the horse's tail. "Whatever he gets, he cleans. That's the rule," Rudy said.

After Rudy built the solar panel to heat the house water, he put together a smaller solar tank on the roof of an outbuilding where they wash and clean clothes and food. Rudy has a workshop where he can make replacement parts for things that break. If both propane and gasoline get scarce, they have a small motorcycle that will extend their mileage on available fuel. Carol can cook with gas, or on the woodstoves that heat the house, or in a Dutch oven that fits into the fireplace.

As an economy measure, they never use paper towels and napkins, only cloth, which can be washed and reused. "You finally begin to realize that labor and time are what run costs up. We have the time, and we don't mind the work. It makes a big difference in the amount of money we need," Rudy said.

After about four years, when their living pattern stabilized, Carol toted up their expenses and found that they were spending about $3,000 a year to cover the bare cost of living. As inflation has influenced that upward, new knowledge and skills have been able to compensate and bring it back down. The total includes no extras, no capital purchases. It means wearing hand-me-down clothes (exchanged with family and neighbors), making sacrifices, bartering work or produce for goods, harvesting the surpluses (you-pick-'em opportunities) of other farmers at bargain prices. They tailor their income to their needs, and the $3,000 is not a rigid budget but a guideline. Extra money goes toward accumulating things that increase self-reliance, but they discipline themselves not to want too much. When possible they buy second-hand and rely on Rudy's skill or Carol's inventiveness. If for some reason expenses go up, Rudy dips into his bank account of things or works extra at off-farm jobs.

"The secret," said Rudy, "is to change your way of thinking, to not feel like you need to have everything. It's a swap. You sacrifice one thing to gain another." Some call that poverty; they call it freedom.

"We don't owe anybody any money and we don't buy anything on credit," Carol said. "If we need something, we save until we have enough to pay for it. That solves a lot of problems. We have found that money creates needs. If we made a lot, it would destroy the way we live."

The annual budget guidelines break down this way: property taxes $200, life and house insurance $300, $120 for a telephone ($10 a month), $240 (or $20 a month) for food and staples, $330 for power ($26 to $28 a month for between 300 and 400 kilowatts), $800 for fuel (transportation and heat), $200 for personal items and $600 for health insurance. The health insurance, however, does not go to a company but into a separate bank account for medical expenses. Confident in their health and their resourcefulness, they assume the hazard of self-insurance. It is part of their new philosophy that no one has absolute security, so they choose their risks deliberately.

If the children did not share their love of the farm, the dream might collapse. That could change, but for now Dory and Jeff are as enthusiastic about their home, school and friends as their parents are. They talk about growing up, getting married, picking out their own patch of the 30 acres and continuing to live here.

"Jeff wants to be an electrician, like I am," Rudy said. "There's a good vocational school in Chipley where he can go and learn the trade without leaving home." Dory is too young to do anything other than generalize about her ambition to remain on the farm forever.

For the children, the farm is both entertainment and education. Dory once explained to Rudy that a favorite game of hers was to catch one of the roosters. He asked if that was hard to do, and she replied that she could manage it if she waited until the rooster was trying to mate with a hen. "Yes," Rudy agreed, properly serious. "That would keep his attention diverted." On a farm, the natural processes take the trauma out of developmental crises.

Wilbur, the red-haired hog, was an example. The children had let Wilbur roam the yard as a little pig, running with the dogs, chickens, ducks, turkeys, geese, guineas and even over into the pasture with the horses, cows and goats. Wilbur discovered the milk-goats' teats, and the goats tolerated it until Wilbur's appetite for warm milk exceeded their capacity to provide it. To protect them, Rudy built a wooden yoke that fit around Wilbur's neck. Because the yoked little pig looked so much like a penitent pilgrim placed in the stocks for public censure, Rudy painted across the yoke: REPENT. Wilbur's mischief was history, recorded in the family picture album.

When Wilbur reached the weight of 200 pounds, however, none of this was enough for reprieve. Wilbur's mission was to furnish meat for the table. The hog-killing accomplished that, and the children accepted it.

The first time the Flachs tried to kill a hog themselves, rather than paying the local slaughterhouse 15 cents a pound to do it for them, the event was more a trial than a celebration, but it illustrated how the Flachs attack each problem with a certainty that somehow they can defeat it.

Rudy prepared by reading all the publications he could find on the subject, including an advisory from the Morton Salt Company on slaughtering and curing. Carol consulted old-timers in the area, and together they devised a plan for the basic steps: killing the hog, bleeding it, scalding, scraping, final butchering.

That morning the weather was 10 degrees. Following the consensus of instructions, they heated the water in an old washpot and poured it into a drum half-buried in the dirt at the prescribed 45-degree angle. When they threw the hog in, most of the water splashed out. They scalded half the carcass at a time and laid it out on the cold ground for scraping.

The job took all day and the process became so laborious that the hog stiffened from rigor mortis or cold. Two carloads of neighbors, coming over to celebrate success, found the Flachs still struggling with a bloody, half-hairy hog strung from the limb of a tree and Rudy standing underneath consulting his books while Carol urged him to read faster.

Later, Rudy reviewed that experience and set up his own system. Rather than a half-buried drum, he found an old cast-iron bathtub and cemented bricks around it to form a fireplace underneath. The water could be heated and the hog scalded in the same tub. He rigged a block and tackle under the tree and built a worktable nearby so the hog could be hoisted and easily shifted between the tub and the table. With those adjustments, the operation became manageable in two hours or less.

The Flachs hardly notice the sacrifices in their lifestyle until family or friends from south Florida come visiting. "Sometimes the water pressure (supplied by the windmill) gets low or we'll have to wait awhile for the solar panel to get the water hot again after it's been used for a while, but we don't think anything about it," Rudy said. "We've learned not to take long showers and things like that. But a visitor will notice right away if the pressure gets low, and want to know why. The next thing he'll do is tell me how I can get an electric pump that will kick in at a certain point and keep the pressure from getting low. Well, I know that, but where is it written that you've got to have 40 pounds of water pressure all the time, or unlimited hot water all the time?"

"Yeah," Carol said. "We get that. We mention to a visitor that we can sell our extra eggs, and right off, she says, 'You know, you could get yourself a couple hundred laying hens and . . . ' Well, that misses the whole point."

"Two other families from Broward County, friends of ours, moved up here because of us," Rudy said. "They wanted to live like we did. After a while, one of the men took a full-time job and went back to work. The other started going back and forth to south Florida, working three or four months there and then coming up here for a month or two. But you see, neither of them changed their lifestyle. You can plant a garden and buy a side of meat, but that doesn't make it. You have to live a different life."

"The thing is," Carol said, "if you don't get away from the spending of money, the man's got to go away to make it. If he goes away regularly, you can't live like this."

The Flachs' standing was elevated late in 1978 when Holmes County wanted to have an antique farm show. The plan was to exhibit old farm implements and demonstrate how grandma and grandpa churned butter and ground their own flour and baked their own bread. So few of the natives could do those things, or even could remember much about them, that the Flachs were asked to put the show together. It was a success. The south Floridians showed the Panhandle folk what old-time farming was like. After that, Thorneycroft became a place of local pride as well as curiosity.

Where the Flachs have not fit local custom, or have not wanted to fit, their differences have been tolerated amiably. Because they are divorced and Catholic, they have no current church affiliation, but they count themselves among the religious anyway and regard their singular path from urban unhappiness to rural satisfaction as a blessing from God.

"Sometimes I think some of our friends are disappointed that we don't go to church with them, but it hasn't made any difference in our friendship," Rudy said. "A lot of people in south Florida have this picture in their mind of rednecks living up here. That's understandable but it's not accurate. These people are farmers, simple people; some of them are unschooled, but they know how to do things and they're smart about what holds a life together. What they have is what a lot of the people in the cities are searching for."

The Flachs are not politically active, but their private preferences run toward the Republican Party or toward an independent stance. Early in their time here they thought that might mark them as outsiders, but they discovered that although voter registration in the county is dominated by Democrats, in presidential elections a Republican often gets the majority.

In their nearly seven-and-a-half years at Thorneycroft, the Flachs have turned their lives completely around. Once they might have looked back on a similar period and remembered the vacations they took, the new cars they bought, the shows they saw. Now they care about different things.

Rudy remembers getting up one cold morning to milk the cows. "I was sleepy and I just leaned my head over against that old cow. She was warm and smelled good, and I could hear all those rumbling noises, things churning around in there while I was milking. Something about that seemed so right. Now I do it all the time."

He remembers when Carol came running into the house and announced a calf was being born. When he got there, he found the new calf had stuck one hoof out first, as though testing the world.

Carol remembers the first time she made homemade soap. Rudy took a shower with it, and went around all day complaining that he smelled like bacon. She remembers the first freeze in the new house. She and Rudy kept running in and out getting firewood and stuffing it into three little stoves. "Rudy," she finally told him, "this won't work. What'll we do when we get old?" He bought a big, centrally heating wood furnace.

She remembers the time when she was learning to cure hams, and visited the mother of one of Dory's teachers, looking for advice. Next thing she knew there was a story going around the school about poor Mrs. Flach who did not have enough money to refrigerate her meat.

They look back now and see more realistically the great gamble they took. They remain a little in awe of what they did. "It was the right thing for us," Rudy said. "Maybe we were just lucky, but I don't think so. We had plenty of problems. But what we couldn't solve, we learned to accept. It worked not just because of what we did, but because we were committed to changing our lives, no matter what it took."

The Flachs do not regard the adjustments as sacrifices but as improvements. "For the first couple of years, we kept waiting to get homesick or for something to go wrong," Rudy added. "We kept wondering, what if we have to go back to south Florida? One moonlit night we went out for a walk, and I told Carol, 'You know, we just couldn't go back'. We accept that now. I could never again live in a city anywhere. If we lost all this for some unknown reason, I'd get a little old shack and we'd live out in the country somewhere, any-where, because it's so much freer and easier.

"If the cities were bombed away, we could survive up here, unless the fallout got us. We could get by with just what we have. But if that doesn't happen, and we hope it doesn't, it's still a wonderful way to live. When I wake up in the morning, I'm anxious to get out and do things. It was never that way before."

The Flachs have discovered a different way. "Nobody should mis-take it as an easy life, or a simple one, either," Rudy continued. "In a lot of ways it's really more complex than living in the city and work-ing at a job. We've had to spend a lot of time studying, learning how to do all these things. We're still learning. Not everybody ought to try this. They might not be emotionally suited. It's hard. You have to change your lifestyle. To make it work, you have to stay right here and stick with it. The responsibilities never let up."

Carol agreed. "Sometimes we wonder how we've done what we have. We really do. But whatever comes up, we've found we can find a way to handle it. For us, it's very satisfying. On a job, you might get a feeling of satisfaction every now and then about something special. But here, we have those feelings every day. Everything is so real. We can see that the things we do make a difference."

The Flachs gambled on a dream and won. For them, it was real.

—*February 8, 1981*

The Inn: The Passing of a Place

Snowbirds come to Florida to escape the cold but often find much more than higher temperatures. They become attached to a place and its people, and the happening is mutual. The burning of a grand old inn in Lake Wales illustrated that in 1979. With it passed a piece of old Florida.

A tall brick chimney stood in a circle of ashes where one tiny arena of life had been cremated. From the burnt-out center, the heat had radiated to damage a part of everything that was close. Some of it showed—tree trunks scorched up one side, shrubs shriveled brown on just one side—and some did not.

Perry Littles, tall and dignified, napped and fretted in the living room of his house over on North Avenue. He fought the heat with a fan and an air conditioner. He had waited tables in that old hotel since 1938. At age 70, what would he do now?

James Kahler, young and athletic, poked around in the ashes trying to save some of the old bricks. His family had owned the hotel under the tall oaks along Scenic Highway (u.s. 27A) all his life and he had taken over the management a year earlier. But insurance for the old building had been too expensive. At 28, he had no plans.

The old Plantation Inn was in Lake Wales, the heart of Florida, away from the crowded coasts, just below the frost line. A minister from Minnesota had been spending his winters there for years, ever since he retired. He tipped the waiters at the end of each season, rather than at the end of each meal, and they kidded him about how he would handle parishioners who skipped the collection plate four months at a stretch.

A widow from Wisconsin called The Inn her winter home, the guests and staff her family away from the family. During the off-season, she wrote them "wish-I-were-there" letters.

There were others, lots of others. Kahler worried about them. "Everything burned," he said. "Even the guests' histories, the names and addresses, everything. We have not been able to tell everybody. When they get in touch with us, we try to find them someplace else to stay, but it's hard to get something they want."

"Those old ladies didn't have a lot of money," Littles explained. "Some of 'em won't come. They won't be able to find another place like we had. It was a good old place, good to all of us. People are different now. They won't have places like that anymore."

The Inn was like a club for the elderly, permitting a sprinkling of the younger. There were bingo nights, card nights, a big fireplace in the television room, a sharing of problems and limited joys. Waiters wore red jackets and short pants with long white stockings, and governed the high-ceilinged old dining room with genteel authority. They chatted with guests about the weather, exchanged advice, laughed at jokes, looked at family pictures. The meals came from an old-fashioned kitchen where one family, its members passing on the jobs from one generation to the next, had been doing the cooking since 1919.

One night, fire flickered alive in the closed and shuttered old inn, whose sturdy heart pine floors and walls had been sawed and planed when Taft was president of the 46 states. Flames rushed across the old boards and turned them into ash and smoke. In just two hours everything was gone.

The founding Lake Wales Land Management Company built it as the Wales Hotel in 1911, the first real structure among a landscape of piney woods and canvas tents, so guests would have a place to stay while they came and looked at lake country land they could buy cheap.

The 25 rooms and 11 fireplaces were palatial then, costing $20,000 and offering hot and cold running water. Broad piazzas overlooked Crystal Lake, and a private plant furnished power for lights. The hotel became the social center where clubs met, governors and senators came to speak, the high school held its proms and celebrities stayed. Gen. George Custer's widow, for example, preferred it.

Lake Wales developed variety and range as it grew into a city of 10,000. Citrus and recreational opportunities bloomed in this almost exact center of Florida. The Passion Play and Spook Hill (where cars seemed to roll uphill) and the Marketplace Mall and the Depot Museum added sparkle.

The famed Singing Tower and nature sanctuary at Iron Mountain, created by magazine editor Edward Bok and dedicated in 1929 by Calvin Coolidge, marked its golden anniversary with an address by Bok's grandson, President Derek Bok of Harvard University. Meanwhile, the grand dragon of the United Ku Klux Klans of America cut hair as usual at his local barbershop.

Amid all this, the old Plantation Inn had remained a special place that offered a certain charm and refreshing familiarity, a thread maternally wound through the intricate new patterns of community life. It recalled the reason and the style that gave birth to Lake Wales. Maybe its loss was not a tragedy in the modern dimension of tragedies, but maybe we are being robbed of the fullness of life when it takes so much more to make us cry, or to laugh, than it should.

"I don't know," Jimmy Kahler said. "I was planning for what I might be able to do in 10 years. We can't build another place unless we get some partners. Otherwise, we'll sell, I guess, and that'll be the end of it."

Perry Littles was discouraged too. "Have to get me a job somewhere," he said. But he and the others do not expect to need their red jackets or white stockings anymore. "Maybe," he said sadly, "maybe there'll be something at one of those fast-food places."

—*August 18, 1979*

Horse Passion: Tenderness Plus a Whip

At 7 A.M. on a chilly spring day in 1981, the horse farm looks ghostly. Fog settles over the barns and the hot-walkers and the mile-long track. Wooden rail fences, soft green hills and live oak trees frame and punctuate an ethereal scene.

A sudden rataplan of hooves, thumping heavily in soft dirt, grabs your attention as a horse gallops out of a cloud, breathing hard, lathering, a small man perched high on its back, talking to it, sounding as though he would not be surprised if he got an answer.

Junior Serna rolls up in a pickup truck with his guest of the day, Jimmy Jones, a short, 74-year-old, storied horseman in a coat and tie. Serna, a slim man marked by a blaze of gray hair sweeping back from the temples, wearing jeans and a cap, points his binoculars into the fog, and he and Jones begin to talk horses.

It is a kind of happy, casual talk that drifts off in all directions until hooves sound and an excited, big-eyed animal pounds by, and then they cluck and point and speculate as though it were a baby at grandma's house.

Serna is trainer at this farm, 360 beautifully greened and shaped acres northwest of Ocala in Marion County. He works with young horses, some of them sensitive, skinny-legged foals dropped into the world only a few months before. With a daddy-like combination of tenderness and firmness, he teaches them the elementals of horse racing in a course that lasts six months to a year. "When them horses leave, we want 'em to be educated," Serna said. "We don't want to send a delinquent to the racetrack."

"A lot of people send their babies here for Junior to get 'em broke, get 'em ready to go to the races," said 28-year-old Bob Murty, Jr., who joined Serna and Jones at the rail. This is a training farm, owned by the Murty Brothers of Oklahoma, Bob's father and two uncles. The Murtys also own a breeding farm in Kentucky.

Under Serna's care this day were 300 horses stalled in nine barns posted like small settlements around the hills. A few of them belonged to Col. Mitchell Wolfson of Miami. Jones, who once saddled eight Kentucky Derby winners for Calumet Farms—including the famed Citation—was an adviser to Wolfson.

Jones has been leaning on an aluminum track rail, slowly sliding along it until he rubbed against an automobile tire that cushioned a gate pole. The tire turned one arm and one side of his shirt black. He was telling stories about the old days, of the big names in racing, missed investment opportunities, blending bloodlines, why benign climate and limestone in the soil made Marion County such good horse country, and his phenomenal years at Calumet. He was wearing a watch on each wrist ("Just got this good one repaired, and it's easier to wear it than to carry it," he explained), plus a copper bracelet on the left one.

"They laugh at me about that, but it works," Jones said of the copper bracelet, citing aid for a wrist and once for an ankle. "It's not a hoodoo," he said. "It actually works. I swear I think it would work on horses. Sometimes I'm gon' try it."

Serna, avoiding either endorsement or rejection of that notion, responded with a story. "I remember back home in Texas some of the old-timers used to have some quarter horses, and when their fillies come in season, they would throw pennies in the water bucket. I don't know the answer, but I know the old-timers would do that and they thought it would help those fillies." Jones added, "I used to see that, too. There'd be 15, 20 copper pennies in the water bucket."

The sun melted the fog, the horsemen continued to explore the frontiers of truth and knowledge and the horses galloped in twos and threes. Serna sent them to the starting gate and around the track, calling out names, alerting Jones to sounds and qualities, answering questions.

Serna's life has been all horses. Now 42, he was born Julian Serna, Jr., in Alice, Texas, grew up around quarter horses and rode them in Texas and Oklahoma. He switched to Thoroughbreds, followed them to Arkansas and Ohio. He galloped horses and became an exercise boy, a foreman and in 1962 a trainer. He was a trainer for Walnut Hill Farms out of Pennsylvania until about five years ago, when he joined the Murtys and came to Ocala. "I wanted more of the farm life," he said. He lives on the farm with his wife, two sons and a daughter. One son gallops horses in the morning workouts. The daughter works in the stables.

"The thing to remember," Jones said, "is that all this is supposed to put 'em together so that they're a good athlete when they're through. It's a short time to do a lot. That's the horse business. Life is short. You got to figure when he's six years old, he's beginning to get over the hill, possibly."

"What we try to do," Serna added, "is to give 'em tender loving care, like a child, but not let 'em get away with too many things. You can correct 'em early, get it out of their mind. He'll understand. In young horses, you're going to find so many different attitudes, like in humans. They've got to get individual treatment, but still you can't ignore the fact that they're animals. It all revolves on judgment. You have to be around 'em all the time."

Jones kept remembering things. "That big old docile horse," he said of one he had. "You could run him a mile and whip him every step of the way, and he'd go back to the barn and go to sleep." He crossed its blood with one "so wild you couldn't catch him with butterfly nets. They mixed good."

"You've got to watch for that willingness out there on the track, see whether they act like they're enjoying it," Serna said. "A certain amount of training will help, but they've got to have class. It'll be in the bloodlines, somewhere. You can see a horse look super-beautiful, doing things right, run well as a two-year-old, but then you'll see those class horses catch up with him come three-year-old time."

On a horse farm, it is a different world. Rugged morning gallops work off the tensions. The men raise the babies into sensitive, responsive, big-eyed beasts with long, skinny legs and gracefully powerful chests, and love them just short of the mating passion. The horse world combines tenderness and the whip. There is a kind of royal fiber running through it all that sanctions male emotion.

Horse racing is a curious, beguiling world, rich in many ways that have nothing to do with wagering.

—May 24, 1981

Apalachicola Feast: The Annual Festival

Somewhere in Florida, a festival occurs almost every weekend. The state hosts 500 or more of them, and at least 5 million people attend. They put folk culture and local pride on display. One of the oldest is the Florida Seafood Festival held at Apalachicola the first Saturday of November. In 1915 there had been an Apalachicola Carnival, and though not continual the seafood festival evolved out of that beginning. I have attended it many times. Typical was the one in 1973, my first.

For eight solid hours, Grandma had been cooking, and the Apalachicola sunset was still an hour away. A flour-streaked hand briefly touched her forehead in a gesture of weariness. "There's no end of the mouths," she said.

For Apalachicola on its day of days, it seemed so. Cars began to flow across the Gorrie Bridge not long after sunrise. By midmorning, they had jelled into long lines that stretched back two miles along the bay.

For a week, the ladies of the church had prayed it would not rain while they worked to get ready for Apalachicola's annual seafood festival. For most of Friday night, townspeople had worked to set up the booths and displays and the deep-fry cooking vats. Saturday morning had been cool and clear, and the people kept coming to tree-shaded Battery Park by the bay. Late in the afternoon, clouds developed and breezes picked up, but the crowds never slowed.

"They're so thick now you can't stir 'em with a stick," said Grandma at midday.

Apalachicola's population had quadrupled for the day. From 7,000 on Friday, it exploded to 28,000 or maybe even 30,000 on Saturday, depending on the enthusiasm of the estimator. Cars snaked round and round the park, people milled past the booths of balloons and dolls and handcrafts and simply awesome arrays of seafood. Some walked two blocks into town past sidewalk art shows, tables of cakes and pastries and more handcraft displays lined along 100-year-old storefronts.

"Every bit of our living comes from the water," said Grandma, the cooker. For all of Apalachicola, the percentage was not quite so high, but oysters, shrimp and mullet hauled out of the water each year still made up 60 percent of the economy.

The seafood festival was created to honor the industry and attract visitors to sample its delights, but it had begun to emphasize as well the statewide benefits of preserving Apalachicola Bay from pollution or other alterations.

Just last summer, the Army Corps of Engineers proposed spending $200 million to turn the river into a barge canal. It wanted to build dams, locks and dikes. Area protests shouted that idea down.

The festival was all hurrah—from bands to oyster-eating contests to oyster-shucking contests to a crab race to a parade and floats to a tour of old homes to a blessing of the fleet. The atmosphere was delightfully small town, circa 1890. But the core of it all was the food booths, where the ladies from the local churches and civic groups, like Grandma (friendly and talkative but too shy to give her name), applied their skills to the fruits of the sea.

There were oysters on the half shell (shucked before your eyes), seafood gumbo, fried oysters, fried mullet, fried mullet roe and grits, hush puppies, boiled shrimp and pastries and sweets, including sweet-potato pie. The aroma from it all floated over the whole town. The high school band tootled, kids climbed trees and everything else in sight, politicians sang the national anthem and pledged the flag and prayed before they got up to speak under a spreading camphor tree.

Using natural gas fires, heating open vats of corn oil, an army of grandmotherly types along with a few men dipped oysters or mullet into ponds of canned cream, rolled them lightly in flour, and then lowered them on huge trays into the boiling oil. The transformation was magical. They came back up browned and crisped, surprisingly light and delicious.

The mouths ate all this and wanted more, even though some had to stand in line for an hour. At the main booth alone, 4,500 pounds of dressed mullet were sold. One booth sold 90 gallons of seafood gumbo, cup by cup, and the lines were still long when they ran out.

No one ever managed to count the total amount of food consumed, except at the oyster-eating contest. In that, six eaters lined up at a table, armed with Tabasco, crackers, soft drinks and hollow stomachs. They had 15 minutes, and all they had to do was eat raw oysters—and hold them down. Otherwise, disqualification (two failed the test).

In 10 minutes, Gary Shiver of Apalachicola had eaten 264 raw oysters and was well ahead. Keeping a careful eye on his competitors and rolling his eyes up at the trees, an understandable exercise in view of the numbers he was gulping into his belly, he forked down four more in the last five minutes, and won easily. Later, nobody saw him standing in line at any of the seafood booths.

"This is the place where you eat fish and live longer, eat clams and last longer and eat oysters and love longer," said Mayor Jimmie Nichols in his welcome address. The mayor called Apalachicola Bay "the last large clean body of water remaining in Florida that has a tremendous shellfish-producing capacity." He said with care and development it could grow up to five times as many as it does now (6 million pounds of oysters and shrimp and nearly 2 million pounds of fish from the 270-square-mile bay and adjacent waters).

On this particular day, the biggest Apalachicola seafood festival yet, the crowds spent some $100,000 for their day's pleasures. As large as that might have been for Apalachicola, the townspeople were more concerned with protecting their way of life. As Grandma cooked and visitors gorged themselves, that was the plot behind it all.

"We don't have much money," Mayor Nichols said, "but we think you'll find we have big hearts. All we want to do is save our river and bay so that all of us can enjoy seafood another day."

—*November 26, 1973*

LeRoy Collins: A Gentleman's Campaign

Few things more strongly suggested the changes taking place in Florida, and in the conduct of political campaigns, than the 1968 election for U.S. senator. Former Gov. LeRoy Collins, a man who believed politics should be practiced with courtesy and dignity, campaigned on his record and lost to Congressman Edward J. Gurney. As Collins' last campaign, it was historic.

LeRoy Collins had the air of a self-made prince who inherited additional royalty from his wife's great-grandfather. He was a silver-haired gentleman with the classic manners of the Old South, and he saw a distinguished record threatened by notions he considered inferior, if not dangerous.

Edward J. Gurney questioned neither his knowledge of self nor his adopted state. He was a lieutenant colonel in a world of many enlisted men. He fought and suffered, discovered the Right, and saw his cause as a restoration of order lost by men like Collins.

*   *   *

Collins was taping a televison address in Fort Myers, five minutes of comment on local subjects to substitute in an already prepared half-hour show. He was worried about the impact. He had been soliciting opinions. One problem had been that he looked down as he spoke. That was because an aide held the cue cards too low. This time, care was taken to hold the cards higher.

Collins was nervous. He fluffed lines, restarting twice. "I've got it now," he said. "Let's go." He went through it nicely, bobbled just once, and then waited to watch the rerun. It was well done. Collins spoke casually as a long camera shot tightened to a closer one. But a technical assistant commented that the whole half hour would have to be retaped, and he expressed concern about its quality. "This is already a second generation [tape of a tape]," he explained.

"Good gracious," Collins exploded. "How many generations of this thing are we going to have to go through?"

Collins even lost his temper in genteel language.

*   *   *

Gurney was in a short-sleeved shirt when aide Jim Martin picked him up at home in Winter Park. He brought along a coat and a tie on a hanger. Martin commented about Collins' techniques on the professionally produced half-hour show. Gurney said detachedly, "Half hours. I didn't know anybody still did that." Gurney believed in short speeches, demanded the camera move in quickly for a tight, intimate shot. He almost came out of your screen.

Gurney noted that *The Wall Street Journal* considered him the favorite to win. He seemed to regard this as natural and proper. Someone remarked that in Collins and Gurney, the voters would have a clear choice of philosophies. "I hope so," Gurney said. He did not like the way Collins expressed conservative positions. He did not want the clear choice to be fuzzed up.

At the televison station, Gurney taped two shows—one for five minutes, one for two. Aides set up the stage with an American flag at Gurney's right, lots of books behind him. "Want to run through it for timing, Ed?" a technician asked. It sounded a little too familiar, as if he should have said "sir."

"No, I'm ready. Give me a sign at one minute." He had rehearsed at home. The TelePrompTer was loaded so the speech would roll before his eyes in easy-to-read type while he seemed to look at the camera, but Gurney didn't need it. When the red light came on, he spoke earnestly, firmly, as though he were scolding a younger man for entertaining doubts. His timing was seven seconds off. The television men were impressed.

"All right, let's do the other one," Gurney said. This was for two minutes. He missed by five seconds.

LeRoy Collins was a slim, tanned man with a heavily lined face. His wife, Mary Call Darby, was the great-granddaughter of Richard Keith Call, twice territorial governor. They lived in the Call family home, called The Grove, near the governor's mansion in Tallahassee. When he first announced his return to political candidacy, some assumed the office was his by right. He had earned it with long years of public service.

At 59, Collins was five years older than Gurney. His political credentials were near legendary. About him there was the aura of being both classic and timely. His campaign themes always went to the positive. "At the core of every problem there is an opportunity," he said. He did not believe he was either liberal or conservative. "I think of myself as a constructive," he said.

One of his favorite stories dealt with a piece of traditional furniture, an old-fashioned light fixture that held candles. When the days of kerosene lamps arrived, there was argument the fixture should be discarded, but because the piece was so beautiful it was saved and adapted for kerosene. The argument was repeated when electricity came, but again its beauty won, and it was wired.

"This is what I believe in," Collins concluded. "The value of the old . . . the responsibility of adding new lights to old lamps. Every generation has this responsibility. Don't listen to them when they say we should throw the old system out."

He had served in the state legislature, held the governor's office for six years (Florida's 33rd governor), had been chairman of the Southern Governors' Conference, chairman of the National Governors' Conference, permanent chairman of the 1960 Democratic National Convention. He had been president of the National Association of Broadcasters, the first director of the federal Community Relations Service created by the 1964 Civil Rights Act. He had been undersecretary of the Department of Commerce, had practiced law privately with a distinguished firm. If Florida ever had a statesman-politician, it was LeRoy Collins. His record was admirable and there never had been a taint of scandal associated with him.

Collins seemed vigorous but not athletic. There were special personal qualities about him of dedication, sincerity, gentleness. He had an air of the Sunday school teacher, perhaps a lay preacher. Once, in

Moscow, he did substitute for Billy Graham in a Baptist church, and he often talked of that to add international emphasis to his state and national stature. He was a family man.

A favorite Collins campaign story involved his wife, Mary Call, and younger daughter. He told it to the ladies, and they loved it. In the story, Collins had on his old tuxedo and was waiting to take his wife to a party. As she came down the stairs in a new gown, the little girl said, "Oh, Mama. You're beautiful." Then, not wanting to slight her father, she added, "and Daddy, you look so *clean*." The ladies always laughed in a comfortable and satisfied way, and you could see it register with them that this was Mr. Clean Politician. A nice man.

Collins inspired confidence, perhaps because his six years as Florida governor had been called the best administration Florida had had in modern times. In the primary, his opponent Earl Faircloth accused him of being too old to serve more than one term, of wanting to retire to the U.S. Senate and write his memoirs. That hurt. People had been telling Collins he should write his memoirs, because as a Southern politician his contributions had been unique, particularly in civil rights. It was on his mind a lot.

Collins often spoke with concern about "artificiality, superficiality" in government. He deplored those who seek "reputation without character" and "power without responsibility." He frequently closed a talk with the comment, "And if I am elected, I will always conduct myself in such a way that you will never mind saying, 'That man is *my* senator'." His campaign dwelled on questions of conscience. "I am never going to retreat from my conscience, what I feel to be my principles," he said. "I don't care what happens in politics." But there were light moments.

During one handshaking tour of a shopping center, Collins gave a pretty young girl a casual hug. "When they tell me I'm too old, I always remember what Oliver Wendell Holmes said when he was 85. When he saw a pretty girl he said, 'Oh, to be 75 again'." Collins laughed.

While visiting a factory in Plant City, an elderly woman's question was almost indistinguishable in the noise. It sounded like, "When you were governor, did you accept bribes?" Collins blinked. "I don't think I understood your question," he said. She repeated it. "If I understood your question," Collins said patiently, "the answer is no." The woman was obviously disappointed. Collins tried again. "I don't think I understood you." This time the woman shouted it more clearly. "When you were governor, did you accept Christ?" He gave her an intelligently affirmative answer, and later shook his head. "I'm so glad I asked again," he said.

He liked to use a Greek quotation that said, "You can never remove injustice from a land until people who aren't hurt by injustice are just as outraged as those who are."

* * *

Edward J. Gurney was taller, at six two, and also slim. He limped, had a Silver Star on his war record and carried a cushion because a German sniper had shot him during the closing days of World War II. Humor for him did not seem effortless, but when it came it was clear and direct. At other times, you had the feeling of reserve, as though there was another thought in the back of that mind while he talked. Perhaps it was the distraction of the war wound.

He was a loner. Newsmen, sometimes grumbling that he was hard to see, nevertheless came away charmed by his frank and cordial manner. About him there was a certain respectability at once aloof and admirable, safe and proper as a bank. He admitted conservatism in the manner of a man confessing honesty, and quarreled only when critics called it negativism. His answer to that was simple enough to please Barry Goldwater, whom he supported for president in 1964. "I like the historic free enterprise system." It was a brief discourse for a graduate of both the Harvard and Duke law schools, but typical. Three other friends, Richard Nixon, Ronald Reagan and U.S. senator John Tower, also would approve.

At a free beer party at Cocoa Beach one Saturday, Gurney was at his best. The beer taps opened at 11 A.M. There were straw hats, hot dogs and loud music. At noon, with his usual superb timing, Gurney stepped to the back of a truck fashioned as a speaker's stand. He told one joke and then delivered a rousing, old-fashioned political speech that drew cheers. He spoke once of "LeRoy" with unusual glee. In 10 minutes he quit. The stage had been set; Gurney delivered his message quickly, entertainingly, forcefully.

It was like the story of two men who knew each other's jokes so well that the stories were numbered, and they laughed just when the numbers were called. Perhaps there was no real discussion of issues, but each time Gurney mentioned a political catch label, the crowd responded. Not even his children had a chance to be bored.

*　　*　　*

Collins avoided fanfare as though he felt it to be undignified. He liked to stroll unannounced into shopping centers, stick out his hand and say, "I'm LeRoy Collins. I used to be your governor." He talked to each person singly and attentively. Just as he did on TV, he entreated his listener with reason, apparently sure in his mind that the wisdom and record of LeRoy Collins would be persuasive if the message were understood. When there was doubt, he tended to talk on and on, saying the same things in different ways, using illustrations, as one might who implored a child to learn.

A government class at a St. Petersburg high school invited Collins to speak. It was a school tradition to schedule political celebrities. A year earlier, Gov. Claude Kirk had spoken and explained government finances. Luckily, it was not a mathematics class, for the governor left behind an error in calculation on the blackboard.

The class was excited and Collins seemed stimulated, though only the teacher could vote. Collins sat on a high stool and began to talk. He told them about himself and his ideas on government. There was that familiar entreaty to understanding. It was as though Collins represented society, and the class represented youth. It was his obligation to make them understand.

Collins' soft voice went on and on. The class, at first eager, began to drowse. Heads nodded. When Collins finished, they revived to ask questions, but only a few minutes were left.

Before a gathering of campaign workers in Miami one night, Collins was at his best. He was sure of the crowd. They understood. He spoke eloquently of the need for ideals and dreams, and closed with a simple thanks. The impact was great. The room and the people were his, but they had been his before he entered.

Another day in Broward County. The Collins campaign bus had an enthusiastic driver. The bus was decorated and some workers wore Collins hats and ribbons. Getting into the spirit of things, the driver blew the horn loudly at each stop. You could see Collins wince. Finally, he leaned over to the driver and said quietly but firmly, "Don't blow that horn anymore."

Newsmen traveling with Collins called it the Non-Campaign, or the Quiet Campaign.

*   *   *

A Gulf Coast radio announcer asked Gurney, "Would you call yourself a liberal or a conservative?" Gurney would have been excused a smile, but he smoothly explained that though labels were elusive, yes, he could be called a conservative. It was like Mickey Mantle saying, yes, he did play baseball, but only in the summer.

Gurney directed his campaign like an army maneuver. It was not complicated. Newsmen traveling with him frequently didn't see him between public appearances. He traveled in one plane or car with his family, the newsmen in another. On days of little activity, he might stay home and have his aides distribute a statement for the day. One day, aide Martin hauled out a statement that criticized the federal poverty program "except for HeadStart." The next day Gurney said that was a mistake, and criticized HeadStart, too.

Martin, the press aide, watched reporters for signs of prejudice. He kept a sharp eye out for liberals. "Ed thought that was pretty good, pretty straight reporting. He didn't even say much about that where you called him an elderly version of the all-American boy," he commented to me one day.

Martin praised straight reporting, without interpretation or analysis or even correction. He wanted reporters to be more like parrots. He particularly did not like it when Gurney was called a right-winger. "If you call him a right-winger, you ought to call Collins a left-winger," Martin argued. But it was not that neatly divided. While Gurney consistently voted the conservative line in Congress, Collins did not consistently stay on the liberal side. Still, it was an argument Martin used well. Even though it rarely resulted in Collins being called a left-winger, it probably reduced the number of times that Gurney was called a right-winger.

When Gurney traveled from Winter Park to Pasco County on the west coast, he and his family flew to St. Petersburg and drove the rest of the way. Newsmen and Martin drove all the way and arrived an hour early. A group of senior citizens gathered in a little park by a river. Gurney arrived, mingled for five or ten minutes, spoke for 10, and left. His message: he had learned in Washington that this was going to be a Republican year. Nobody ever got a chance to grow tired of Gurney.

*　*　*

The two candidates seemed eager for battle. Collins swung at Gurney early, even before the primary ("that lone, negative voice") and took a stab in return that hurt. Gurney told his people to campaign for Collins in the primary ("I don't want to lose him; he's a great target for November"). Collins attempted to reply with the Uncle Remus tale about Brer Rabbitt and the Briar Patch. He got it mixed up ("Like Brer Rabbit, he says that because it's what he doesn't want") but everybody understood.

Collins would not debate Faircloth in the primary, accusing him of being irresponsible. But he readily agreed to take on Gurney in a series of televised debates. Collins thought Gurney could be flustered if forced away from scripted answers. Too, each man considered the other his opposite in political theory, and conviction brought confidence that the other was wrong and therefore vulnerable. It was a collision of styles as well as philosophies—Collins an old Southerner with new ideas, Gurney a new Southerner with old ideas.

The winner went to Washington; the loser—perhaps Florida's most distinguished public servant ever—went to pasture.

—*July 28, 1968*

Retirement: The End Game

Retiring to Miami Beach was the classic dream of the Snowbird, but the reality of it could be daunting. In 1980 Gloria and I tried it, an experiment in retirement for Tropic *magazine. We gave ourselves a budget of $700 and off we went into the South Beach of that time, a mecca for the old, not yet transformed into an internationally famed place of youthful fashion and entertainment. Then, South Beach was a place where old folk grappled with the issues of making life meaningful until death.*

Two old men sat on a curb at Lincoln Road Mall, talking. "A little money? Yes, I have a little money," one said. "But I must make it last. It will not come again." He spoke of a dream he had, of taking a plane west and seeing California.

The friend urged, "So go to California. Why not?"

But he could not decide. "The trouble is," he explained, "I don't know how soon I will die."

Retirement days can be lonely and dull, yet full of anxiety. It is a curious combination. Shadows that we have held distant all these years become so real and present that we can sit down at the kitchen table and calculate them with a pencil and pad. Death becomes an item to be considered in the budget.

"I thought every day would be like Sunday," said a woman in a coin-operated laundry, remembering when she began retirement. "It isn't." There is not the ease and the comfort there should be. Time blurs. The days and the weeks string together with trivia while fear grows that you are no longer important to anyone.

Like most, my wife and I had rejected the mirror of old age as distorted, somehow not applying to us. After experimenting with retirement for one month on Miami Beach, we felt differently. The month was both enriching and disturbing. I doubt we ever will be quite the same again.

We borrowed 30 days out of our future and tested our readiness. It was like flipping ahead on the calendar, scouting that last big hill on the horizon so we could see where the rainbow ends, and discovering that the pot is not gold but ceramic. Only the most practical and courageous can celebrate the discovery.

The elderly understand all these things, for they have traveled the road. They perceive our disbelief in this reality the way a parent perceives a child demanding the right to make a mistake. They try to warn us, to share their pain and their truth, and they are frustrated when we only humor them or simply ignore them. They are hurt when we do not help them by letting them help us.

We, as Victor and Gloria Burt, explored this different world long enough for us to realize, not just to know intellectually, that retirement and old age are a Pyrrhic reward for a long life. An aura of grace and strength radiates from those who handle it with good spirit. The alternative is a pathetic desperation that soils not just one life but all those around it.

We moved to the south stretch of Miami Beach, a place renowned as an inexpensive staging area for the next life. In Florida, it was the ultimate urban situation for a retiree, a multiethnic setting that could have been lifted out of old New York when its neighborhoods were at peace. For the elderly, it had everything but a cemetery. They gathered along the beach, feeding the pigeons, talking, staring out at the ocean as though awaiting a ship and a long voyage.

Our second-floor, back apartment looked out on a square patch of weeds and grass, an untended courtyard bounded by the rears of pastel buildings weathered gray. Boards nailed across doors, lower windows wired shut, assured security. It was a scene we shall not forget.

On sunny days somebody always washed, and damp clothes hung out of windows or from lines strung on poles. Utility wires crisscrossed the buildings. The back side of a billboard facing Washington Avenue and the white tower of the St. Moritz Hotel on Collins Avenue topped our skyline.

The days all seemed the same. We woke each morning to the sound of an old man's long coughing spasms. Finally, he would spit and be quiet. Then, in this neighborhood tight with apartments, a baby would cry and a Spanish voice would croon to it. Then cars would begin to hum along the streets, the horns honking and sirens signaling the emergencies of the day. Neighbors came out. "Raining, already. When will it stop raining?" a woman would say. As the sun came up, an ocean breeze flapped the drapes. We would hear the televisions snap on, one by one.

There was a feeling that the lives here mixed as did all this, into a human tossed salad, that we became part of one life pattern. If the neighbors cried or laughed or cursed, we could hear it. At mealtime, we could sniff the air and guess what they would be eating. We knew their television, their music, their life's rhythms.

In one month, we knew the tastes of our neighbors in all these things without knowing for sure which names and which faces went with those tastes. Many of the neighbors remained essentially strangers, but we had the feeling of bosomy familiarity.

For this experiment in retirement, I used my middle name, Victor, and grew a mustache and beard. It came out streaked and gray, and kind friends assured me I looked far older. I was a disabled early retiree from north Florida who walked with a cane. Gloria was my younger wife, my nurse and my keeper.

We made the arbitrary decision to give the two of us an income totaling $700 a month. This, we knew, was neither the lowest nor the highest on South Beach, but we believed it would be representative. We assumed in our budget the typical expenses of established retirees. As nearly as possible we wanted the budget to represent an average month.

Finding the apartment was not easy, but our search led to a manager named Sam who took care of it. He was a small, weary man with a distinguished Old World accent. "I manage five buildings. I could manage 20, but I don't want it. Ya know what I mean?" he explained. He showed us a plainly furnished but comfortable apartment that, he informed us, was the best in the neighborhood. He said there was a perpetual breeze and fine neighbors. We would be very lucky if he decided to let us have it. "What do we have to do?" I asked. "It all depends if I like you," he said, pausing. "But it's okay. I like you."

We paid him one month's rent, two months' security deposit ($750 total) and he congratulated us on our good fortune. We had a place to live and, despite the shortage of apartments on Miami Beach, it had taken only three days. GOD BLESS OUR HOME, said an inscription on the light-switch panel. A restaurant place mat, made of paper and bearing a map of Florida, was taped to the bathroom wall. A calendar in the living room advertised vitamins. Any worries about security vanished quickly. Tenants before us had left two extra latches on the front door, three extra latches on the back door. Gloria cleaned up the dust, wiped the dirt out of the corners and announced we could start living.

The location was ideal. Everything was close. We were one block from shop-lined Washington Avenue, two blocks from Lincoln Road Mall, six blocks from Lummus Park on the beach. Even for a man with a cane, there was a handy answer for every conceivable need. We could walk to the grocery store, coin laundry, library, civic centers, bank, restaurants, movies, doctors' offices. We could eliminate the expense of owning a car. Sam was exactly right.

We hardly knew where to begin, but hunger advised us. In a grocery store on Washington Avenue, which offered one of the world's fine collections of prunes and raisins, we checked prices and stocked up a cart with minimum necessities. We noticed that cat food, the storied diet of the South Beach poor, cost more than beans. Stocking the cupboard took an alarming $63.87, and small necessities (napkins, a can opener, dish towels, etc.) at Woolworth's added another $31.36. The first day staggered the budget. We would have to try harder.

We walked the mall, opened a checking account, visited the library, toured the beach, located the movies, and were pleased to find the Lincoln Theater offered double features for $1.50. We walked Washington Avenue south to Fifth Street, from there over to the beach and back. There were disabled cars on the street, disabled humans on the sidewalk. Everyone jaywalked, making drivers angry and honked-at pedestrians fearful, but they kept jaywalking anyway. My feet and legs hurt, and a few pounds rolled off me in sweat, but the outlines of our world took shape.

We thought we knew Miami Beach. In two decades of living in the Miami area, and a half century in Florida, we had accepted the beach's reputation as a rude, uncaring place. It is not. We experienced things that tended to confirm that reputation but, gradually, we began to see a different community, not just a transient playground elbowing a near ghetto. We liked it, even though the experience left few illusions.

Nothing disconcerted us more than the desperation that grips some of the old. It stems from fear. They know that the simple frailties of age sometimes make them targets. They become very sensitive to the possibility that someone might cheat them, rob them, deny them benefits. Some, trying to overcome their fears, become so aggressive that they inspire similar behavior in others. The defensiveness on both sides finds cause and grows.

In the grocery stores, shopping carts become weapons for wedging into line, holding someone else off while the day's bargain specials can be picked over. Brief, loud arguments flared quickly and faded.

At the produce market, fruits and vegetables are pinched, squeezed, bounced. Bruised items are triumphantly presented to the clerk for a discount. At a Washington Avenue bakery, where the old folk lined up for day-old bread and pastries, six cents became a major issue. A clerk charged 75 cents; a woman thought it should be 69 cents. "You trying to cheat me?" the woman said in a rising voice. "Yesterday she charged me only 69 cents." The clerk replied flatly, "So she made a mistake yesterday." The woman erupted. "Cheating, cheating," she said loudly. The clerk did not budge and the woman walked away muttering, "Such an attitude!"

It happened often, in the grocery store and bakery, in offices, waiting to get on the bus, wherever there was competition of any sort. Standing in line at the bank, leaning on my cane, two people pushed in ahead of me, knocked my cane aside and to my surprise nearly floored me. They simply wanted to be next. A woman in the grocery fretted because the line was irregular, and there was some confusion about who had priority position. She nudged the man ahead of her. "Stand over there," she said, pushing. "You're not in line." The man shook her off angrily. "I stand where I want to," he said tightly.

Antagonism sets up between elderly customers and clerks, salespeople, cashiers. In a clothing store, I held up a shirt to see if it fit. Inadvertently, my cane touched the saleslady. "No, no," she said, shoving, "you hurt me with that." At one office, a young clerk berated a doddering Cuban because she could not speak English. In a department store, as a covey of elderly crowded in disorderly fashion around a cash register, the cashier threw up her hands and grimaced. "And it's not even full moon yet," she said. The customers, listening, did not move or blink.

In some cases, the suspicion was policy, not just incompetent personnel. Sometimes it seemed that old age was regarded as a state of disgrace, and there seemed more concern about guarding against the possible than with being fair toward the probable.

A sign was posted in the window of a small store: "If you value your life as much as I value my merchandise, you won't steal here." In a grocery: "Thought for today and every day! Don't embarrass your family and friends by shoplifting. Think!" In a seafood market, a straight defense: "Our fish NOT caught in Biscayne Bay." A cafeteria had signs that forbade loitering after eating, warning there would be a charge for cups of hot water with small orders.

We saw elderly outcasts without pride digging into the garbage daily, sifting and choosing, not caring who saw. The overtly handicapped ventured out on canes, in wheelchairs, on walkers. But with some the handicaps did not show. They walked down the sidewalk twitching, muttering to themselves, walking blindly into the streets without noticing traffic, bumping into others on the sidewalk. Beggars, some ragged and some well dressed, asked for quarters and complained bitterly if they got nickels.

But those were only the things that snagged in the memories of those who moved in the surface streams of Miami Beach. They were too numerous not to notice, but not numerous enough to be regarded as typical. They were the stereotypes that created the misleading impressions. For us, the balance tilted far to the other, more positive side.

On a broiling hot day, we walked a half dozen blocks to place a deposit for gas service, arriving at 12:30, and were told customer service was closed until 1:30. We sat down, distressed. What should we do? Sweat poured off me, and I wondered whether a sunstroke might be the reward of a return walk. We could not decide. (Ours was a dilemma we saw replayed on the streets of Miami Beach a dozen times. Exhausted, despairing old folk, not knowing what else to do, sought shelter and rest as randomly as did the pigeons.) A clerk put down her lunch, called us over, took the deposit and cautioned us to walk on the east side of Washington Avenue, where there would be shade. We went away enamored of the gas company.

Our neighbors made us understand, though, more than anything else, that the clichés about Miami Beach rested on exaggerations of truth. Old age and a deteriorating South Beach imposed limits, but within them there is the same variety you find at any age and at almost any other place: the greedy and the good, the desperate and the serene, the grimy and the neat.

Most of the elderly we met, in fact, behaved with higher standards than did the young. They dressed more neatly, spoke more courteously, were quicker to offer assistance and conversation, and turned away in embarrassment from those who did not.

Though South Beach bumped elbows across Lincoln Road, the Mason-Dixon line of the beach, with a more glittering scene of tourists and the moneyed, that was another world from the one we lived in, and there was little exchange. The South Beach old folk overcame transience with a sense of community that sprang from the common problems of old age.

As we came back from our walks, neighbors would stop us to talk. They were interested in where we had been, what we did, how we felt, whether we were happy. It was easy, therefore, for us also to be interested in them. We heard about their families, their ailments, the bargains they had found, the entertainment that was available.

They would dress up to sit on the patio and talk. This was a formal entertainment, and they wanted to look nice. They advised Gloria about shopping, inquired solicitously about my health, explained Jewish customs and expressions we did not understand, encouraged us to feel at home and to visit, seemed truly pleased to have us as neighbors. We developed real affection for them and felt it was re-turned. In few other places we have lived did we find so quick and warm a response.

It was the custom to retreat first to the patios and then inside to apartments when the sun went down. While they did not dwell on it, the neighbors cautioned us that there were predators abroad at night. Doors were latched three and four times, ground-floor win-dows on exposed sides bolted. We heard stories of muggings, beat-ings, robberies, always with old folk as victims.

We followed that custom, rarely venturing out at night. On our budget, there was nothing to do at night that we could not do in the day, and it was easier to stay home and read or watch television. Our neighbors found this no bother, and neither did we. We could hear them playing cards and talking. The practice was simply an ac-knowledgment of fact: night involved risk. All of us routinely avoided it, just as we might avoid rush-hour traffic.

One neighbor laughingly told us about a bold old gentleman who regularly walked four blocks to join them playing cards and often returned home alone as late as 11 P.M. He never had a problem, they said, except that other pedestrians would walk across the street to keep from meeting him on the sidewalk. It was a popular story.

After one week, Gloria was getting nervous. Fidgeting, she dropped one of our four water glasses and broke it. That did not help. She thought she should be doing something, but there was nothing to do. It took half an hour to clean the apartment. She read and exercised, and we walked. Everything was different—the pace, the people, the scene. The south end of Miami Beach seemed for-eign and exotic compared with the village where we lived in rural north Florida. We were expatriates, living in a world where almost everyone was old.

We walked out of an ice-cream parlor on Lincoln Road Mall, and an old man confronted us, begging. "Help me," he said, "I'm hun-gry." We gave him nothing, and it bothered Gloria. Later we saw him using the same tactic in front of a short-order restaurant. He worked the crowd until dark, with small success, and then took a booth, smoking a cigarette while waiting for a waitress to take his order.

All this was tougher on Gloria than on me. Sympathy wrings easily from her. I just sweat a lot. She liked to believe in people, as I do, but she was less accustomed than I was to genial fraud. We had not been to church and she missed that. Easter morning we went for a walk in the oceanside park and found it crowded. For Easter in Miami Beach, that was not so unusual, but for her it was disquieting not to hear a hallelujah on this special day. We grumbled about the hot sun, but the old folk were wearing shawls and jackets.

Little things emphasized the strangeness. At the laundry, a woman pushed Gloria's clothes off a table used as a folding area. The deliberate rudeness surprised her. She was not used to that. Some older women, embarrassed by it, sat down in chairs and talked sympathetically with her.

Gloria quit going out wearing shorts or with curlers in her hair, even to the corner to buy the morning *Herald*. At first, that had seemed permissibly casual in a retiree's neighborhood on Miami Beach, but the women in our building were so neat and prim that she decided to be a little less casual.

The neighbor women enjoyed conversation with a new face. They showed Gloria pictures of their grandchildren, told family stories, shared chocolates. One told Gloria she would like to move into a hotel, but her husband refused. They were veteran retirees. He liked to clean the apartment, to fiddle around in the kitchen cooking. It gave him something to do. What, he asked his wife, would he find to do if they lived in a hotel?

The women talked about shopping, sewing, going to movies. They agreed that X-rated movies were shocking. They seemed so anxious for Gloria to be happy in the building, which heightened her distress. She felt overcome by conscience that she could not tell these nice ladies we had not retired but were only experimenting with the idea. She felt sneaky about it.

The first week went quickly, and at its end we reviewed the business of retirement. The first seven days had cost us $126.42, most of that coming on the first day. It was too much. From the $700 total, we subtracted the rent ($250), an estimate of $100 for the month's utilities (power, phone, gas) and the first week's expenses. With 23 days remaining, we had $223.58 left, or an average of less than $20 a day for food, entertainment, laundry and whatever else came up. We had not been to the movies, had not eaten in a restaurant, and had enjoyed a diet more filling than satisfying: mostly black beans and rice, with occasional stew beef or sausage tossed in. We knew the challenge better now, and we felt restless with it.

We had learned a little about the way to meet a retirement budget. To be successful, we could not concentrate solely on counting the money, for that nourished the idea that only money counts. Eventually our appetites would break loose. We had to change our values. We had to find pleasure and significance in other coin. We had begun to see how others managed. But could we?

A tanned old man in brief trunks sat on the edge of the green-slatted public bench, his Buddha belly rounding out smoothly, and gazed across the littered sand at the ocean. He came to the park on Miami Beach every morning to read the paper, to think and to deepen that tan.

He talked to Gloria and me, a couple of strangers, as though we were rookies entering the major leagues. We had confessed to him that we were experimenting with retirement, testing ourselves for 30 days on a budget of $700. But in this, our second week, we still were uncertain. We did not know whether we could make the abrupt change to retirement.

Immediately he understood better than we. "It takes a while," he said. "Do not give up too much too fast. Save what you can of the old life. See what will fit, and keep it. You must remember that you have not become new people. You have only changed circumstances.

"Life is like a Turkish pastry—layer upon layer. Old age doesn't change you. It limits you. Everything goes on. But you can't have any fun if you are a sissy about being old. You cannot begin by deciding that you have been defeated."

That day became a turning point. The old man accelerated our learning process. It was as though we had ripened under the sun and relaxed into a new normality. Retirement seemed easier.

As a morale booster, we went out to lunch at El Choclo, an Argentine restaurant on Lincoln Road Mall. We spent $7.42 gorging ourselves on *ropa vieja*, a dish of chili beef, rice and beans that had us smacking our lips in celebration. With a promising Buddha belly of my own, I headed back to the apartment for a nap, a practice that I came to regard as one of the superior joys of retirement. Gloria wanted to go window-shopping, arguing that it did not cost anything to look.

Remarkably, this small change in our approach and attitude made a big difference. Evidence came two hours later when she returned happy and smiling. She did not look like the anxious person who had been dropping glasses and getting homesick a week earlier.

An encounter on the mall confirmed the new direction. An old man wearing coat and tie had tried to establish a romantic liaison. He had walked alongside until she looked at him in the window reflections. "Hi, dolling," he said. "It is hot enough for you?"

This struck Gloria as funny, not threatening. She assured him pleasantly it was indeed hot, and hurried home to tell me about the courtly old flirt. A week earlier, it would have distressed her. Not now. "Oh," she said airily. "That's just Miami Beach." From then on, all was well.

Routine evolved. In the morning we would take a long walk, return to the apartment for the noon movie on our little black-and-white television set that had a picture that curled on the bottom, and eat lunch. Later we would nap, read and get ready for the afternoon walk. I found a trade-'em-in paperback bookstore on Meridian Avenue and ran up a string of five books for the month.

If we went to the mall in the morning, we would go to the beach in the afternoon and return along Washington Avenue, where shops offered everything from shoe repair to jewelry to kosher meat. Some mornings we switched to the library. One afternoon a week we took in a movie. Once a week we ate lunch out, either at El Choclo or at what became our favorite, Mi Bohio, a fine little hole-in-the-wall Cuban-Colombian restaurant on Española Way. Sometimes we ate at the somewhat more expensive Concord Cafeteria and walked back along Collins Avenue gawking at the once-grand hotels. Nights, we continued to stay at the apartment. It fit our schedule, pocketbook and inclination.

It became easier for us to budget by averaging daily costs, and so we began to shop for groceries daily. Not only was that convenient, but it gave us something else to do. Shopping was a money game.

Our daily ceiling was $9. If we went over, we trimmed enough off the next few days to make up for it. When we went under, we gave ourselves an extra lunch at Mi Bohio. As we went along, we learned better how to manage.

The second week's expenses totalled $75.02, a nice drop from the $126.42 we spent the first week, but still a little high. We adjusted again. With 16 days remaining, we had $148.56 left in the budget. There would be fewer frills, no more sweet rolls or pies from the bakery, for example. We would preserve our restaurant option as essential entertainment, but in general we would walk more, talk more, read more, eat less. I was beginning to feel that I would remember this experiment as a 30-day walk.

The mall and the beach offered diverting contrasts. On Lincoln Road, we could ride the curb and take the sun and the breeze and talk with strangers and see an incredibly varied human parade moving along the fine shops, the discount stores, the ice-cream parlors, the electronics shops. They walked with canes, they rolled in wheelchairs, they strode like executives, they dawdled and they daydreamed. They looked in the windows at Japanese trinkets, coyote furs, guayaberas, books, wood carvings, Korean textiles.

Most mornings at the beach, we found a few drifters still sleeping on the sand. The renowned cart ladies, who lived from grocery carts stacked with all their belongings, moved up and down the sidewalks, checking the garbage. We had thought we would enjoy swimming, but a TV show about sewage-dumping offshore effectively killed that appetite.

On the beach the scene was equally varied: withered and pneumatic limbs, bloated and flat bellies, old men exercising (bicycling upside down on the sand, jogging along and wrestling the air), younger men puffing strange cigarettes and tilting bottles, younger women sunning themselves, seminude and occasionally topless, old women a few feet away shivering in the faint breeze. Couples played cards under the sea-grape trees. Individuals sat alone in folding chairs, staring at the ocean for hours. Young men whistled at girls and called, "Hey, sweetie." Old men sidled up to the same girls on benches and whispered, grinning big. The girls enjoyed ignoring them. The young were a minority, encountered in the stores or on the fringe of retirement life. When moving among the old folk, they were studied as minor curiosities.

An old fellow we called "The Pigeon Man" came out of an old hotel every afternoon, proceeded down the beach sorting through the trash cans, and returned to take a perch on the coral rock wall. Pigeons were the principal animal life on the beach, though we saw a few doves and sparrows and gulls, and a rare cat or dog. Pets were not really a part of life. Pigeons, and The Pigeon Man, were exceptions. When The Pigeon Man pulled out his pouch and began to scatter feed and talk quietly, dozens of pigeons gathered, sitting on his arms and legs, cooing to him, eating from his hand. The Pigeon Man was an erect, gray-haired fellow in glasses who wore his trousers rolled up to the calves. He carried a cane but did not need it for walking. He spoke warmly to no one but the birds, scolding children who frightened them, lecturing loiterers who blocked his way on the sidewalk. He plainly felt that pigeons were the classiest company on the beach, and they reciprocated.

"For all of us it is the same," said a woman, watching the old man and his birds. "We are lonely. We don't hear from the children. They don't have time for us. It is the regular story of the beach. We find somebody we can talk to. So what if he likes pigeons? Can we read and watch TV all the time? No. We must talk." On the green benches, on the coral curbs, waiting in line in the stores, on the patios, wherever they could gather, they talked. Age made everyone kin.

Late one afternoon an old woman rested for a moment in the shade of a palm tree on Collins Avenue. She watched until a young woman sweeping the hotel steps looked up, and she began. "What do you think?" she said, waving her arm. "From one o'clock I have been in the doctor's office. He gave me only an iron shot and it cost me five dollars and fifteen cents. So what do you think of that?" The young woman ignored her.

A line formed outside the library one morning before it opened at 10. One woman went to the door anyway, found it locked. She waved a hand. "So I'm not a member in good standing," she said, smiling. She tried leaning against a pillar, but it was uncomfortable. She tried to sit on a curb, but it was too low. "You know what my grandson always says to me?" she asked. "He says, 'You are up the creek, Grandma'."

The doors opened, and the line spilled toward the newspapers and magazines. Tables and chairs filled up. *The Miami Herald* and the *New York Times* went first. For these, there was a limit of 30 minutes. The library was a cool lounge that served the mind and not the mouth. It was perfect for the budget.

But this library did not have the intimidatingly silent atmosphere of some. As an attendant walked by, a woman grabbed his arm. "Look at this," she said loudly. "All the way over here I walk, on this cane, to get this recipe. She held up a magazine. "And look at this. Somebody cut it out. What do you think of that?" "That's not nice," the attendant said in a soft voice. "No, it's not nice," the woman replied. "It's terrible."

The theater was another cool refuge. For $1.50 each, we could spend an afternoon watching a double feature of recent vintage. The elderly like early-afternoon movies. They commented on what they saw. Talking increased enjoyment. When Lee Strasberg and Ruth Gordon in *Boardwalk* celebrated their golden wedding anniversary, women all over the theater clucked and purred. "Dot's wonderful. Dot's so wonderful," one said. When Strasberg, the old man, throttled a young thug and dramatically vowed never to be forced from his neighborhood, applause broke out. "So good," a man said, filing out after four hours of fantasy. "Such a good afternoon."

When the beach, the mall, the theater, the library, the TV and walks paled as entertainment, we began to attend a class in the philosophy of Spinoza. At Ida Fisher adult education center, large-bottomed students propped up their canes and fitted themselves into desks custom-built for children. The teacher wore a red tam and had a positive manner. "Never quarrel with your life," she commanded, unreeling the wisdom of Spinoza, the 17th-century Dutch philosopher, as it applied to the Iranian crisis. She and Spinoza concluded that President Carter's patience was just the right thing (this was before the aborted commando raid). One woman raised her hand. She wanted to ask what Spinoza thought about Carter not holding Iranian diplomats hostage in this country. Why not hostage for hostage? The teacher ignored her. "Ah, she don't know," the old woman said. That slur offended another student, who noted quietly, "This woman, she is a pain in the neck."

At a later session, Spinoza took on an even more difficult subject, the Cuban influx into south Florida. The class fairly burst with opinions. "We have to understand that we are in the midst of a social revolution," said the teacher. "I think this is the beginning of the downfall of fascism."

Questions and comments began to pop at her like firecrackers. It threatened to become disruptive. "We must remember that we are a generous nation," the teacher said. A woman cracked back, "We are *too* generous." The teacher tried to give a balanced picture of Cuba. A man got up and left. "I am not a socialist," he said. The teacher countered, "I myself am a capitalist. Communism does not work."

The teacher spoke of the pro-te-lariat, pronouncing it that way quite carefully, and defined the class as bourgeois. Someone asked whether Jesus Christ was a socialist, whether a kibbutz was a form of communism. Spinoza, she continued bravely, would have us accept the Cuban influx as an expression of God. A man complained loudly, "But the Cubans, they have the advantage with all this government help. They'll move all the Jews out of here, if this keeps going on. There won't be any of us left. Everybody in the world wants to come to Miami Beach." He drew applause.

The teacher recovered with a speech about the untidy beauty of democracy. A man commented that when he came to this country, nobody helped him. A woman stood up, defending the teacher. "If this country is so much better off now that it can give help, then I'm glad," she said. The invoking of patriotism quieted everyone, and the session ended with individuals reciting poems and singing songs. It was a stimulating hour and a half. Who would have suspected that old Spinoza had the answer to the Cuban problem?

Curiously, time began to get away from us. We had believed that monotony and boredom expanded time, made it seem longer, yet the third week and part of the fourth week passed while we were still planning how we would cut expenses. We were nearing the end of our experiment in retirement, and it seemed too soon.

Regrets began, and we found that this, too, was a standard emotional pull in retirement. So many things seem to end without being finished. Life seems so untidy, distracting. At an age when there is an urge to make the circles complete, to accomplish neat conclusions, the task becomes more elusive than ever. For so many old folk, things seem to ravel away and they cannot get a grip and set them right. They brood about this, knowing that time is short, that the end of life is a reality they must ponder. They sit on the benches and curbs and fret that they will leave so many loose strings, unfinished thoughts, unrealized ambitions. Everything they ever dreamed of doing, and never did, becomes a burden. They talk of this, and their faces show how hard it is to surrender.

The third week cost us $61.94, the least and best yet. We felt we were beginning to learn, but we had only nine days left. With the experience of another month or two, each day learning more about reorienting values, we felt confident that we could manage a $700-a-month budget more comfortably.

The fourth week cost $67.22, and the last two days added $11.35. At the end of 30 days we had spent $591.95, including the rent. Phone, power and gas bills added $54.12, less than we had feared. Enduring those warm nights without using the air conditioner paid off. Deducted from $700, that left $53.93. We thought it had been a good month, but clearly it was experimental. Adjustments would have continued. We think the first week's expenses, $126.42, were less typical than the last two weeks. If the entire month had averaged as low as the last half, we could have put aside at least another $50 for emergency needs that inevitably would arise. We were satisfied, but realized that one month did not produce final answers. Permanent retirement would require great determination and flexibility.

Two days before we moved out, we called Sam, the apartment manager. He expressed great regret at our departure and explained that a return of our deposit would depend on how soon the apartment could be rented again. "I told 'em over there that in you we got the finest people. But, regardless, you gotta go, you gotta go. That's that." Sam, like Spinoza, did not quarrel with fate.

The neighbors were curious but understanding. "So much trouble you went to, and now you leave," one said sympathetically. "We were hoping you'd change your mind," another said. One asked confidentially, "What happened? I know something happened." We tried to explain, and they tried to understand. One neighbor said, "I tell ya what I'm gonna do. You leave me your address, and I write you when the apartment is rented. That way, you get some of your deposit back. I write you a secret letter, so you'll know. Just don't mention my name."

On that strain of conspiratorial goodwill, we moved out. We confess to feeling relief that the retirement was unreal, but we also felt concern for the good neighbors, the kind strangers. The Pigeon Man, The Beggar, The Old Russian Woman and all the others. For them, there was no easy escape.

We look back at that month with wonder. We learned so many things, some of them we really did not want to know just yet. We had a troubling glimpse ahead and we know that life, if we can hold on to it, has some stiff challenges left for us. It will be like growing up again, reaching another majority and facing another difficult set of responsililities, without that exhilaration of youth to carry us forward.

We know that if we are not careful, retirement one day will come as a surprise, like the end of a journey we never expected to finish. Rather than a climax, a public sounding of trumpets, it is more likely to be a whispered command—right in the middle of some job you are doing—to sit down and let someone else take over. If we are to succeed as retirees, we must be prepared to accept that command as a reward, not as a banishment.

Only the good die young, it has been said, and if that were so it would explain a lot about the rest of us, but it is not. What dies young is freshness and innocence; what replaces it becomes the mold of your life, and that is what will chafe you or comfort you in old age. Personal defenses must be ready for long hours of contemplative argument with yourself.

The old want to be loved and sustained by the young, yet the key to that may lie in their own ability to bear the pressures of age so well that the young themselves are sustained by the example. When that desperation of the aged breaks into the open, it becomes a curse to all. The young are repelled by it, for their brains are not wrinkled enough to know better, and nature is rarely kind to that which upsets its plan.

We understand these things a little bit now, and we are not entirely comfortable with them, for they tell us that retirement does not mean the end of the fight. It is not really a time when we can quit working and relax to spend our days in ease and serenity. The fight just shifts to new ground and new rules. Retirement is a totally different demand on our balance and will. We get that reward of serenity only if we earn it with courage and moral stamina. The terrors—of physical infirmity, loneliness, despair, senility, death—are inevitable; the test is how we deal with whatever number of those that become our lot.

The marvel is that so many do this so well. They handle the terrors, and they spare the rest of us full knowledge of their anguish. We have fresh, deep admiration for those who make the late years the blessing we always have imagined they should be. They add incomparable stature to their lives and hope to ours.

Our month on Miami Beach was a rare opportunity to intern for the future. We learned that there is no trick, no secret that will help. With retirement, you do not get a set of answers to go with the company watch. Time is short, yet you have no significant way to spend it. Money is short, and needs for it besiege you. You must dig answers out of your head and your emotions. We discovered that it will be very late if you do not begin the search early.

When our real time comes, can we do it? Can we face those stark practicalities with enough courage and grace to achieve serenity? We cannot be sure, but we think a month on South Beach, where youth is recognized as an unearned virtue, has improved our chances.

—June 29, 1980, and July 6, 1980

PART 4 **THE NEXT FLORIDA**

John DeGrove: From Mule to Megastate

Probably no individual better represented the stretch from the past to The Next Florida than John M. DeGrove, a Cracker like no other. He could remember when his family lived on a backwoods farm, and for their best cash crop cut the hearts out of palm trees and sold them. He could tell stories about feeding dried moonshine mash to the mules and cows. Over the years I talked with him many times, and in 1998 he talked about The Next Florida, a subject that had always preoccupied him professionally. He knew it better than most.

DeGrove speaks Cracker creole fluently. It is his native language. He loves fried mullet, the Cracker caviar. He hobnobbed with governors, became the father (or grandfather) of growth management in Florida, but never drifted away from his proud Cracker beginnings.

He had rare links to old Florida, even while he was mired up to his eyebrows in trying to shape the new one. He followed a long, long road trying to do his Cracker duty. He wanted to blueprint the future. He evangelized in the state university system, served in important planning jobs under three governors, became a powerful figure in civic and environmental circles. He wrote a book called *Land, Growth and Politics*, which gave more details about how a state could grow without turning trashy than anything else any library ever had seen. Along the way he picked up that description that would forever define him: he was the "father of growth management" in Florida.

When he looked back on all that, he was not totally satisfied, yet there was satisfaction that many good things had happened. "Maybe

John DeGrove. Photo by the author, 1998

it would be better if I were called the grandfather [of growth management]," he said. "A grandparent doesn't have quite as much responsibility for some of the details of how things work out." He did not disown his growth-management baby, but it hadn't grown up exactly as he had hoped.

DeGrove is a tall man with the weary face of a diplomat accustomed to hearing angry arguments. All his educational training, from B.A. to Ph.D., zeroed in on the growth dilemma. He spoke in the soft, true accents of Florida: a subtle blending that is one-part Southern, one-part Snowbird and two parts rebellion against the other two. His family stretched back five generations in Florida, and his demeanor had the kind of unpretentious yet complex quality marking native things that have the ability to survive adverse conditions.

The family came over from Holland (after having left France) in the mid-1600s and settled in New York. The name then was Vandergruff. The family once owned land in New York City where the city hall later stood. One notable incident involved the loss of their family lawyer, Alexander Hamilton, who was killed by Aaron Burr in a duel that became celebrated in American history. The DeGroves migrated first to Kentucky and then to Florida. Most of what John remembered began with his grandfather, who was involved in many things, including running steamboats on the St. Johns River. He operated ferries across the river at Mayport and at Jacksonville. He worked on the St. Johns River Dayline that ran steamboats between Jacksonville and Palatka.

"Grandpa had orange groves around what is now Mandarin [south of Jacksonville on the east bank of the St. Johns River]. They were wiped out in those famous back-to-back freezes in the winter of 1894–95," DeGrove said. Grandpa then looked at a place nearby called Mineral City, where the National Lead Company was mining trace elements out of beach sand. When perhaps the first environmental lawsuit in Florida history put the mining company out of business—for blocking a public highway, the beach—the DeGroves passed up Mineral City. The soil was no good for farming. They moved a few miles inland, off the coast between the Jacksonville beaches and St. Augustine, to an area of good black soil that became Palm Valley. The DeGroves thus established kinship with many other pioneer Florida families by missing out on the real-estate pot of gold. Mandarin became an attractive part of metropolitan Jacksonville, and Mineral City became the nationally famed resort Ponte Vedra Beach.

"Grandpa set up a truck farm. He raised vegetables and things. He had cows. Grandma's brother was the fire chief in St. Augustine. He had ties to the Minorcan colony there. When Grandpa ran for the state legislature, there weren't enough votes in Palm Valley to elect him, so Grandma's brother rallied the Minorcans. With that support, he won," John DeGrove said.

Grandpa, or William DeGrove, became the patriarch of Palm Valley. He served in the state legislature from 1918 to 1922, while Sidney J. Catts was governor. In early Palm Valley there were no paved roads, no stores. The Intracoastal Waterway had not yet been cut through. The nearest railroad came to Pablo, later to be Jacksonville Beach. John's mother and father met in 1920 when she, a 17-year-old high-school graduate from Hawthorne (east of Gainesville) with a teacher's certificate, came to Palm Valley to teach, and they married. (His mother later earned undergraduate and master's degrees from the University of Florida.)

Special arrangements were made when John was born. "Mama wanted it to happen in a hospital, and so she got her brother [the St. Augustine fire chief] to get her into the Florida East Coast Hospital in St. Augustine. I was the first one of my family ever born in a hospital," he said. He grew up in Palm Valley on what he calls "a one sick mule farm."

"Mama quit teaching for three years to stay with me. Then she started back and she took me with her. I started the first grade in a one-room schoolhouse when I was three years old," John said. The school didn't have classes beyond the sixth grade, so his mother got a job teaching in St. Augustine so she could carry John with her and let him continue his education.

The family farm was memorable. "Not a very prosperous deal, but we never felt deprived. Mother's teaching job brought in some money." he said. To supplement that, John turned to what he said was one of the area's two best cash crops—"cutting buds." This involved carving out the buds or hearts of palm trees. "If you did it carefully, it wouldn't kill the tree," he said. "We sold them to brokers. I'd wander through the woods and try to fill up a croker sack with buds. There was a pole bud [harvested by a cutting device rigged to a pole and used for tall trees] and an axe bud [for trees short enough that you could reach them with an axe]."

The other cash crop, one he remembers as being pursued mostly in a wild area later to become the Guana State Park, was moonshine. "We weren't in moonshine, but we knew some people who were," John said. "One guy had a still out back of his place. For security he kept a bunch of guineas. They're good watchdogs. They make a lot of noise when someone comes around. He also had nine daughters." For good measure, in times of concern, the moonshiner would post his daughters in the trees to warn him if anybody was coming. John had the job of going out there to collect the free mash.

"I'd tell 'em when I was coming and then I'd get on a mule and go over and get it. We'd dry it out and use it as feed for the stock," he said. When John was 15, his father died. The Atlantic Beach Elementary School opened in 1940, and his mother became its first principal. Atlantic was one of the Jacksonville beaches. In 1998 she died at age 94. "I remember a lot about those days," he said, "but I

The DeGrove family in Palm Valley, circa 1927. John, about three years of age, in foreground. Photo courtesy of John DeGrove.

deeply regret never sitting down and talking with her and recording the details of that time."

For one of the most influential public servants of his time, all that amounted to an extraordinary background—a full-blooded Cracker who became a major league bureaucrat, a modern man who tasted pioneer Florida and had a personal sense of how this state's history developed. In response to those sensitivities, growth management became his signature preoccupation.

He was a leader in the 1970s struggle that awakened Florida to its environmental jeopardy. He was director of the Joint Center for Environmental and Urban Problems at Florida Atlantic and Florida International universities. When Bob Graham became governor (he served from 1979 to 1987), DeGrove had known and worked with him for a quarter century, since the years when DeGrove was a professor at the University of Florida and Graham an undergraduate.

Governor Graham, long a believer in new towns or urban clusters as the way for Florida to grow, drafted DeGrove to become head of the Department of Community Affairs (the land planning agency that administers growth management laws). They had shared this vision of the future for a long time. The heart of the commitment that DeGrove took with him to Tallahassee was nothing less than the birthing of *The Next Florida*. He took a leave of absence from his post as director of the Joint Center for Environmental and Urban Problems at Florida Atlantic and Florida International universities.

DeGrove had spent much of the previous 10 years studying the strategy of growth management in seven states: Hawaii, California, Colorado, Oregon, Vermont, North Carolina and Florida. Out of that study came his book. In it he expressed conclusions about how Florida should compartmentalize if it were to survive in an attractive form. Oregon tried it, with success, and DeGrove wanted to adapt that experience to the Florida realities. "But our growth pressures were greater and we needed more imaginative ideas here," he said.

He did not talk of limiting growth—calling that impossible—but of managing it. He advocated an idea then just becoming popular among planners: the designation of urban areas into which all new development would be squeezed. He wanted to accommodate the growth pressures by permitting (in those urban areas) greater density in housing, more people per acre, cluster and high-rise dwelling units. The idea was to force urban redevelopment by denying space for development to sprawl across the countryside.

In effect he wanted to challenge directly one of the nation's greatest problems: the structural blight, the strained public services, the social rootlessness that burdened the cities. It was monumental stuff but, in his view, a tight urban focus would lead to an easing of a range of those problems.

In return for that, he wanted to bar development from prime agricultural lands, wetlands and other environmentally sensitive or unique areas, and he pledged the retention of open spaces and natural vistas. With this, he believed developers and environmentalists might realize a mutuality of interests, as happened in Oregon, and create an coalition of public support. It was an optimistic view.

He wanted to couple this with statewide taxes, or standards, that made growth pay for what it demanded in community services. For example, he recommended state standards for locally applied impact fees. DeGrove estimated that in the early 1980s new growth paid for less than 40 percent of what it required in public services. He was saying, in other words, that for years Florida taxpayers had been subsidizing new residents.

"Reshaping the urban development pattern was a very controversial matter with citizen groups," he said. "What they feared was that they would get the higher density but in the long run they wouldn't get the trade-off of open space and protection of environmental areas. They were afraid that the system would finally break down, and they'd get the high density everywhere."

That was the nub of the DeGrove vision. He understood that The Next Florida, whether his innovation or somebody else's, would begin arriving only when Floridians' anger at what they saw exceeded their fear of what they later *might* see.

The future he blueprinted had some intriguing theoretical answers, and he understood that it scared a lot of people. He was patient about that. He knew that there were not any really popular solutions to Florida's flash-flood population growth.

Simply put, he wanted to reshape the state. He wanted to make it more focused, more orderly. He wanted to make sure that space always would be left for agriculture and wetlands and Florida's unique natural vistas. He wanted to bend still more the honored but already bent old dream of living in a single-family home. He wanted to dampen the newer, escapist Florida dream of living on five rural acres. Virtually everybody would live in a city. DeGrove was the messenger with news about what the future would do to us. He was more matter-of-fact than enthusiastic about it. He did not argue against the inevitable, but argued that we should be prepared to cope with it.

The experience in state government jolted him a bit, but he kept it in perspective. As he remembered it, he had things going nicely there in his branch grove of academe until Governor Graham called him. He knew Florida and he knew the governor, and occasionally he would enjoy lofting from his Boca Raton office an avuncular complaint toward Tallahassee. "There I was," he said, "comfortably giving advice to the governor, telling him how I thought things could be done differently."

The governor invited DeGrove to demonstrate his expertise. "He put the arm on me to get up there to Tallahassee and help him do it right, if I knew so much. Somewhat to my surprise, he persuaded me," DeGrove said. He entered the trenches.

Becoming a bureaucrat proved to be more entangling and bruising than he had imagined. Both poles of the growth dilemma peppered him thoroughly, either for doing too much or too little. He learned why the full term usually has been "harried bureaucrat," spoken as one word. "It was a shock," DeGrove said. "I had been involved in government before [particularly with the landmark environmental legislation of the early 1970s], but this was the first time in the full and complex sense of running an agency at the center of a maelstrom of controversy. It was much more difficult to organize and implement than I thought."

Bureaucrats today routinely face an assumption of incompetence or guilt. It puts a touch of mean-spiritedness into political dialogue at the same time that it increases public protection. DeGrove understood the necessity of that, but when it happened to him personally, the experience still came as a shock. Back in academia, the view was never quite the same again. "Being responsible for the myriad of decisions was far more demanding than I anticipated," said the educator. People got madder at him than he ever expected, too. "It was the educational experience of my life. But it also was the most satisfying and inspiring experience I ever had."

Reviewing his long service, DeGrove had no regrets about what he tried to do. "It didn't play out exactly as I had hoped, but it had impact," he said in a 1998 conversation. "Three governors—Reubin Askew, Bob Graham and Bob Martinez—gave me opportunities. All we were trying to say was that we needed to manage the growth pressures. On balance, any rational and reasonable person looking at how that played out would say two things—one, that we did a lot of good; and two, that we didn't achieve as many of the goals as we had hoped. I have to say the state is worse off for not having achieved them. We were not as effective against growth sprawl as we needed to be. It still spreads out and eats up the natural landscape. But the concepts were sound and solid. Developers need incentives for doing the right thing."

A key setback for growth management came during the administration of Gov. Bob Martinez, according to DeGrove. "Things had been going well. Martinez helped pass a sales tax on services that would have channeled billions of dollars to local governments for growth management." The state collected that tax for six months, and then Martinez backed off. There was vocal opposition in the state, and some polls showed the tax was unpopular. DeGrove believes pressure from his national party, which had a presidential election coming up, prompted Martinez to support repeal of the tax. After several special sessions of the legislature, it was voted out. "That was not only a tragedy for growth management but also for Martinez," DeGrove said. "I think he might have been reelected if that tax had stayed in place."

Still, whatever had gone before, DeGrove deliberately chooses to be hopeful about Florida's future. "I cling stubbornly to the optimistic view," he said. "I think we can still back off and figure out how to grow smart rather than grow dumb. Florida doesn't need a wimpy tax structure to grow. It'll grow anyway. The climate is enough. But that's the argument.

"Growth pressures continue to build, even though they are not at the old peak. We'd be smart to have a tax structure that guarantees the quality of life. I'll tell you, though, that if I weren't an irrepressible optimist, I'd be pretty damned worried. Unless that changes, Florida can't be competitive on a sustained basis."

That is John DeGrove's vision, his worry.

* * *

Each of us has his own. Most of the time the future creeps up on us quietly, like a new habit—arriving not on a thundering spaceship or a roaring jet-ski, but more like an old man out on his daily walk, coming at us step by slow step. The Next Florida probably will arrive that way. We see the old man approach way yonder in the distance, and watch him getting closer, yet chances are that we still will be surprised when he gets here.

If we just look at those steps one at a time, though, we might be able to understand them. Some of the mystery might fall away. We might at least have a better view of where that old man came from, and if we pay close attention we might even be able to guess where he's headed, what this future might be that he is bringing so deliberately. Think of me as that old man for a moment, toddling out of the past, mumbling about how it used to be. Throw away the statistics and the charts. This is about memories and visions.

Maybe you have not seen Florida in the days when a 50-foot oceanfront lot at Flagler Beach could be bought for $25 down and $10 a month, and there were few takers. Maybe you don't remember when Naples was a remote place and property sold for the price of a dinner in a fine restaurant there today, or when Destin was a long stretch of unbroken dunes, and you could stand out in the Gulf chin deep and see your feet in the clear water, wondering why so magnificent a beach had so few people.

Maybe you don't remember the days when you could meet strangers in Florida and they probably would be Floridians. Maybe you don't remember the lean-to shops at citrus groves along the highways where mom-and-pop owners would go out back and pick some rust-streaked oranges and squeeze the juice out of them for you—all you could drink for a dime. Most of the moms and pops got squeezed out of that business, and the scientists did away with those rust streaks because the tourists preferred oranges that were perfectly orange.

Maybe you don't remember those tacky roadside stands that would sell live baby alligators to tourists for one dollar each, and the wild stories that later developed of baby gators being flushed away and growing up to be scary monsters in distant city sewer systems. Maybe you don't remember those huge piles of Conch shells pyramided out front of those stands, pretty skeletons of marine life being sold as doorstops, and stacks of coral broken off live reefs waiting to become dust-catching knickknacks on the shelves of any who wanted to take home some of the wonders of Florida, no matter how repulsive the idea.

Maybe you don't remember the days when you looked at a restaurant menu and could recognize the names of all the fish, and you knew that they came out of Florida waters. Maybe you don't remember the days when Floridians could go out on the beach and dig buckets of donax and make soup any night, or net blue crabs nibbling at a piece of meat tied to a string and dipped into a briny creek, or stand knee-deep in the surf and cast out, any day of the week, and fill a frying pan for lunch.

Maybe you don't remember when you could drive along A1A and almost anywhere find a place to pull off and park while you went down on the beach for a swim. Maybe you don't remember the days before I-95 and the turnpike, when the traffic moved easily on U.S. 1, and the drive along the Indian River was among the prettiest in Florida.

Maybe you don't remember any of that, but those memories suggest the way it once was. They could go on and on, but you get a picture, an impression, of the contrasts between then and now, an idea about the range of what we have gained—more convenience, greater diversity, greater comfort, more jobs, the enlightenment of wider horizons—and the range of things we have lost to pay for it. You can decide for yourself whether it has been a good swap, but in any case these memories tell you where this mile-weary old man came from and you can tell, from the way that history is blowing, the direction Florida is heading.

It's a success story, with loss and created vulnerability as part of the reward—the continual division and dilution of natural treasures. Many good things have happened, but accumulated science and social experience tell us they can and need to be achieved in better and less damaging ways.

*   *   *

Cracker Florida probably lives most visibly in those weathered old frame houses with the rusting tin roofs, wraparound porches and the overhangs that still grace some rural parts of the state. We like to call them Cracker houses. They are practical and unpretentious, built to harmonize with the Florida climate and environment. In his book *Classic Cracker*, author and architect Ron Haase defined them as having pure form and classic simplicity. Cracker houses are wedded to their place.

A hopeful sign for The Next Florida was the development of a Panhandle community that elevated the old Cracker style and its basic ideas into a respectability that seemed to insure this was one bit of old Florida that would survive as something more than a museum exhibit. Seaside was a community born out of the boyhood experiences of Robert Davis, who grew up in Birmingham, Alabama, but made his way in the world as a major builder with different ideas. On a barrier island between Panama City and Destin, on land he had inherited from his grandfather, he created an internationally celebrated revival of the concept that small towns with distinct character were good places to live. A building code insured that the yards had picket fences, the houses had porches and pitched roofs, many of them metal. The fundamental concept invited community and aimed for livability. Seaside was the Cracker philosophy amplified and brought forward, a place with an aura of the Tropic of Cracker, one that fit and belonged as well in The Next Florida.

*　*　*

When I was young my family, which lived in Jacksonville, liked to go for weekend drives in the old Model A. Sometimes we would drive over to the beach and go for a swim, or maybe down to the jetties at the mouth of the St. Johns River and watch the boats and the fishermen. Maybe we would go sightseeing at Fernandina or Green Cove Springs, or drive down to Palatka when the azaleas were in bloom at Ravine Gardens. Sometimes we would just drive out to wooded areas on the edge of town, look for a pretty spot by a creek, and picnic. On some memorable Sundays we went over to Macclenny and ate fried chicken. There would be long lines of cars traveling the 25 miles from Jacksonville to line up at the Morris House or the Annie Hotel for chicken, all you could eat for 50 cents each, served on tables covered by white tablecloths. Florida was like that then.

One Saturday afternoon in 1935 (September 19, 1935) was bigger than most. My folks wanted me to see history in the making. They packed a picnic lunch, and we drove across north Florida to some place south of Palatka, near Ocala, I can't remember where, to watch some men set off an explosives charge that would blow a hole in the ground.

Someday when I grew up, they said, I could tell people that I had seen the beginning of the cross-state barge canal. I would be proud. Someday great vessels would sail right through the Big Scrub on a canal cut from the Gulf Coast to hook up with the little Ocklawaha River, which would be properly reamed out to facilitate the traffic, and then to the St. Johns River. The tides of the Atlantic and the Gulf would rise against each other. This would open up economic vistas so great they strained the imagination.

The details of that fine day in 1935 become dim more than half a century later, but nevertheless for that first glorious blast we were somewhere nearby, probably cheering. About all I remember clearly was that we never got close enough to see anything, but we did hear an explosion. Nevertheless, the glowing promises went, I was witness of a sort to a grand event. I was treading among the low-numbered pages of a significant chapter in American history. It didn't turn out that way, of course.

In his 1974 book *The Florida Experience*, author Luther J. Carter put it in better perspective. President Franklin D. Roosevelt, without the authorization of Congress, allocated $5.4 million to the Army Corps of Engineers as permitted by the Emergency Relief Act and got the canal started with a flair. From his home in Hyde Park, FDR pressed a telegraph key mounted on a gold nugget and set off the explosion. The *Jacksonville Journal* reported that FDR had blasted his name into history. That was the historic explosion we heard.

By 1998, after 63 years of controversy and an extraordinary tapping of taxpayer monies, the uncompleted canal had been called off as an unworthy project and discontinued, but there were still arguments about whether a dam constructed in 1968 to be part of the canal project should remain because it created a pond that fishermen liked.

My folks were both right and wrong: I saw the beginning of something bigger than it should have been, but remembering it now does not make me proud.

For Florida, it turned out, that was not so unusual. There have been many false starts, corrections or half-corrections, and restarts. Progress has been ragged and incomplete, but it continues. Grandiose schemes came along with regularity, new things or new ideas with an appetite for eating away at things natural for dubious gains, but each marvelous new answer seemed to bring with it a set of three or four new problems, each requiring another new answer that also carried multiple problems. As we made progress, sometimes it seemed we fell further behind.

The barge canal had recognizable cousins. The Everglades was diked and drained, and its wild edges suburbanized so primly that its great natural systems of flow were kinked. That created the near endless task of unkinking them.

The Kissimmee River was efficiently ditched, generously treating Lake Okeechobee to neat, straight shots of pollution to go with those being back pumped into the other side of the lake. That created the project of putting the meanders back into the river.

Along our coasts, where some 80 percent of Floridians live, castles went up on the sand pleasantly close to the water, and persistent erosion made them less pleasantly closer. If a hurricane came, they would topple, be built again, and be toppled again by the next one. The congested cities struggled with traffic, crime, vulnerable water supplies, public services, the assorted ills of growth that come too fast for accommodation.

Crotchety old-timers wondered. In the old days down in the Keys, the wreckers posted false lights so ships would crash against the reefs—and the wreckers then could come out and salvage the ships' cargoes. Were we still sending out deceptive signals? Were we luring people to Florida with bright lights and advertising and other messages implying Florida was safer and more attractive than it really was? When just a heavy rain or mild storm could necessitate a disaster call, when the streets seemed so clogged they hindered transportation rather than speeding it, when public services were staggered just by the routine burdens, the question was legitimate.

*　　*　　*

Maybe nowhere else in the world did muck have a more honored place in polite company than it did in Belle Glade, south of the great lake (Okeechobee) where the mythologized Everglades becomes domesticated to a degree, where muck in a fictionally classic way turns into treasure. There, muck was appreciated as one of Florida's greatest wonders, a kind of super earth that had a rich, black, potent look. When tender green things burst out of it, the ancient miracles of growth seemed somehow fresh and surprising, almost miraculous, especially during winter when snow and ice shut down farmers in less benign climates.

The organic Everglades soils, or muck, developed from decomposed vegetation over a period of 4,000 years. Once farmers learned the right combination of soil additives to harness the muck's explosive richness for crops, they wanted to drain more and more swampland to take advantage of it. Trouble was, when the muck dried, it oxidized. Around Belle Glade, it literally burned away. In 1983 Dr. George Snyder, a soil scientist at the University of Florida's Institute of Food and Agricultural Sciences substation at Belle Glade, told me that the muck was subsiding roughly at a rate of one inch per year. Measurement is not precise because depth varies from one place to another, as does the rock level. The earth seemed to melt away around houses and road foundations. In 1998, reviewing the process again, Snyder said the muck continued to disappear but at a slightly slower rate. Surveys over the years confirmed it.

Before the draining of the Everglades began (in the 1880s), explained Snyder, there had been about 10 feet of muck above the limestone rock base. In 1912, measurements showed that 95 percent of the 680,000-acre agricultural areas had five feet or more of muck; a survey in 1988 showed half of the agricultural area having soils three feet or less in depth; by the year 2000, the muck was expected to subside to such an extent that half the area would have two feet or less of muck above the bedrock. "Those predictions remain pretty much on target," Snyder said.

Some things have changed, though, Snyder added. The old prediction had been that when the muck subsided to three feet, agriculture there would end. That did not hold. As the state buys agricultural lands for environmental reasons, there is less farming, especially in sugar, but farmers now grow crops on thinner layers of muck. Some farming continues on muck soils no more than six inches deep. "They are farming shallower now. The water table also is being kept higher and that slows subsidence," Snyder said. Still, in some areas, the rock base has come all the way to the surface.

The muck gave Palm Beach County the oddest wrappings of wealth and lifestyle in all of Florida. In the west, the county rooted in the lush, productive muck and in the east it crowned in the upper-crust glitter of Palm Beach. Like much of the rest of the state, this classic Florida stretch was also compromising and changing. In terms of the future, the disappearing muck pointed a direction.

* * *

Everything happened in one month for Nathaniel (Biddy) Thomas, father of 14. The doctor discovered he had diabetes, the dentist said all his teeth had to be pulled, and he lost his job at Rainbow Springs. The park, a commercial attraction since 1936, closed in the spring of 1974 because its owners said they were losing money on it. "All this, and I can't even take a drink," Thomas said. "All I can do is pour."

Rainbow Springs sits just off u.s. 41 about four miles north of Dunnellon in north central Florida's Marion County. Ocala, 35 miles to the northeast, was the nearest population center. Thomas had been hired in 1937 as a waiter. In 1968 he began piloting the river raft. He had not decided what he would do.

Around Dunnellon, people thought that these were the prettiest springs in Florida. The National Park Service in 1973 added them to its list of Registered National Landmarks. The grounds were beautiful. Seven miles of walkways wound through giant oaks, magnolias, redbuds and dogwoods, plus clusters of azaleas.

In 1972 the springs drew a record 335,000 visitors, but after that the crowds dwindled. An energy crunch was part of that but the trend was down. The state bought Rainbow Springs in 1990 and made it a park. With an admission charge of $1, the park drew 100,000 visitors in 1997. For tourists, apparently, it was too quiet, too remote, too natural. They preferred Mickey Mouse, putting up another road sign on the way to The Next Florida.

* * *

Small squalls of rain swept over Windley Key that Saturday morning, January 24, 1998. The gumbo limbo and poisonwood trees dripped on the trails through the old quarries. In a rocky clearing, a small band of the faithful, perhaps as many as 70, gathered to hear Alison Fahrer read Psalm 30: "You have turned my wailing into dancing." It did not matter that the rain diluted the limeade and made the chocolate-chip cookies and Key lime bars limp, for it was a happy occasion—groundbreaking for the Alison Fahrer Educational Center at the Windley Key Fossil Reef State Geologic Site.

Not only Alison and her husband, Bill, were there, but other folk who either were key to the founding of that historic park as well, or later had become one of the faithful who believed in its value and helped make its vision a reality. There were Ed Kloski, the ranger Pat Wells, representatives from the state, locals including the Reverend Ralph Johnson, Eileen Sylvester, Megg Mabbs and many more. The building's architect, Bill Bean, had been unable to make it.

"Since 1981 Bill and I, and Ed Kloski and many others, have worked to bring this event to pass," Alison said. "These 32 acres are now a thriving part of the Florida Park System. So this is indeed a day to celebrate. Feel free to dance."

The Russell family homesteaded Windley Key in the 1800s. They were an extraordinary family whose history included flight from North Carolina after the American Revolution to settle in the Bahama Islands. They left the Bahamas in 1860 to come to the Florida Keys and homestead 162 acres in the Islamorada area that included Windley Key. The Russells were Conch royalty. Descendants of those original settlers still lived in the Keys.

The Russells sold Windley Key property to the Florida East Coast Railroad in 1908. The key then was used as a stone quarry during the building of Henry Flagler's Overseas Railroad, the stone being used both for the rail bed and for bridge approaches. Later, the stone was also sheared off to make decorative building facades. In 1980, a developer was dickering for zoning variances that would permit him to buy the quarry property, blast out the old quarries for a kayaking pool and build condominiums. Alison Fahrer moved to stop him. By then the old walls of the quarry had become the equivalent of laboratory specimens of reefs—a place where fossilized reef life could be studied in much the same way that doctors study bone structure by using a CAT scan. The site was historic, and the quarries were a valuable tool for geologists.

The Fahrers, Ed Kloski and a coalition of Keys environmental organizations mounted a crusade that finally resulted in the state buying the site as a park, and then appropriating the money to build an educational center that would be named for Alison Fahrer. In The Next Florida, more and more, prime natural or historical areas needed governmental sanction for preservation.

*   *   *

Grapefruit and swamps contribute to expectations about the next Florida. Oranges always got the glory; grapefruit were among the underappreciated things. Like mullet, muscadines and in-laws, their supply historically has been plentiful, their taste distinctive if not peculiar, and their real value widely uncertain. That changed.

Grapefruit proved full of surprises. In the old days, the first wry taste brought a pucker and a grimace. That merely weeded out the undeserving. Grasping the truth about them was a benchmark in the mature appreciation of Florida. In them you could find something loftier than conventional sweetness, if you worked at it. They had a challenging, tonic taste that startled the palate and curled down the gullet somewhat like a green wine, awakening the body and suggesting there would be adventure in the day.

The grapefruit put loads of vitamin C and potassium into the system and, according to research on pigs, fought against cholesterol. Eating it could almost be considered patriotic. Florida, the grapefruit daddy of the world, had more than 9 million grapefruit trees and raised more grapefruit than anybody else, almost half the world supply.

Despite all this, the grapefruit lagged behind the orange in popularity, as Dr. Poonam Mittal told me in 1986. She was marketing director for the Florida Department of Citrus. "There is a lot we still need to know," she said.

In the early 1970s, Florida marketing strategy called for gymnast Cathy Rigby to rave wholesomely on TV about grapefruit juice as a diet and fitness product. Rigby and the ads were a great hit, but grapefruit sales did not increase. Later there was an ad campaign to expand customers' perceptions, changing them from grapefruit juice as only a health drink to grapefruit juice as a beverage for all times. That did not work either.

Many other things have been tried. In the early 1980s promotions switched to a combination approach that pushed both juice and fresh fruit, with success, and then a series of winter freezes came along and crops were diminished.

The citrus department once tried an experiment at the welcome stations along the major highways coming into Florida. It had been the custom to serve both orange juice and grapefruit juice, but the grapefruit juice usually was passed up. For three years, the welcome stations tried serving only grapefruit juice. "People continued to ask for orange juice," Dr. Mittal said. Thirsty visitors, with no choice, drank the free grapefruit juice but did not seem happy about it. "It was not good public relations," Dr. Mittal said. In 1984 orange juice went back into the welcome stations.

As new varieties of grapefruit were developed, things changed a bit. With seedless (six or fewer seeds) and pink varieties of grapefruit, fresh grapefruit started to become more popular. The pink grapefruit, especially, were more attractive and seemed to be sweeter.

Dr. David Tucker, grapefruit specialist at the University of Florida's Institute of Food and Agricultural Sciences at Lake Alfred, suggested the same year that this was more a matter of illusion and laziness than taste. He made the case for the old grapefruit, the Cracker equivalent of the grapefruit. He personally preferred the white, seedy (30 to 70 seeds) grapefruit known as the Duncan, which sprang from a seedling in the original tree in Florida. The public might find the newer pink grapefruit prettier and sweeter, but he found no evidence that it actually was. "The Duncan is recognized as having the best taste, but the public is so finicky that it doesn't want to bother with seeds, and so it is used less and less," Dr. Tucker said.

That was how it was with grapefruit. In the modern marketplace, illusion and ease counted for more than value, and the grapefruit ethic sometimes went uncelebrated. Crackers understood the feeling. True Floridians and others did what they could to change this.

They ate more grapefruit, gladly puckered and spit seeds. They ate pink, too, and swore that all grapefuit tasted good and was good for you, too. From their low point in the early 1980s, the figures for grapefruit began to move up again. In the mid-1990s, they were as high as ever.

Cheryl Pepper, director of Florida's Visitor Services, said in 1998 that the state now served both grapefruit and orange juices in their four highway welcome stations. "We served 2.5 million cups of orange juice—excuse me, citrus juice, both orange and grapefruit—last year," she said. There is a fifth welcome center at the capitol in Tallahassee, which doesn't serve citrus juice because it might stain the marble floors.

Whatever, it appeared that in The Next Florida grapefruit would have status equal with orange juice. Crackers cheered.

*   *   *

With swamps, too, it was a matter of understanding the value of gifts already in hand, so they would not be lost. In The Next Florida swamp appreciation, like music appreciation, might be part of every Florida child's education. The children need to be able to recognize swamps as biological headquarters for the land, the life generators, both reservoirs themselves and cleansing entrances for water filtering into the aquifers.

Mark T. Brown, "The Swamp Doctor," was a leading advocate of swamp education. He loved swamps, and he practiced what he preached. He had a Ph.D. in swamps. In 1986 Brown lived at the edge of a swamp. He and his wife raised two daughters there. He nurtured swamps, lectured about them around the state, formulated laws for them, even created them. Swamps were his life's work.

Brown said the state needs a new generation of swamp lovers both to nurture and protect its old swamps, and to establish some new ones. Ideally, more of Florida's children would grow up near swamps, he said, so they could taste the wild appeal of these curious places before the prejudices of habit and convenience blunted their sensitivities. Perhaps, then, they could love a swamp properly, as a birthright and a blessing, the way real Floridians should.

His ideas would have the old-time Crackers slapping their knees in laughter and shaking their heads in wonder, but Brown was representative of the new Cracker. "If people had the right appreciation of them, there's no reason why we couldn't think of swamps as being suitable landscaping," he said. "Swamps can be beautiful things, as well as useful."

Brown prized swamps not only for the state's health but also for the personality they brought to Florida's flatlands and sandhills. From the aristocrat of Florida's swamps, the Everglades, to the smallest backyard marsh, they added substantive character. He thought all Floridians ought to have a chance to know the mysteries and benefits of swamps but, especially, the children should know.

It takes an open mind to grow fond of swamps. They have a peculiar smell. They send out fleets of mosquitoes and other less famous insects, and all manner of other things that crawl and bite. Adults cannot always learn. They just can't do it. To love swamps—really love them—said The Swamp Doctor, you have to learn as a child.

He was realistic about what this meant to a man in his business. In Florida, where the number and the quality of swamps were diminishing, where millions of newcomers without swamp experience have taken up residence, he pursued what sometimes seemed to others a limited crusade. Still, he was confident the future would confirm his answers.

Brown grew up in south Florida, in Miami and Pompano Beach, but by 1986 had retreated down a two-rut dirt road in north central Florida east of Gainesville. There were no close towns. The road wound through tall pine trees to the edge of his natural habitat, and there on semi-damp ground rose a house that had grown with each child. He built much of it himself, with lumber from area forests.

He enrolled at the University of Florida in 1965, and never left. "They call me the only student with tenure," he said. After he earned a B.A. and an M.A. in architecture, for his Ph.D. he joined the university's Center for Wetlands (the academic word for swamp) at the time it was being founded by Dr. Howard T. Odum, a world-class visionary who was both celebrated and controversial.

The Swamp Doctor was an ace Odum disciple, a professional colleague and assistant, working as a research scientist at the center. Most of the work there related in some way to Odum's conclusion that one day the world would have to gear down to accommodate energy shortages. Odum dismissed growth philosophy as a "false god."

Brown's research revolved principally around Florida swamps, but his range had been wide. He had studied the ecological effects of war in Vietnam ("A bombed-out landscape recovers faster than one that has been paved over"), analyzed energy perspectives of the Amazon River for the Cousteau Society, assisted Dr. Odum in a 1976 study on the carrying capacity of man and nature in south Florida that forecast an inevitable leveling off of the economy, assisted in a 1975 study that recommended de-channelizing the Kissimmee River (an experiment then under way).

Another project, for the state, pursued the re-creation of wetlands—literally, the making of swamps—on lands reclaimed from phosphate mining. In both, as in much of his other work, Brown's goal dealt in the reversal of history, a change of attitudes and the development pattern. He and Odum called it, in their research papers, the quest for a system of appropriate technology symbiotic to the future of both humanity and nature. They would maximize the vitality of both humans and nature by building protection of the environment into the economy.

"We're looking at a low-energy future, but no one wants to recognize it as that," Brown said. "Everybody thinks we'll just go on and on, but we can't. As individuals, we are willing to buy insurance, just in case. But society won't do that. We're sitting here in this state saying we're gonna grow forever and everything's going to be great. But what if we don't? There needs to be a tiny fraction of our money, at least, going into strategic planning for that possibility. If we stop growing, what's the landscape, the culture and the economy gonna look like in a low-energy world? What will life be like?"

One thing The Next Florida would need, The Swamp Doctor said, was more swamps. He will be ready.

*   *   *

Floridians sit on their dune ridges and peer across the state and hope that dizzying combination of beauty and mess they see out there is not really The Next Florida, even though they know it might be—unless, as growth management expert John DeGrove warned, we quit growing dumb and learn to grow smart.

Part of the problem, beyond the daunting numbers, is human nature. Most of us look across a pristine dune, where only the wind has rippled the sand, where there is no sign of human meddling—not even a beer can—and experience a childlike urge to walk across it, to make a mark on this unmarked thing. We feel the need to put footprints, or worse, on the virginal treasures that nature leaves. We want to skip stones across placid ponds, just to see the splash; we want to pluck wildflowers out of the fields, just briefly to capture that beauty even though we are causing it to perish; we want to grab up live shells along the seashore, just to possess these marine jewels, condemning them to death on a dusty shelf.

Strange are the ways of professed nature lovers who become nature killers. We have become conquistadores in Disney-like wildernesses, survivalists in a country where survival has been insured for most, eager to tame what's already tamed, to conquer what's already conquered.

*   *   *

So, with all these bits and pieces and hopes and fears, The Next Florida begins to take shape. The rustle of a palmetto frond gives way to the exotic blossoming of an oleander, the dark water of Florida creeks washes not against sandy white shorelines but against concrete bulkheads. The Mineral City where the DeGroves passed up real-estate fortune turns into a wondrous resort with internationally attractive tennis and golf and vacation complexes.

The new contours of Florida can be traced by following the tidal ups and downs of places like Miami Beach, rising out of mangrove swamps into one dazzling incarnation after another, but with disappointing dips in between; by the story of Miami itself being transformed from a village bounded by beanfields, swamps, barrier islands and the sea to an ambitious international city with no limits except those of self-penalty, sometimes viewed from afar as a Babel without a common language and a proud Gomorrah; in the transformation of St. Augustine from a centerpiece historic shrine into

tourist attractions that cluster distractingly around historic treasures, making history an accomplice; by small places looming big
such as Eatonville and Cross Creek, each celebrated not for what
they are but for what the visions of writers Zora Neale Hurston and
Marjorie Kinnan Rawlings made them; by the fortunes of Sanibel
Island, which went from a true island to a bridged resort; and by the
meteoric rise of Destin from a fishing village to a Panhandle version
of Miami Beach; in the rise of Jacksonville from historic Cowford
and a Georgia refuge to the beautiful city it is now, with the St.
Johns River winding through its high-rises, laced dizzyingly by
interstates.

In Defuniak Springs, the Confederate flag still flies at the Walton
County Courthouse on working days. Nearby is a white marble
monument erected in 1871 to honor the Confederate war dead, a
stone hand atop it thrusting an index finger upward, perpetually
making a point. Near the other end of the state, at Cocoa, rocket
ships blast off to the moon and other places. In Tallahassee, the two
capitols rise single-file, symbolically suggesting the old and the new
Florida coexist.

Across the middle, a megacity grows, Florida's largest, spreading
from Tampa Bay along I-4 past Lakeland and Disney World and its
Orlando suburb to Cocoa and the Space Center. It begins to link up
with another one, down the coast through Melbourne, Fort Pierce,
Stuart, West Palm Beach, Fort Lauderdale and Miami, with an ex-
tension into the Keys. Ambitious Gainesville and important Tallahassee become jeweled fobs on the interstate chain along with
Pensacola at one end and Naples and Fort Myers at the other.

The beginning of The Next Florida is in sight, though perhaps
dimly. Crystal balls, tea leaves, hog entrails—or even dreamy-eyed
mediums in Cassadaga communing with another world—can only
tell us for sure that it must begin with the present. The future is
happening now. Whether The Next Florida will evolve as a true de-
scendant of the old one remains a matter for hope, not prophecy.

Bibliography

Barbour, George M. *Florida for Tourists, Invalids and Settlers.* Appleton, 1884.

Bellman, Samuel I. *Marjorie Kinnan Rawlings.* New York: Twayne, 1974.

Bigelow, Gordon E. *Frontier Eden: The Literary Career of Marjorie Kinnan Rawlings.* Gainesville: University of Florida Press, 1966.

Bigelow, Gordon E., and Laura V. Monti, eds. *Selected Letters of Marjorie Kinnan Rawlings.* Gainesville: University Presses of Florida, 1983.

Blake, Nelson M. *Land into Water—Water into Land.* Gainesville: University Presses of Florida, 1980.

Brooke, Steven. *Seaside.* Gretna, La.: Pelican Publishing Co., 1996.

Burt, Al. *Al Burt's Florida: Snowbirds, Sand Castles, and Self-Rising Crackers,* Gainesville: University Press of Florida, 1997.

———. Articles and columns in *The Miami Herald* (including *Tropic* magazine) from 1973 to 1996.

———. *Becalmed in the Mullet Latitudes.* Port Salerno, Fla.: Florida Classics Library, 1984.

Burt, Al, and Heinz Erhardt. *Florida: A Place in the Sun.* Offenburg, West Germany: Burda GmbH, 1974.

Carter, Luther J. *The Florida Experience.* Baltimore: Johns Hopkins University Press, 1974.

DeGrove, John M. *Land, Growth and Politics.* Washington, D.C.: Planners Press, 1984.

Douglas, Marjory Stoneman. *The Everglades: River of Grass.* Coconut Grove, Fla.: Hurricane House Publishers, 1947.

———. *Florida: The Long Frontier.* New York: Harper & Row, 1967.

Federal Writers' Project of the Works Project Administration for the State of Florida. *Florida: A Guide to the Southernmost State.* New York: Oxford University Press, 1939.

Gannon, Michael. *Florida: A Short History.* Gainesville: University Press of Florida, 1993.

Haase, Ronald W. *Classic Cracker.* Sarasota, Fla.: Pineapple Press, 1992.

Hanna, A. J., and Kathryn Abbey Hanna. *Lake Okeechobee*. Indianapolis and New York: Bobbs-Merrill, 1948.

Kennedy, Stetson. *Palmetto Country*. New York: Duell, Sloan & Pearce, 1942. Reprint, Gainesville: University Press of Florida, 1973.

Morris, Allen. *The Florida Handbook*. Tallahassee: Peninsular Publishing Co., biennial editions from 1973 to 1998.

Rawlings, Marjorie Kinnan. *Cross Creek*. New York: Grosset & Dunlap, 1942.

———. *The Yearling*. New York: Scribner's, 1938.

Tebeau, Charlton. *A History of Florida*, rev. ed. Coral Gables: University of Miami Press, 1980.